D0788983

CALGARY PUBLIC LIBRARY

MAR   2015

HOW THE WILD WEST WAS WON

BRUCE WEXLER

Skyhorse Publishing

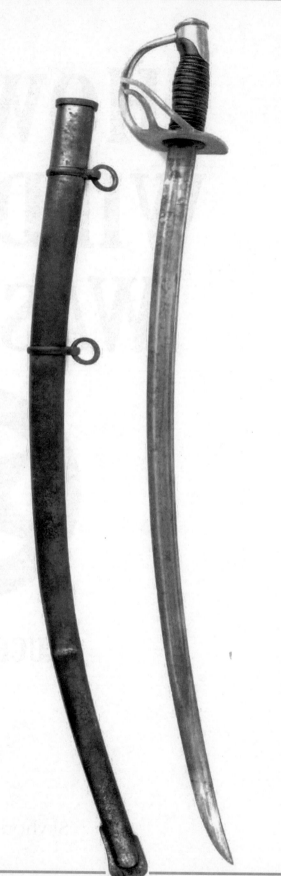

Copyright © 2013 by Bruce Wexler
All Rights Reserved. No part of this book may
be reproduced in any manner without the express
written consent of the publisher, except in the case
of brief excerpts in critical reviews or articles.
All inquiries should be addressed to Skyhorse Publishing,
307 West 36th Street, 11th Floor, New York, NY 10018.

Skyhorse Publishing books may be purchased in bulk at
special discounts for sales promotion, corporate gifts,
fund-raising, or educational purposes. Special editions can
also be created to specifications. For details, contact the
Special Sales Department, Skyhorse Publishing,
307 West 36th Street, 11th Floor, New York, NY 10018
or email: info@skyhorsepublishing.com

Skyhorse® and Skyhorse Publishing® are registered
trademarks of Skyhorse Publishing, Inc.®,
a Delaware corporation.

www.skyhorsepublishing.com

10 9 8 7 6 5 4 3 2 1

Library of Congress Cataloging-in-Publication Data on file

ISBN: 978-1-62873-654-0

Printed in China

Contents

Introduction to the Wild West

*B*ut the West of the old times, with its strong characters, its stern battles, and its tremendous stretches of loneliness, can never be blotted from my mind.

– Buffalo Bill

*T*he West is color. Its colors are animal rather than vegetable, the colors of earth and sunlight and ripeness.

– Jessamyn West

*O*nly remember, west of the Mississippi it's a little more look, see, act. A little less rationalize, comment, talk.

– F. Scott Fitzgerald

Opposite page: Monument Valley, Utah. The dramatic red color of the buttes is derived from iron oxide deposits exposed in the weathered siltstone. This iconic western landscape appears in many movies, including John Ford's *Stagecoach* and *The Searchers*.

America without the West in unthinkable, but its assimilation into the nation was by no means inevitable. The integration of the West into the United States took over a hundred years to complete. The chronicle of this epic achievement is the story of every settler that made it to the region, those that died on the way, and even those that left it empty-handed. It is also the story of the original peoples of the West, the Native Americans, who paid such a devastating price for its settlement.

The legend of the West is woven from the lives of millions of rugged individualists, who made their way there to live freely. It is a fantastic drama with countless players: farmers, preachers, saloon girls, prostitutes, ladies, businessmen, gunslingers, lawmen, Mormons, gamblers, trappers, ranchers, medicine men, and cowboys.

Without a doubt, the most fascinating period in the history of the Western frontier is the century between 1800 and 1900. This was the era of the Old West, and a time of fundamental change. During this time, the West evolved from a wild and untamed territory into an integral part of the modern world. From being virtually uninhabited, apart from the nomadic tribes, the West became somewhere that Americans could put down roots in their own land. Some Westerners became rich beyond the dreams of avarice, while others scratched out the toughest living imaginable from the virgin terrain. Others went completely to the bad, and preyed on their fellow settlers. But even the criminal element of the Old West was somehow larger than life, and more fascinating, and has left a legacy of extraordinary stories.

N. C. Wyeth's atmospheric painting of a stagecoach holdup. He depicts a gentleman bandit asking the passengers for their valuables.

The history of the West is packed with an infinite variety of human experience, which has left a huge impression on the region. As well as mass migration, the nineteenth century also saw the indissoluble linking of the Atlantic and Pacific coasts. Connected in turn by the pioneer trail, the stagecoach, the Pony Express, the railroads, and the telegraph wire, a single nation was gradually forged from two distinct regions. But just as progress pulled the nation together, it also spelled the end of a valuable way of life that had existed unchanged for thousands of years. A human price was paid for every gain.

With the benefit of our modern sensibilities, we can acknowledge that this century of change was one of the most explosive in the nation's history, especially that of the West. As well as bravery, ingenuity, and determination, the nineteenth century witnessed violence, genocide, and environmental disaster.

In the past, the story of the West was told as a string of simple triumphs: the defeat of the Indians, the building of the railroad, the taming of the region by white settlement. Predictably, this was followed by a revisionist backlash spotlighting the dark side of westward expansion: the murder of the native peoples, the decimation of the region's wildlife and natural resources, the triumph of mighty capital over the plucky individual. Today, we seem to have a more balanced view of the complexities of Western integration, while appreciating the mythology of the West and its timeless appeal.

If America has changed the West, the West in its turn has had a massive impact on America. When the United States became a continental nation, it was transformed into a far bigger and more powerful country with greater resources of every kind. The West has also permeated the very fabric of American cultural life. Its wild and beautiful landscape is familiar to millions of people who have never breathed its free air. Through its portrayal in the movies, literature, television, fashion, and even toys, the West has become a familiar concept. It has come to represent the very best of America itself: freedom, courage, and self-determination. It is both a unique part of America, and a metaphor for the country as a whole.

With all its mixed bag of courage, violence, creativity, and exploitation, the West has a compelling charm to almost all Americans and to millions of people in the world at large.

To anyone with an interest in the Old West, *The West* is a virtual tour of the most extraordinary century in the region's history. The book recreates its drama, iconography, atmosphere, and its cavalcade of legendary characters.

Native Americans in the West

Opposite page: Magnificent regalia of pierced shells, ermine, and feathers.

Native Americans first came to America around forty thousand years ago over the frozen Bering Strait, known as Beringia, which formed a land bridge between Siberia and Alaska. These people came from Asia, and were of Mongolian origin. The abundant livestock of their new homeland sustained these new

Above: White settlers began to arrive in North America in the sixteenth century and immediately began to influence the native tribes.

Americans, and attracted further immigrants. They arrived in waves, and pushed the earlier incomers further and further east and south until the entire continent was thinly populated. When the first white settlers arrived, there were around ten million Native Americans in America. The tribes had hugely diverse cultures and lifestyles, and a complicated oral and pictorial culture. Some were hunter-gatherers.

Right: Sauk chief Black Hawk. Black Hawk did not believe in ownership of land, and fought to maintain tribal traditions.

Opposite page: The nomadic tribes of the Great Plains used teepees winter and summer. This one is covered in buffalo hide.

Others were farmers. Many had long traditions of producing exquisite artifacts from natural materials. It was Christopher Columbus who coined the term "Indian" for these peoples, under the misapprehension that he had reached the Indies. It was actually San Salvador on which he landed in 1492. The new white settlers had a devastating effect on the indigenous population. The European diseases they carried (typhus, smallpox, influenza, measles, and diphtheria) infected and killed

as many as ninety-five percent of them. Perhaps the one positive consequence of the incoming Conquistadors was the introduction of horses to America. This had a huge impact on life on the Great Plains, enabling the Native Americans to kill buffalo and other game far more effectively. It also led to the invention of the travois to move their camps and possessions more quickly and easily, by dragging them along the ground. Horses were also used in inter-tribal warfare.

The completely opposing beliefs held by the white settlers and the Native Americans soon became a source of conflict. The indigenous people were nomadic, and believed that the man belonged to the earth, not the other way around. By complete contrast, the Europeans were bound by the conventions of property ownership, and had a settled, cooperative style of living, and organized religion. This gulf between beliefs was well put by the famous Sauk chief, Black Hawk,

Above: Apache scouts, armed with rifles. They were photographed in Arizona in 1871.

speaking in 1831. "My reason tells me that land cannot be sold; nothing can be sold but such things as can be carried away." As more and more white settlers arrived, the process of American settlement began again. European settlers arrived in the East, and gradually pushed the Native Americans further and further west.

Completely out-gunned by the white Americans' superior weapons, the Indian stood no chance against them. Although different problems sparked conflict between the races, the Indian Wars were fought over land rights. The United States government believed that buffalo-hunting Plains tribes were preventing white settlement across swathes of western territory, including Kansas, Nebraska, the Dakotas, Montana, Wyoming, and Colorado. It was generally believed that the Indians were hindering the "Manifest Destiny" of white people to "overspread the continent." President Andrew Jackson set out the agenda of the U.S. Government in the Indian Removal Act of 1830. Many Americans held the same view as General William Sherman, who asserted, "All Indians who are not on reservations are hostile, and will remain so until killed off."

Native Americans saw things completely differently. The famous Sioux chief and negotiator, Spotted Tail, countered, "This war did not spring up on our land, this war was brought by the children of the Great Father." The first of these land wars was the Arikara War of 1823. The Arikara tribe were semi-nomadic farmers living in South Dakota who were attacked by the Sioux and the U.S. Army (under the leadership of Col. Henry Leavenworth) and driven into the North of the state. The conflict set the tone for many future encounters. The Indian Wars rumbled on for decades, and encompassed hundreds of attacks, fights, and skirmishes between the Native Americans, settlers, and the U.S. Army. The most devastating period of hostilities took place between 1866 and 1890. Geographically, the conflict spread over most of the western states: Arizona, California, Colorado, Montana, North Dakota, Oklahoma, South Dakota, Texas, Utah, Washington, and Wyoming.

Opposite page: Arikara warrior Bear's Belly, wearing a grizzly bearskin. The Arikara were close cousins of the Pawnee, and were a nomadic and agricultural tribe.

Above: A necklace of eagle talons that belonged to Rough Hair.

Overleaf: A map showing the distribution of the Native American tribes before westward expansion.

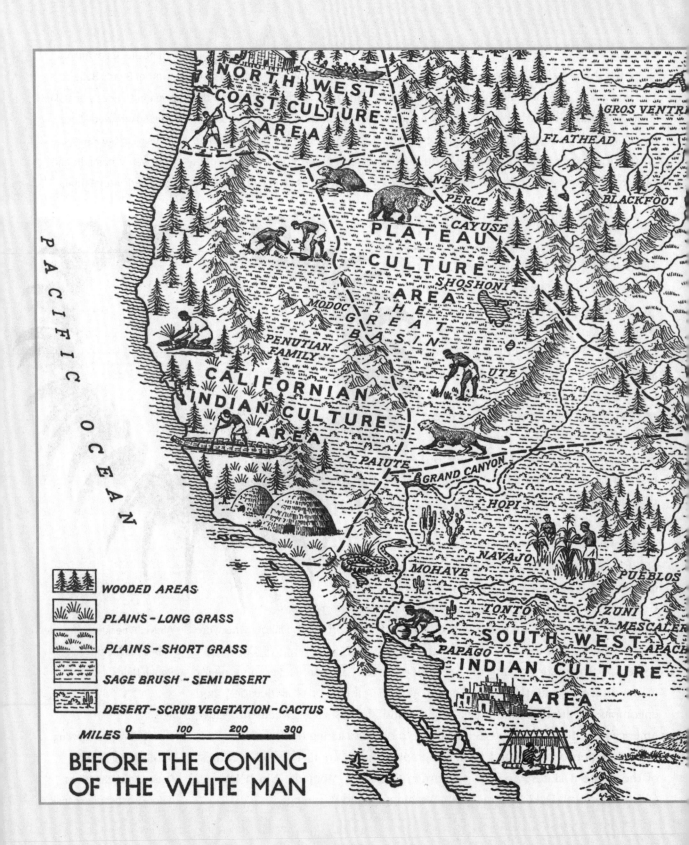

PACIFIC OCEAN

NORTH WEST COAST CULTURE AREA

GROS VENTRE

FLATHEAD

BLACKFOOT

NEZ PERCE

CAYUSE

PLATEAU CULTURE AREA

SHOSHONI

MODOC

THE GREAT BASIN

PENUTIAN FAMILY

CALIFORNIAN INDIAN CULTURE AREA

UTE

PAIUTE

GRAND CANYON

HOPI

NAVAJO

PUEBLOS

MOHAVE

ZUNI

MESCALERO

TONTO

SOUTH WEST INDIAN CULTURE AREA

APACHE

PAPAGO

WOODED AREAS

PLAINS — LONG GRASS

PLAINS — SHORT GRASS

SAGE BRUSH — SEMI DESERT

DESERT — SCRUB VEGETATION — CACTUS

MILES 0 100 200 300

BEFORE THE COMING OF THE WHITE MAN

Above: Comanche chief Quanah Parker. Parker was the son of Chief Peta Nocona and Cynthia Ann Parker, who had been captured by the tribe at the age of nine.

Right: A Navajo mother and child wearing traditional silver and turquoise jewelry.

Opposite page: This beaded buckskin jacket was produced by Lakota Sioux craftspeople in around 1890.

There were many famous battles and countless attacks, but the Indian tribes scored very few serious hits against their white opponents. One of their few victories was at Custer's Last Stand. Far more common were massacres of the tribespeople, like that perpetrated at Wounded Knee in South Dakota, and terrible treatment, such as the infamous Trail of Tears. The Trail of Tears was the forced removal of the Cherokee Nation from Georgia to Oklahoma, under the terms of the New Echota Treaty of 1835. A string of forts was built along the route to corral the Indians and protect the troops who forced the thousand-mile march to the West. The sophisticated Cherokees, who had been so tolerant of the white settlers arriving to

Opposite page: Chief Geronimo was a Chiricahua Apache who fought the Apache Wars to preserve tribal lands. He surrendered in 1886, and died in 1909.

share their homeland, were herded like animals and died by the thousands, particularly during the savagely cold winter of 1838 to 1839. Among the victims was Quatie, the wife of tribal chief John Ross, who died just outside Little Rock.

Estimates of casualties in the Indian Wars vary, but a reasonable approximation would probably be around forty-five thousand Indians and nineteen thousand whites. These casualties included many women and children on both sides, many

Right: A Navajo war captain. He wears a war hat of tanned leather, and carries a lance and rawhide shield.

of whom perished in bloodthirsty massacres. Both sides were extremely violent and destructive. Despite this, remnants of the native inhabitants survived, but they account for only around two percent of the modern population of the United States. The descendants of over five hundred different tribes endure, but most have lost their distinctive languages and culture.

Even a brief analysis of a few of the most prominent tribal groupings gives an insight into the great variety of traditions and lifestyle.

Opposite page: A painting by John Hauser Jr. depicts Sioux Chief Iron Tail wearing his spectacular war bonnet (below). He was a survivor of the Wounded Knee Massacre.

APACHE

Apache is the Zuni word for "enemy," but the Apache called themselves the Dine, "the people" in their Athapascan language. The Apache were the major tribe of the American Southwest. Made up from nine distinct sub-tribes, they populated Arizona, New Mexico, Oklahoma, and Texas. Related to the Navajo and enjoying a similar way of life, their tribal deity was known as Yusan or Ussen. Despite a fairly unsettled lifestyle, the tribe often lived in wooden huts or adobe structures rather than under canvas. They had a reputation for being fierce warriors. They had enthusiastically adopted horses from the Spanish invaders, and were experts in horsemanship, using the animals for both hunting and raiding other tribes. Geronimo was one of the most famous Apache chiefs. His capture in 1886 was hugely symbolic, and signaled the end of the Apache warrior culture. In fact, they were the last tribe to surrender to the United States government.

COMANCHE

The word "Comanche" comes from the Spanish phrase *camino ancho*, meaning "wide trail." Their mother tongue is derived from Aztec and is related to the languages of the Shoshone, Ute, and Paiute. Originally from the Rocky Mountains, the Comanche moved onto the Plains to hunt buffalo, and became a nomadic tribe. The tribe emerged as a distinct group before 1700, when they broke away from the Shoshone tribe. The Comanche existed in dozens of autonomous groups, and expanded by capturing women and children from rival groups and assimilating them. The horse was pivotal to their lifestyle, and the Comanche introduced the animal to other people of the Plains. They had originally used dogs to pull their travois, but moved to using horses. The Comanche people had a traditional division of labor; the men hunted and

fought, while the women brought up the children, cooked the food, and made clothes from buckskin, deerskin, buffalo hide, bearskin, and wolf skin. The tribe tended not to eat fish or fowl, preferring game meat flavored with berries, nuts, honey, and tallow. The Comanche were a very hospitable tribe who worshiped the Great Spirit. The tribe was run by a council of ministers, which included both a "peace chief" and a "war chief." Medicine men were also influential; their duties included naming children. The Comanche were indulgent parents who cherished their progeny. Retired warriors gathered daily in the smoke lodge.

Unfortunately, like many other Native Americans, the tribe fell victim to European diseases such as smallpox and cholera. Their population crashed from twenty thousand people in the mid-1800's to a few thousand by the 1870's. By the 1860s, many Comanche were confined to reservations. Their condition had deteriorated dramatically. The buffalo was virtually extinct, and their skirmishes with the U.S. Army had been devastating.

Above: Jenny LaPointe made these Lakota Sioux moccasins. They date from around 1900. Jenny LaPointe was a member of Buffalo Bill's *Wild West Show.*

Opposite page: Ahfitche, the governor of San Felipe Pueblo, New Mexico uses a drill to make holes in shells for use in jewelry. The photograph was taken in 1880.

Right: This rawhide dance rattle belonged to Crazy Crow, a member of the Plains Crow tribe.

CHEROKEE

The Cherokee were one of the largest tribes of the Southeast, known as the "Tsalagi" in their own language. Cherokee comes from the Creek word for "people of a different speech." They had migrated from the Northwest following defeats by the Iroquois and Delaware. They became a settled agricultural people, who lived in around two hundred villages. Typically, each of these consisted of between thirty and sixty dwellings, together with a large council house where the sacred fire was kept. The tribe cultivated the "three sisters" of corn, beans, and squash. They were also hunter-gatherers, with a highly sophisticated standard of living. The Cherokee were heavily influenced by white settlers, and invented their own written language consisting of eighty-six characters in 1821. The Cherokee also traded with the British. But a devastating smallpox epidemic in 1753 killed half the tribe. They also fell out with their British allies and, in 1760, the Cherokee warriors massacred the garrison at Fort Loudon in eastern Tennessee.

Trying to protect their valuable lands from white settlement, the tribe sold the land of other tribes. An honest Cherokee chief took Daniel Boone aside and told him, "We have sold you much fine land, but I am afraid you will have trouble if you try to live there." But fighting between the tribe and white settlers continued unabated, exacerbated when gold was discovered on their lands. The Indian Removal Act of 1821 stripped the Cherokee of any legal rights, and they became the victim of every kind of theft and violence. They were finally driven to surrender their homelands in return for $5,000,000 and seven million acres of land in Oklahoma. But the treaty proved to be a fraud. The Cherokee were driven out of their lands by force, and embarked on the infamous Trail of Tears. Many died of measles, whooping cough, and dysentery, while others perished from exposure. In the end, they were forced to abandon even the Oklahoma territory they had been awarded. The tribe was finally compensated by the U.S. government in 1961 with a payment of $15 million.

Opposite page: Sioux warrior Yellow Shirt holds a sacred horse dance stick in his right hand. In his left, he holds a beaded pipe and a tobacco bag.

THE NAVAJO

The Navajo remain the largest Native American tribe, with around two hundred thousand surviving members. Navajo comes from the Spanish for "people with big lands." The tribe called themselves the "Dine" or "people." They originally came from Northwest Canada and Alaska, but traveled to the Southwest part of America. The tribe grew corn, beans, squash, and melons and wove attractive rugs and fabrics. The Navajo lived in fairly substantial circular dwellings called *hogans*, made from wooden poles, tree bark, and mud. Traditionally, the doors always opened to the east. When the white settlers arrived, the tribe stole their sheep and horses and integrated both animals into their tribal lives. The Navajo nation now extends into Utah, Arizona, and New Mexico. It extends over twenty-seven thousand square miles, and is larger than several U.S. states.

Opposite page: A Cheyenne warrior wears a war bonnet crafted with ermine drops and a beaded brow band. His sash is decorated with a star motif.

Above: Sioux Chief Hollow Horn Bear, who as a young man fought with Sitting Bull at the Battle of Little Bighorn.

THE SIOUX

"Sioux" is the name given to the tribe by French fur traders who had close relations with them in the late seventeenth century. It was the traders' diminutive of the tribe's Indian name, "Nadouessioux," or "the adders." The tribe was a large and disparate racial group, composed of three distinct ethnic strains. The Sioux migrated to the Plains in the late eighteenth century, and substantially changed their way of life from being canoe men and gatherers of wild rice to horse-riding hunters. Largely through trading with the French, many Sioux braves also became armed with guns. The Sioux involved themselves in many struggles with other tribes, but also began to attack settlers to the area. The "Minnesota outbreak" of 1862 resulted in widespread Sioux violence, and several hundred settlers were brutally murdered. A court marshal condemned three hundred tribesmen to hang for their part in the killing spree, but President Lincoln spared all but thirty-eight. Despite this, the resulting hanging at Mankato, Minnesota, remains the largest mass execution in American history. A vicious cycle

Opposite Page: Hunkpapa
Lakota Sioux tribal chief
Sitting Bull routed Custer's
Seventh Cavalry at the
Battle of the Little Bighorn.
Later, he appeared in Bill
Cody's *Wild West Show*.

Left: Red Cloud was the
head chief of the Oglala
Lakota Sioux. Between
1866 and 1868, he waged
Red Cloud's War, fighting
for control over traditional
tribal lands in Powder River
Country. He died in the Pine
Ridge Reservation, South
Dakota, in 1909.

of murder and revenge continued. Red Cloud's War raged for two years starting in 1866. Subsequent hostilities broke out in the Black Hills, including the killing of Custer and his men. In 1890, the tribe's famous Ghost Dance ritual culminated in more murder and mayhem, and resulted in the death of Sitting Bull as he tried to protect the tribe's independence. This in turn provoked the fight at Wounded Knee Creek against the forces of the U.S. Seventh Cavalry.

Beaten by U.S. government forces, the Sioux were mostly confined to reservations by the end of the nineteenth century. Confined, the tribe reverted to the farming traditions of their past, raising cattle and corn rather than hunting the almost extinct buffalo. Most famous Sioux, including Little Crow, Crazy Horse, Red Cloud, and Sitting Bull were known for their fighting prowess, but the tribe was also noted for its dancing and fine craftwork.

Cavalry Regiments of the Indian Wars

Below: An early cavalryman with a saddle-mounted holster.

Of all the institutions of the Old West, the cavalry is surely one of the most iconic. From 1865 to 1890, the cavalry played a huge role in western expansion, patrolling the frontier and protecting would-be settlers from Indian attack. Effectively, the frontier started west of the Mississippi River, and as western settlement became increasingly widespread, the cavalry became responsible for a huge area of territory.

The cavalry also became a major enforcer of the civil law in the region, and became involved in many actions to bring lawbreakers and gunmen to justice. A good example of this would be the 1870 shootout between Wild Bill Hickok and riders of the Seventh that took place in Hays, Kansas. Hickok killed one cavalry officer and wounded another.

The role of the cavalry in the post-Civil War period was determined in 1869, when President Grant appointed William Tecumseh Sherman Commanding General of the United States Army and the cavalry also came under his command. At this time, Sherman's major preoccupation was the subjugation of the Indian tribes, which he saw as a barrier to westward expansion. To this end, he created the Plains Cavalry, and recruited an additional four regiments to deal with the so-called "Indian problem." The Indian Wars raged until the Massacre of Wounded Knee in 1890, and became the focus of the Plains Cavalry for over two decades.

Opposite page: William Tecumseh Sherman became Commanding General of the Army in 1869. He waged the Indian Wars for twenty years. His stated objective was the extermination of the Native Americans.

Each cavalry regiment consisted of twelve troops of approximately ninety-five men. Although recruiting officers was no problem, as many men stayed in the army when the Civil War ended, it proved much harder to engage ordinary troopers. The ranks became filled with many wanted men and immigrants, not all of whom spoke

Several guns of the period became highly
identified with the U.S. Cavalry in the years
following the Civil War.

English. The starting pay was a meager thirteen dollars a
month, and many men in the ranks were malnourished. As well as
patrolling the western territory, many cavalrymen were garrisoned in forts.
These were built across the region, from the mountains of North Dakota and
Nebraska to the deserts of Texas, New Mexico, and Arizona.

Begun at Sherman's instigation, the Indian Wars were the focus of cavalry action
for over twenty years. The General used the same scorched earth tactics against the
Native American tribes as he had employed in the Civil War. Not only did he seek
military victory against them, he also wanted to deprive them of their means of

Above: A Model 1865 Spencer carbine. The gun was chambered for the .50 caliber rimfire cartridge. Many Buffalo Soldiers of the Ninth Cavalry stationed at Fort Davis, Texas, were armed with the gun.

Above: A Springfield Model 1873, recovered from the battlefield at Little Bighorn. Custer's Seventh Cavalry were armed with the gun. It was ineffective because the Indian braves rarely came within its range. The gun was nicknamed the "Trapdoor" after its Allin breechloading system.

Above: Standard Model 1873 Springfield carbine. The Springfield was the first standard-issue breech-loading rifle adopted by the United States Army.

survival. In the case of the Plains Indians, this meant the decimation of the buffalo.

The Seventh United States Cavalry was undoubtedly the most famous regiment to fight in the Indian Wars. Constituted in 1866, the regiment was made up of twelve companies, or "troops." Like most of the post-war cavalry, its troopers were armed mainly with single-action Colt .45 revolvers and modified single-shot .50 caliber Model 1865 Spencer carbines. These were based on the Spencer Model 1863 of the early Civil War era, but had shorter, twenty-inch barrels. These guns were finally replaced by the Springfield Model 1873. Although sabers were still issued, these were now largely ceremonial.

Above: The single-action Colt .45 revolver was adopted by the U.S. Cavalry in the postbellum era. It became known as "the gun that won the West."

Until 1871, the Seventh was based at Fort Riley in Kansas. Its mission was to enforce United States law in the subjugated South. But the regiment was also involved in anti-Indian action, including the famous 1868 Battle of Washita River. Commanded by General Custer, the 7th attacked Chief Black Kettle's Cheyenne village. Even at the time, Custer's attack on a sleeping village was controversial. The general was accused of sadism, and his men of killing women and children.

In 1873, the Seventh U.S. Cavalry moved its base to Fort Abraham

Lincoln, in Dakota Territory. The regiment's initial brief was to reconnoiter and map the Black Hills mountain range, which stretches between South Dakota and Wyoming. Custer's discovery of gold in the Black Hills, during his expedition of 1874, had a profound effect on the region. Not only did this discovery precipitate the huge social upheaval of the Gold Rush, but it also exacerbated conflict with the Sioux, Lakota, and Cheyenne tribes, who were under the leadership of Sitting Bull and Crazy Horse. Modern historians accuse President Grant of deliberately provoking war with the native peoples; he was desperate for gold-fuelled growth to lift the economy out of depression.

But victory against the Sioux and Cheyenne peoples was only achieved at a huge cost to the men of the Seventh Cavalry. The Battle of the Little Bighorn (June 25–26, 1876), also known as Custer's Last Stand, saw two hundred and sixty-eight cavalrymen killed, and a further sixty wounded. The death toll included Custer himself and two of his brothers – Captain Thomas Custer, and their youngest brother, civilian scout and forage master Boston Custer – and Custer's nephew, Autie Reed. Not only were the cavalry outnumbered by two thousand braves at Little Bighorn, but they were also out-gunned. The U.S. forces were armed with newly issued single-shot Springfield rifles, while many of the Indians had various repeating rifles and carbines such as Henrys, Winchesters, and Spencers. Custer's Last Stand became the most serious defeat inflicted on the cavalry in the Plains Wars. Every man and horse of the Seventh cavalry that fought at Little Bighorn perished at the scene; the single exception was Captain Keogh's famous mount, Comanche.

Below: A cavalry saber from the Indian Wars period, made by Ames.

Opposite page: George Armstrong Custer was one of the most famous cavalry commanders in the Indian Wars. He met his demise at the Battle of the Little Bighorn of 1876 at the hands of a combined force of Lakota, Northern Cheyenne, and Arapaho Indians.

Left: Custer meets with his Crow scouts. His favorite Remington rifle rests on the guy rope.

Despite his complete failure, General Custer's reputation remained strangely unstained by this terrible defeat, largely due to the efforts of his widow, Elizabeth Bacon Custer, and friend, Buffalo Bill Cody.

Several other United States Cavalry regiments fought in the Indian Wars. The Fourth United States Cavalry was formed in 1855, and was deployed to Texas after the war. Its duties were to protect settlers and the U.S. mail from Indian attack. In 1871 the regiment was called to more active duties, protecting the Texas frontier from Comanche and Kiowa attack. In March 1873, a large part of the regiment was transferred to Fort Clark, from where they made forays into Mexico to prevent highly destructive Apache raids into Texas. In 1880, the Fourth was transferred to Arizona

Above: Custer's Seventh Cavalry unit on their way to Little Bighorn.
Opposite page: Indian chief with Winchester Trapper carbine.

Territory, where they continued to pursue their nemesis, the Apache. Six years later, in 1886, the Fourth was instrumental in the capture of Geronimo. In 1890, the troops of the Fourth were redeployed to Washington State, and took no further part in the Indian Wars. Over the period of their involvement, the regiment had had many successes against a number of Indian tribes, such as the Comanche (including the Quahadi and Kotsoteka Comanche), Kiowa, Cheyenne, and Apache tribes.

Top: Custer's Last Stand. Armed with single shot Springfield carbines, his forces were outgunned by the Indian attackers.

Bottom: The dreadful scene after the Battle of Little Bighorn.

Opposite page: Custer attired in his cavalry uniform of fringed buckskin.

The Fifth United States Cavalry was formed in Louisville, Kentucky, in 1855, and was originally designated the Second United States Cavalry Regiment. In 1861, this regiment split between men loyal to the Confederacy and those who supported the Union. The Union cavalrymen were re-designated as the Fifth, and these men were instrumental in saving their artillery at the Battle of Gaines' Mill in 1862. In the post-bellum Plains Indian Wars, the regiment's main duty was to recapture escaped Sioux and Cheyenne and repatriate them to their reservations. They were also instrumental in the defeat of the Miniconjou Sioux at the Battle of Slim Buttes, which took place 1876 in Dakota Territory. Colonel Wesley Merritt led the troops in this engagement. This victory was of huge psychological importance, as it was the first significant defeat of the tribes since the annihilation of Custer's Seventh.

The Sixth United States Cavalry, also known as the "Fighting Sixth" also took a major part in the Indian Wars. It was raised in 1861, and became part of the Union Army of the Potomac during the Civil War. Between 1865 and 1871, the regiment was deployed to Texas during Reconstruction. The regiment also fought in the Indian Wars, and clashed with Geronimo and his Apache braves on more than one occasion.

The Eigth Cavalry Regiment was formed in 1866, and organized at Camp Reynolds, in Angel, California. Unsurprisingly,

many of its recruits were disappointed "forty-niners," and were reputed to be pretty wild characters. The regiment's first duties were to protect the settlers and travelers of Nevada, Colorado, Arizona, and New Mexico from opportunistic attacks from Apache and Navajo tribesmen. They often provided armed escorts. The Eigth also fought in the Apache Wars of southern New Mexico, and engaged with warriors from the Navajo, Comanche, and Kiowa tribes. As more settlers moved into the

Above: The Sixth U.S. Cavalry training their horses at Fort Bayard, New Mexico. Opposite page: A saddle-mounted carbine boot for the 1873 Springfield.

Above: Custer's favorite gun, a .50 caliber Remington single shot rifle.
Custer wrote to Remington praising the gun.

Left: The Sixth U.S. Cavalry practice saber exercise at Fort Bayard. The Fort was established in 1866 to protect miners and settlers along the Apache Trail.

Right: The Seventh Cavalry surrounded the Indian camp at Wounded Knee Creek with four of these Hotchkiss guns.

Below: The aftermath of the Wounded Knee Massacre that took place on December 29, 1890.

Northwestern states, the Eigth also undertook the longest-ever cavalry march in May, 1885. The march was two-thousand six-hundred miles long, to their two new regimental headquarters at Fort Meade, South Dakota, and Fort Keogh, Montana.

The involvement of the cavalry regiments in the Indian Wars ended in 1890 with the Massacre of Wounded Knee. During this period, the cavalry had mounted many protective operations for the people of the West, but had also been an instrument of United States Government policy. As well as facilitating the settling and civilizing of the western territories, their role had also included the dispossession and subjugation of the native peoples of the region.

Above: At least one-hundred and fifty men, women, and children of the Lakota Sioux tribe were killed at Wounded Knee. Another fifty people were wounded. Many of the casualties were fatally injured.

Left: Captured Apache warriors (including Geronimo) surrounded by cavalrymen. Geronimo gave himself up to First Lieutenant Charles B. Gatewood, but officially surrendered to General Nelson A. Miles on September 4, 1886 at Skeleton Canyon, Arizona.

Winchester 1873

Above: The heavy-duty steel frame and receiver enables the 1873 to use heavier centerfire ammunition.

Along with the Colt Peacemaker, the Winchester 1873 shared the reputation of being "the gun that won the West." A third weapon, the Springfield Model 1873 has also been awarded this sobriquet by some commentators. This reflected the large numbers of Western settlers that owned these three famous rifles. In reality, the frontier was all over by 1890 while the Winchester 1873 remained in production until 1919. This put the greater part of the model output well outside the period on which its fame rests. Nearly three-quarters of a million examples of the gun were manufactured during this time.

Horace Smith and Daniel Wesson formed the Volcanic Repeating Arms Company in 1855, in Norwich, Connecticut. Volcanic moved to New Haven, Connecticut in 1856, but the firm had become insolvent by the end of the year. Oliver Winchester purchased the bankrupt company and re-launched it as the New Haven Arms Company in April, 1857. After the Civil War, the company was re-named again, this time as the Winchester Repeating Arms Company. The first Winchester rifle, the Model 1866 was launched that year. It was a repeating rifle that could fire a number of shots before it needed to be reloaded. The Model 1873 was a steel-framed version of the earlier gun, lighter than the earlier brass-framed model. Gone was its pretty "yellow boy" appearance. Its extra strength also meant that the rifle could use more

Above: This example of the gun is embellished with nickel tacks.
This was a form of decoration favored by Native Americans.

A fine example of a handmade, hand-tooled, leather saddle scabbard.

powerful .44-40 inch centerfire cartridges. Each bullet was propelled by a cartridge that contained forty grains of black powder, which gave the Winchester excellent stopping-power. The popularity of the gun led Colt to manufacture a version of their famous Peacemaker chambered for the same powerful round. This meant that their ammunition was interchangeable, and a man only needed to carry one kind of cartridge.

Winchester produced three variants of the Model 1873: the rifle, carbine, and musket. The rifle version had a twenty-four inch barrel, while the carbine barrel was only twenty inches. This meant that the carbine became the most popular variant of the gun, because it was the most portable.

In 1950, Jimmy Stewart starred in the Anthony Mann movie, *Winchester '73*, which was inspired by the legend of this popular weapon. The character of Wyatt Earp also makes an appearance in the movie. Stewart's character, Lin McAdam, wins a Winchester rifle in a shooting contest by shooting through a tiny stamp. The film is set in 1876, and the shooting competition takes place just as the news of

Custer's Last Stand is spreading across the West. The movie was so successful that it was credited with reviving interest in antique firearms.

SPECIFICATIONS

Caliber: 0.44-40 inch

Length of barrel: 24 inches

Barrel shape: octagonal

Finish: blue/casehardened

Action: 15 shot lever action

Year of manufacture: 1890

Manufacturer: Winchester Repeating Arms Company, New Haven, Connecticut

Buffalo Soldiers

Opposite page: An immaculately-dressed African-American buffalo soldier, complete with bugle. The photograph dates from the 1870s.

African-American soldiers formed a significant part of the United States Cavalry in the post-bellum period. They became widely known as the "Buffalo Soldiers." "Colored" regiments were constituted by a July 1866 Act of Congress, which set out how segregated regiments would "increase and fix the Current Peace Establishment of the United States."

The term "Buffalo Soldiers" was coined by the Cheyenne tribe in 1867. It was inspired by their admiration of the fighting ability of the black soldiers, which they said matched the courage and stamina of the buffalo. The term was also a reference to the men's close cropped, curly black hair. There were four buffalo regiments; two cavalry (the ninth and the tenth), and two infantry (the Twenty-fourth and the Twenty-fifth). These soldiers became the first African-American soldiers to be recruited to the United States Army in peacetime. The men were mostly freed slaves, and many were Civil War veterans. Over one-hundred and eighty thousand black men had fought for the Union, and thirty-three thousand had fallen. These African-American soldiers were highly motivated by a desire for respect and for recognition of their first-rate soldiering. They won great admiration for their courage, and eighteen black combatants received the Congressional Medal of Honor for their part in the Civil War. These men wore the "Buffalo Soldiers" tag with pride.

Ironically, strict segregation meant that black soldiers constructed many forts and facilities that they were forbidden to use. Ultimately the Buffalo Soldiers formed twenty percent of the post-war cavalry and fought a hundred and seventy-seven engagements in the Indian Wars. Thirteen enlisted men and six officers from the Buffalo regiments won the Medal of Honor during this period. During the decades of the Indian Wars, the Buffalo Soldiers' uniform consisted of a flannel shirt worn under a dark blue blouse, light blue trousers tucked into over-the-knee boots, and a kepi cap decorated with the crossed saber and their regimental motto. The motto of the ninth was "Ready and Forward." That of the tenth was "We Can, We Will." When mounted, the cavalrymen wore a slouch campaign hat. Initially these were black, but became grayish-brown after 1874. Although the Buffalo Soldiers were not issued with regulation neckerchiefs, these were vital to protect them from the dust of the Plains, so most wore their own. These were usually yellow, red, or white. Like their white counterparts, the Buffalo Soldiers were armed with Springfield carbine rifles, Colt Single-Action Army Revolvers (Model 1873) in .45 caliber, and traditional cavalry sabers.

Above: A group of Buffalo Soldiers pose for a casual photograph.

The army's black cavalry and infantry regiments numbered around five thousand men, and formed at least ten percent of the soldiers who guarded the Western Frontier, which ran between Montana and Arizona. This duty lasted for a quarter of a century, between the end of the Civil War and the end of the Indian Wars (1891). By this time, the West was considered to have been "won."

Day-to-day life for Buffalo Soldiers was tough. Their rations were limited to beef, bacon, potatoes, beans, and a few fresh vegetables, with fruit or jam as an irregular treat. The men were on duty for seven days a week, with only the Fourth of July and Christmas Day given as holidays. Their living conditions were also grim, during the early post-Civil War years, most of their barracks were little better than dilapidated huts, poorly ventilated and full of vermin. These unhyginic surroundings led to outbreaks of dysentery, bronchitis, and diarrhea. Despite this, morale and standards of military discipline remained very high in the black regiments. When on duty, the men were drilled, paraded, and inspected regularly. They were also noted for the great pride they took in their uniforms.

On the positive side, Buffalo Soldiers were often offered a rudimentary education, and their poor living conditions were broadly similar to those endured by their white counterparts.

The Ninth U.S. Cavalry regiment was raised in July 1866, at the instigation of General Phillip Sheridan, as a segregated African-American unit. It was raised in Louisville, Kentucky, and consisted largely of men who had fought on the Union side during the Civil War. They were paid a salary of $13 per month, with their living expenses covered. The regime placed under the command of Colonel Edward Hatch. In June 1867, the regiment was ordered to Texas, charged with protecting the stage and mail routes, building and maintaining forts in the area, and establishing the civil law. The regiment was also involved in the famous Battle of Beecher Island, which took place in Colorado. Answering a call for help from Colorado's acting governor, Frank Hall, fifty handpicked men overpowered a combined force of over six hundred warriors from the Arapaho, Cheyenne, Brule, and Oglala Sioux tribes. The regiment suffered only six fatalities.

Between 1875 and 1881, the Ninth became increasingly involved in the Apache Wars. Their distinguished service included the heroic Battle of Tularosa, where

Left: A highly-decorated group of Buffalo Soldiers from the Tenth Cavalry Regiment.

Left: A standard cavalry uniform.

twenty-five cavalrymen fought off over a hundred Apache warriors until reinforcements arrived.

The Tenth Cavalry regiment was also a segregated African-American unit, and was also founded in 1866. Its headquarters were at Fort Leavenworth, Kansas. The regiment drew its recruits from Missouri, Arkansas, and the Platte. (The Platte was a large area of territory that was made up from Iowa, Nebraska. Dakota, Utah, and

Idaho.) The men of the Tenth Cavalry were of a notoriously high caliber. The regiment was led by white officers, and led by Civil War hero Benjamin Henry Grierson. Grierson had a great belief in the black soldiers he had recruited. For the next eight years, his men were based at several different forts in Kansas and Oklahoma. Their duties included protecting railway workers as they built the Kansas and Pacific railroad (between Kansas City and Denver). The railroad had a huge impact on the life of the West, and greatly increased the flow of settlers into the Great Plains. Grierson's men also built a considerable part of the region's telegraphic network, and Fort Sill, in Oklahoma. But they were also involved in direct combat with various Indian tribes, including the Cheyenne, Comanche, and

Above: The Buffalo Soldiers served cheerfully in a variety of roles. This troop is guarding Yosemite National Park around the turn of the 20th century.

Arapaho, and supported Sherman's winter campaigns of 1867 and 1868.

In 1875, the regiment was moved to Fort Concho in Texas. This was a return to their former role in the area: protecting the state's infrastructure, scouting unmapped territory, opening up new roads, and extending the telegraphic network. In other words, their job was to help civilize and tame this new territory, making it suitable for settlement. They were also the main law enforcers in the area, controlling outlaws, Indians, and Mexican revolutionaries.

Between 1879 and 1880, the Tenth was heavily involved in the Apache Wars, especially against the warriors of Apache chief Victorio, a violent protégé of Geronimo who was credited with the Alma Massacre of several settlers in April 1880. The regiment's most notable engagements took place at Tinaja de las Palmas and Rattlesnake Springs. They forced Victorio to retreat into Mexico, where he was finally killed by Mexican troops on October 14, 1880.

Despite the harsh discipline and conditions to which the men of the Tenth Cavalry were subjected, the regiment had the lowest desertion rate in the United States Army. The general level of desertion was extremely high at this time (in 1868, it stood at around twenty-five percent), but desertion was four times higher in white regiments than among the Buffalo Soldiers. Alcoholism was also much less common in black regiments.

Above: Victorio was the chief of the Chihenne band of the Chiricahua Apaches. He died on October 14, 1880.

Opposite page: A private from one of the six U.S. colored cavalry regiments raised by the Union to fight in the Civil War.

The Taming of Texas

Above: Stephen Austin recruited ten good men to protect the new territory of Texas. They were the nucleus of the Texas Rangers.

From their earliest days, the Texas Rangers were surrounded by the mystique of the Old West. Their role in the taming of the hugely important state of Texas cannot be under-estimated, and they were the closest thing to an official police force in the West. The service countered threats from wherever they arose: villains, insurgents, Indians, and bandits. It was dangerous work, and thirty Rangers fell in the line of duty during the years 1858 to 1901. By enforcing the law of the United States in Texas, the Rangers effectively brought the state into the Union, where it would become a crucial element in the culture and economy of the West. Today, the historical importance and symbolism of the Texas Rangers is such that they are protected by statute from being disbanded.

The origins of the Texas Rangers stretch back to the earliest days of European settlement in Texas, and the organization is now the oldest law enforcement agency in North America with statewide jurisdiction. At the beginning of the nineteenth century, Mexico controlled the territory of Texas. The entrepreneurial Moses Austin was keen to encourage settlement of the state, and petitioned Texas governor Antonio Maria Martinez to allow three hundred settlers into the region. Ultimately, permission was granted. Moses died in 1821, but his son Stephen put his father's plan into action. But Texas's Mexican rulers soon proved to be unable or unwilling, to protect the incomers from Indian attack. To counter the problem, Stephen Austin recruited a fledgling force of ten men in 1823, "to act as rangers for the common defense."

For the time, the idea was revolutionary, as contemporary law enforcement in the West was, at best, patchy and informal. Austen's original force of "ranging" law enforcers is credited as the forebear of the contemporary Texas Rangers. They went on to become not only an effective force for law enforcement, but also a focus of

Western values. They "ranged" the length and breadth of the new colony, protecting white settlers from attack by several Indian tribes, including the Comanche, Karankawa, Waco, Tehuacani, and Tonkawa. When no threat was apparent, the men were allowed to return to their own land and families.

A corps of professional, full-time Rangers was established a few years later. These men were paid $1.25 a day for "pay, rations, clothing, and horse service". In this way, the men were responsible for providing their own arms, mounts, and equipment. Rangers also had to buy their own weapons, and many carried examples of the newly-introduced Colt revolving pistols. Samuel Colt had founded the Colt Manufacturing Company in 1836, in Hartford, Connecticut.

Fewer than a thousand colonists had made it to Texas by 1821 (before the involvement of the Austins). But despite attempts by the Mexican government to

Above: The Gonzales Ranging Company of Mounted Volunteers was the only fighting force to answer Colonel Travis's desperate pleas for assistance in defending The Alamo from over five thousand Mexican troops.

Opposite page: The Battle of the Alamo was fought between February 23 and March 6, 1836. It was a pivotal event in the Texas Revolution. All but two of the Texian defenders were killed at the scene.

limit the number of American settlers, an estimated fifty thousand arrived between 1823 and 1836. Inevitably, this led to a schism of opposing interests opening up between the new American Texans and the government of Mexico. This ill feeling led to the wrongful imprisonment of Stephen F. Austin for over two years in Mexico City. He had been accused of "inciting revolution" against the Mexican regime, when he was actually negotiating for improved rights for the American settlers. Unsurprisingly, this dreadful experience converted Austin (who was to become the "Father of Texas") into a fervent believer in Texan independence. He went on to become a volunteer commander in the Texas Revolution.

When a provisional "rebel" Texan government, (known as the Permanent Council) was established by the Consultation of 1835, one of its first acts was to recruit twenty-five professional Rangers under the command of Silas M. Parker. Their primary duty was to range the frontier between Brazos and the Trinity. This force grew to three companies of fifty-six men, each commanded by a captain supported by first and second lieutenants. The three companies were commanded by a major.

Texan unrest flared into armed conflict on October 2, 1835, at the Battle of Gonzales. The Texas Revolution had begun. Hostilities raged for the following three months, until the Texan forces had defeated the Mexican troops in the region. On March 2, 1836, the Texans issued the Texas Declaration of Independence, effectively creating the Republic of Texas.

But as far as the Mexican government was concerned, the Texans were rebels who needed to be crushed. In early 1836, General Santa Anna led six thousand troops across the Rio Grande into the state. Many Texans fled to avoid his forces in what became known as the "Runaway Scrape." The Tumlinson Rangers fought a famous rearguard action to protect the shattered Texan army as it retreated, enabling it to re-group later, while other Rangers served as scouts for the Texan cause.

Buoyed by his success, Santa Anna headed towards the Alamo Mission. After a thirteen-day siege, his forces finally overcame the two hundred Texans who were defending the Mission. Every single Texan defender was killed, including James Bowie (inventor of the Bowie knife) and Davy Crockett. Santa Anna's army then swept on towards modern-day Houston. But by this time, many more settlers had joined the Texan army, now commanded by General Sam Houston. Houston's men were ultimately victorious at the Battle of San Jacinto, and Santa Anna was captured. He was forced to sign the Treaties of Velasco, which ended the war and granted

Texas its independence from Mexico. "The Last Stand" at the Alamo became a potent symbol of American resistance to foreign domination and was instrumental in Texas joining the Union in 1845.

In the heat of the revolution, Texans had served as both soldiers and Rangers. Some Rangers were drafted into cavalry regiments, where they were called dragoons. The Gonzales Ranging Company of Mounted Volunteers, for example, was the only fighting force to answer Colonel Travis's desperate plea for assistance in defending the Alamo from the overwhelming Mexican forces. The Rangers died heroically alongside the other defenders. Several other Rangers had been captured by General Santa Anna on his way to Houston, and were among the three hundred and fifty people that he ordered to be slaughtered on Palm Sunday 1836, in fields just outside Goliad. Sam Houston's battle cry at San Jacinto had been, "Remember the Alamo, Remember Goliad." Several individual Rangers were also noted for the contributions they made during the war, including Jack Hays, Ben McCulloch, Samuel Walker, and "Bigfoot" Wallace.

The Rangers had played a critical role in achieving Texan victory, and the service gained a great deal of recognition after independence. Government investment meant that Service also became much better equipped. In 1839, the Rangers became the first civilian force to be armed with Colts. Texas bought one-hundred and eighty Colt Patterson No. 5 Holster Model revolving pistols to arm the force. Samuel Colt had patented the gun's revolving mechanism in 1835. The weapon became known as the Texas Patterson. Samuel Walker, a Ranger who rode with Captain Jack Hays, wrote to Samuel Colt, "The pistols which you made... have been in use by the Rangers for three years... In the summer of 1844, Col. J. Hays with fifteen men fought about eighty Camanche [*sic*] Indians, boldly attacking them on their own ground, killing and wounding about half their number... Without your pistols, we would not have had the confidence to have undertaken such daring adventures."

Ultimately, the Rangers' frontier patrols were instrumental in establishing the current border between the United States and Mexico, although there were continual skirmishes along the Rio Grande for the next ten years. The Rangers continued to make punitive strikes in Mexico into the twentieth century. In one 1917 battle, it is thought that the Rangers may have killed as many as twenty Mexicans. Despite this, ethnic Mexicans and Native Americans have both become members of the Rangers Service. An Indian nicknamed Bravo Too Much rode with the most famous early Ranger, Jack Hays, in the 1830s.

Opposite page: A buckskin-clad Texas Ranger from the early years of the service.

Although Texan independence had been achieved, the work of the Rangers was far from over. The state still needed protection from Indian attack, and the rule of law needed to be established. The Rangers proved to be a cost-effective way of achieving both of these aims. Their role became more internal, and although they had been known as "los diablos Tejanos" (The Texas Devils) for their effectiveness against Mexican guerrillas, the responsibility for defending the international border was gradually devolved upon the United States army.

The next great conflict in which the Rangers were involved was the Civil War. Many enlisted in "Terry's Texas Rangers." Commanded by the brilliant Colonel E. Terry, the Rangers became part of the Army of Tennessee between 1861 and 1865, and were a great boost to the strength of the Confederate Army.

In the postbellum period of Reconstruction, the role of the Rangers was assumed by the highly political and widely disliked Texas

Above: Jack Ford led the Texas Rangers in pursuit of the notorious Mexican-American renegade Juan Cortina.

State Police, who were charged with the implementation of the deeply unpopular "carpetbagger" laws. This force was seen as an instrument of the Union, and was highly unpopular with Texans. When Governor Richard Coke was elected in 1873, one of his first acts was to re-commission Texas Rangers. In 1874, the Texas Legislature ordered the formation of two Ranger forces. These were the Frontier Battalion, led by Major John B. Jones, and the Special Force, led by Captain Leander

McNelly. Their formation was to herald one of the most successful periods in the history of the service.

The legislation of 1874 was a defining moment in the history of the service. Rangers became officers of the peace, rather than fighting men serving in a semi-military organization, and their authority was acknowledged state-wide.

Although victory in the Texas Revolution had secured the state's international boundaries, the upheaval of the Civil War had led to a surge in internal lawlessness. The Rangers developed their role as law enforcers while continuing their fight against insurgents. They effectively neutralized the formerly powerful Comanche, Kiowa, and Apache tribes by succeeding in famous skirmishes such as the Battle of Plum Creek. The new Rangers also brought over three thousand Texan desperados to justice, including the train robber Sam Bass in 1878 and the sadistic gunfighter John Wesley Hardin. Hardin was reputed to have killed thirty-one men, but legend has it that he was captured single-handed by Ranger John B. Armstrong. Armstrong attacked him, wielding a long-barrelled Colt .45, shouting "Texas, by God!" Armstrong's hat was pierced by a bullet, but he was uninjured.

Effectively, the Rangers brought Texas under control from internal lawlessness and external threat. This made it possible for law-abiding settlers to make the state their home, and enabled Texas to become an extremely important region of the American West.

Above: This anonymous daguerreotype portrait is believed to be the only one showing a Texas Ranger wearing full battle dress.

Remington Rolling Block Rifle

Below: The distinctive design of the Remington rifle
clearly distinguishes it from other Western arms.

Right: Custom made backsight
is a specialty of Carlos Gove.

Lieutenant Colonel George Armstrong Custer was one of the
larger than life characters of the West. Western novelist Louis
L'Amour tells us how Custer's troops cleaned up towns like Fargo-
in-the Timber, "Destroying local villains like Jack O 'Neil."

Custer's time on the frontier with the US Cavalry was not
just spent quelling Indians. He also took time off to go hunting
in Yellowstone National Park, where he used his favorite weapon,
a Remington Rolling Block Sporting rifle. In a letter written to
the Remington Company on October 5th 1873 from his base at
Fort Abraham Lincoln, Custer claimed that he killed far more
game than all the other professional shots on the trip.

It is easy to think of rifles like the Winchester 1873 as the
standard equipment for Western shots, but the Rolling Block rifle
also made its mark. In the years following the Civil War, Remington

SPECIFICATIONS

Caliber: 0.40-.70 inch

Length of barrel: 30 inches

Barrel shape: Octagonal

Finish: Blue casehardened

Grips: Walnut

Action: Single shot/breech loading

Year of manufacture: 1874

Manufacturer: Remington/C.
Gove & Co., Denver Armory, 340
Blake Street, Denver,
Colorada

was preoccupied with chasing lucrative military contracts, but many rifles were also sold to sportsmen and hunters. They were generally used for larger game, where a powerful, large-caliber weapon was required. "The Remington system" as it was correctly known, was developed by Joseph Rider as an improvement to his split-breech concept, which was used on war models. The gun was a single-shot breech-loader that would take a heavy charge center-fire cartridge, based

But the US Navy did order significant quantities of Rolling Block rifles and carbines, and this contributed greatly to Remington's success. The company must have been particularly pleased when a famed western hero and serving soldier like Custer praised their products.

Our featured gun has been converted to under-lever action by Carlos Gove, the pioneer gun-maker of Denver, and has double-set triggers. Carlos Gove rebuilt guns using this technique from 1873-77. The gun was handed down through a Western family for several generations, having been given to Charlie Robbie, the original owner, for killing an Indian at the Sand Creek Massacre.

Below: Checkered stock and double-set trigger show that this was a real shooter's gun.

on the design of army sharpshooter Colonel Hiram Berdan. Ultimately, however, the US Army decided in favor of rifles with the Allin 'trap door' action. This was a cheaper option, as Allin was a government employee and the government could avoid paying a royalty to use the system.

The Wagon Train

Opposite page: Children formed a large percentage of the pioneers that made their way to the West. Many died on the journey from disease and accidents.

The territory of America was hugely enlarged in the first half of the nineteenth century. Jefferson's 1803 Louisiana Purchase of the land between the Mississippi and the Rocky Mountains River for fifteen million dollars was quickly followed by the acquisition of Oregon (1821), Texas (1845), and a large chunk of the West in 1848. This consisted of California, Nevada, Utah, Arizona, New Mexico, and part of Colorado. Alaska was bought from Russia in 1867. This expansion of American territory opened up great opportunities for settlement in the lands to the West, and inspired the "Great Migration" across the Rockies. This was to become the greatest mass relocation in American history. A steady flow of wagons, carts, and carriages left the eastern states across a network of trails; the Bozeman, Oregon, California, Mormon, Santa Fe, and Applegate. The two thousand-mile long Oregon and California trails were perhaps the best-trodden. In the nineteenth century, over two hundred thousand pioneers followed this route. The first trickle of westward emigration over this land route began in 1841, when fifty-eight settlers set out westwards.

Newspaper editor John O'Sullivan described this phenomenon as America's "Manifest Destiny, to overspread the continent."

Right: Many pioneers travelled to the West in trains of covered wagons. They banded together for safety and mutual assistance.

Before the Gold Rush, most westward emigration was motivated by the desire for freedom and farmland. According to English settler George Fromer, there was "good land dog-cheap everywhere" in the West. Under the Homestead Act of 1862, settlers were allowed to claim one-hundred and sixty acres for around ten dollars if they settled the land for at least five years.

Above and opposite page: These two images provide a stark contrast between a romantic view of the Western wilderness, and the reality of the harsh terrain.

Before they trekked west, most immigrants sold everything they owned – farms, animals, and household goods – to invest the money in their new life. Most were farmers, while some were artisans. James Marshall's discovery of gold at Sutter's Mill on January 24, 1848, was also a great stimulus to the westward diaspora, motivating more than eighty thousand people to hit the trails. Most of these were

Right: Most wagon trains consisted of between forty and fifty wagons. These are being drawn by oxen.

Above: Freezing accounted for around five per cent of emigrant deaths on the trail. The winter of 1856 was notoriously harsh.

single men, but some women insisted on accompanying their husbands, preferring the hardships of the trail to becoming "Gold Rush widows." Many disappointed gold seekers decided to stay in the West, and reverted to being either farmers or ranchers.

The Mormons also made up a large proportion of the westward emigrants. They first proclaimed their intention to "send out into the western country… a company of pioneers" in January 1846. By 1860, of the forty thousand white settlers in Utah, almost all were Mormons. When the railroad was introduced in 1869, their numbers swelled to over eighty thousand.

Preparation for the long and arduous journey could take many weeks and months. The trekkers knew that they would pass no settlements on their way west,

and needed to carry all of their requirements with them for the next four or five months. The typical pioneer's outfit consisted of one or two small farm wagons, six to ten oxen, one or two cows, food for the journey, clothing, and utensils. Heavy possessions, such as pianos, stoves, and furniture were usually shipped to the West Coast. Provisions were perhaps the most critical element of the outfit. Taking enough flour, biscuits, bacon, coffee, tea, sugar, lard, rice, beans, eggs, corn meal, and dried fruit was absolutely critical to the success of the enterprise. The settlers also packed guns, farm and carpentry tools, cooking utensils, and crop seeds. Women pioneers often oversaw the packing of the wagons that were to carry their families to the frontier. Their aptitude for this crucial task could mean the difference between life and death.

Below: Few people actually rode the unsprung wagons. They were too uncomfortable, and the extra weight took too great a toll on the draft animals. Most pioneers walked to the West.

Above and opposite page: The Mormon pioneers left Nauvoo, Illinois on February 4, 1846, under the leadership of Brigham Young. Their destination was the Great Salt Lake Basin in Utah. Brigham Young first reached the Great Salt Lake Valley on July 24, 1847.

Many trekkers also carried one of the many published trail guides, some of which were completely misleading and dangerous.

The wagons themselves were also critical to the success of the enterprise. They needed to be strong enough to haul heavy cargoes over thousands of miles of the road-less wilderness, but light enough not to tire the animals that pulled them. Most were constructed from seasoned hardwood, usually maple, hickory, or oak. Minimal iron was used to keep the weight down. The "lubrication" system for the spring-less wagons consisted of a bucket of tar and tallow dangling from the rear axle. The wagon cover was made from canvas or cotton, and it was designed to shield the wagon from rain, dust, and sun. Another important decision was the choice of draft animal: mules or oxen. Mules were stronger and faster, but unruly. Oxen needed little grazing and were extremely strong, and were the choice of approximately three-quarters of the pioneers. Whatever the pioneers' choice of animal, they became more and more valuable with every mile they covered.

Once on the trail, life was very tough. Treasured personal possessions that had been packed with loving care were often discarded along the trail, and many travelers lost their children or spouses on the journey. Their pathetic graves were often marked only with unnamed headstones. Pioneers died from a variety of causes, accidents, and diseases. The single greatest cause of accidental death was being run over by wagon wheels. Children were especially vulnerable. Accidental shootings were also common. Other deaths were caused by fights between emigrants, lightning, grassfires, snakebites, hail storms, and even suicide.

Opposite page, above: An early photograph of Salt Lake City.
Opposite page, below: Brigham Young established way stations like Cove Fort, Utah to provide shelter to the Mormon pioneers on their way west.

Below: Around ten percent of the Mormon pioneers made their way to Utah pushing a handcart. Lacking the funds for ox or horse teams, over three thousand pioneers joined ten handcart companies.

Disease was also a serious issue on the trail. Cholera was common, and usually fatal. A person could sicken and die in just a few hours, to be buried at the trailside. Smallpox, flu, mumps, measles, and tuberculosis were highly contagious and could wipe out an entire wagon camp.

Indian attacks weren't too much of a problem for the early pioneers, as most Indian tribes were tolerant towards the pioneer wagon trains. Some even traded with the white settlers. It is estimated that only three hundred and sixty-two emigrants were killed by Indians in the years between 1840 and 1860 (while emigrants had killed four hundred and twenty-six Indians). There was much more tension in later years, when the decimation of the buffalo herds left the tribes bitter and hungry.

It is estimated that at least a tenth of the pioneers that set out on the Oregon Trail died on the way west, so there were at least twenty thousand deaths en route. Most were buried at the side of the trail with unmarked headstones.

Camp life soon became routine on the long journey. Typically, a bugler blew a trumpet at four to wake the camp. The pioneers would then round up their cattle and fixed a breakfast of bacon, corn porridge, or "Johnny cakes" made from flour and water. Everything was then packed, and a trumpeter signaled a "Wagons Ho" to start the journey. With a single rest at noon, the wagons kept rolling along the

Right: An abandoned prairie schooner. Wagon productions greatly increased with migration to the West. In the mid-1800s, Studebaker advertized that they turned out a new wagon every seven minutes. Hugely important to so many pioneer families, wagons became one of the most evocative symbols of the American West.

Above: *The Wagons,* painted by Charles M. Russell (1865-1926). A group of Native American braves watch the dust cloud raised by a faraway wagon train.

trail until evening fell. The families then ate supper and settled down for the night. Even in the extremely difficult circumstances of the trail, pioneer women were still expected to discharge their housekeeping duties. Hampered by their long skirts and impractical equipment, the simplest task became extremely arduous. One women pioneer, Lodisa Frizzel, described how tough it was: "All our work here requires stooping. Not having tables, chairs, or anything. It is very hard on the back." Another traveler, Helen Carpenter, complained about the monotony of the trail diet. "One does like a change, and about the only change we have from bread and bacon is bacon and bread."

The harsh journey took its toll on the pioneers. Miriam Davis described how she could hardly recognize herself at the end of it. "I have cooked so much in the sun and smoke that I hardly know who I am and when I look into the little looking glass ask, 'Can this be me?'"

Below: A pioneer family poses by their overturned wagon in east Oregon. They are accompanied by their black servant.

Boomers, Sooners, and Moonshiners

Above: President Abraham Lincoln.

Right: The Land Claims Office at Round Point, Oklahoma Territory, in January 1894.

Over a period of less that a century, the rush to settle the West meant that only a few areas of virgin land survived until the mid-1880s. By this time, Indian Territory had become the final frontier. Although more than fifty-five Native American tribes occupied parts of this designated territory to the west of the Mississippi, the vast majority of the land was uninhabited. This huge area was called the Oklahoma District. *Harper's Weekly* described it as "the last barrier of savagery in the United States."

President Abraham Lincoln signed the original Homestead Act on May 20, 1862. The act stated that any settler could claim one hundred and sixty acres of undeveloped federal land. The army became involved, clearing the land of illegal squatters, and organized the first great land run on April 22, 1889. This was supposed to give every settler an equal opportunity to claim the best land of the Oklahoma District. As the bugles blew at precisely noon on that day, over 100,000 "Boomers" cycled, rode trains, and drove wagons into the territory. Unfortunately, these fair-minded individuals were in many cases pre-empted by the so-called "Sooners," who had already sneaked into the Oklahoma District and

Right: Men from Troop C of the Fifth U.S. Cavalry, photographed with squatters they arrested in Indian Territory (before the area became Oklahoma).

Below: The first blacksmith shop in Guthrie, Oklahoma Territory, circa 1889.

claimed some of the best plots. The unscrupulous Sooners were often deputy marshals, surveyors, or railroad workers whose work had given them access to the district and an opportunity to study the land.

A third category of settlers, the "Moonshiners," also jumped the gun, sneaking through the lines of soldiers to get onto the territory by the light of the moon.

By nightfall on April 22, an amazing 1.92 million acres of the Unassigned Lands had been claimed. At the same time, Guthrie, which was to become Oklahoma's first state capital, was already a tent city of fifteen thousand. Within five days of the land run, the first wooden buildings were already being raised in the town. By September that year, Guthrie had three newspapers, a hotel, three general stores, and fifty saloons. Across the territory, everything necessary for civilized life sprang up almost at once. Tradesmen established their businesses, and three men set up a bank with money they had printed themselves. They used a potbellied stove as their vault.

Within weeks, the Oklahoma District was scattered with embryonic new cities, including Oklahoma City, Stillwater, Norman, and Kingfisher. Under the Organic

Overleaf: The clerical workers of the U.S. Lane Office at Perry, Oklahoma, photographed with the area's U.S. deputy marshals on October 12, 1893.

Opposite page, top: W. H. McCoy's land claim at Perry, Oklahoma Territory. He is photographed with his friends and servants on October 1, 1893.

Act of 1890, the Oklahoma District became the Oklahoma Territory. Further land rushes opened up more and more land to settlement, although the land was now allocated by ballot. The largest of these took place in 1893, when the six million-acre Cherokee Outlet was distributed among a hundred thousand new settlers. This strip of land was fifty-seven miles wide and contained six million acres of some of the best land that the U.S. government ever offered to its settlers. The land grab began the instant that a pistol shot rang out on September 16, 1893. The treeless plains were instantly filled with the turmoil of thousands of thundering wagons, driven by dust-encrusted Boomers sweeping towards the town of Perry. The fastest run into the territory is attributed to Jack Teamey, a tax collector from Guthrie. He

Above: Hell's Half Acre, Perry, Oklahoma Territory. The tent town was photographed in 1893.

Opposite page, bottom: The Wild West Hotel on Calamity Avenue in Perry, Oklahoma Territory. The photograph was taken in September 1893.

made it from the county line (just north of Orlando) to Perry in thirty-one minutes. By four o'clock the same afternoon, he was serving beer at his new enterprise, a tent saloon called the Blue Bell. Beer was sold at a dollar a bottle, and it is reputed that over thirty-eight thousand glasses were drunk after the thirsty work of the day. Perry's recreational district, which soon became known as Hell's Half-Acre soon had no fewer than a hundred and ten saloons and gambling houses.

It was not until November 16, 1907, that Oklahoma became a state in its own right, when President Theodore Roosevelt signed a proclamation to that effect.

In the early twentieth century, the discovery of "black gold" in the state led to a great influx of wealth, and many of Oklahoma's most prestigious families made their fortunes at this time.

Left: Temporary banks and an early lodging house in Perry, Oklahoma Territory.

Colt 1882 Sheriff's (Storekeeper's) revolver

In the 1880s, Colt introduced an extremely wide model range, from concealable derringers to hammerless shotguns. This meant that they had no single competitor. Smith & Wesson produced rival models to Colt's handguns.

The Colt 1882 Sheriff's (Storekeeper's) revolver was a derivative of the 1873 single-action model. The sheriff's revolver is without the ejector rod of its counterpart. This gun was produced by Colt in many versions and calibers between 1882 and 1898, and around 70,000 were made. For a compact weapon it still packed a considerable punch, using the full-size model's 45 caliber center-fire ammunition. Shortened handguns were convenient for concealment and quick to draw, and thus found use for both defensive and offensive firing.

Left: A genuine early example of the gun, with a good original finish, can be worth $30,000.

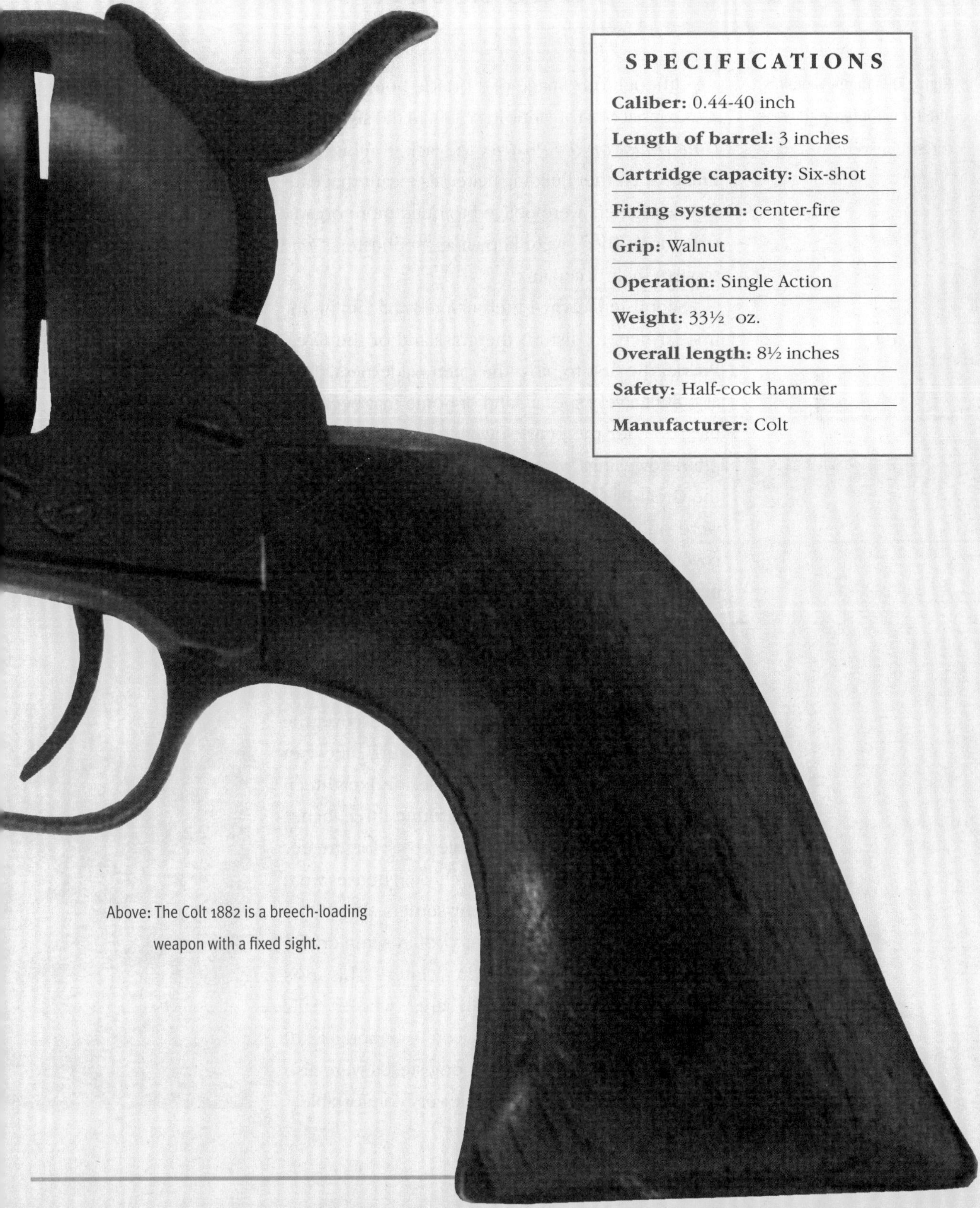

SPECIFICATIONS

Caliber: 0.44-40 inch

Length of barrel: 3 inches

Cartridge capacity: Six-shot

Firing system: center-fire

Grip: Walnut

Operation: Single Action

Weight: 33½ oz.

Overall length: 8½ inches

Safety: Half-cock hammer

Manufacturer: Colt

Above: The Colt 1882 is a breech-loading
weapon with a fixed sight.

Sodbusters

Right: This family's prairie shelter is roofed with grass turfs.

Although our image of a prairie home tends to consist of a romantic log cabin in the style of the *Little House on the Prairie*, the lack of indigenous timber and other building materials meant that early frontier settlers were obliged to build more organic structures. These were known as "sodbusters," and so were their occupants.

Sodbusters earned their name by becoming the first farmers to disturb the grassland of the Great Prairie; the first to plow the open wilderness. They also built a very special kind of home that became a nickname for the prairie-dwellers later. These early prairie dwellings were made from the virgin turf of the Great Plains itself. Some of these "sodbusters" were built into banks and hillsides, "dug in like coyotes," as one woman homesteader described it, but others were freestanding.

In the construction of these unusual homesteads, only the window frames and doors were made using timber. The walls were raised with buffalo grass sods, which were also used to cover the roof. The sods were strips of prairie turf, between twelve and eighteen inches wide, and eighteen inches long. They were usually around three inches deep. They were laid in double rows for greater strength. Even the newcomers' chicken houses were built with these materials. Many settlers also built a "cave" to keep their provisions cool in summer and stop them from freezing in winter. This was particularly important in an area whose daily temperature fluctuates between -30 and +110 degrees Fahrenheit. The sod homesteads were also thermally efficient, and could be very comfortable.

Opposite page: The interior of a large log cabin provides a warm and sociable indoor space.

With an annual rainfall of just fifteen inches, it was very hard to grow grain on the prairie, and the sodbusters' 160-acre plots provided enough grazing for only eight cows. Despite this, many settlers fell in love with the wonderful landscape of the Badlands and their peaceful lives there, with just prairie dogs and gophers for company.

Sod homes may have been the first residences of the new settlers, but the coming of the railroad meant that conventional building materials could be shipped into the area. At this time, many sodbusters were replaced by log cabins. But timber

Right: The first log cabins provided speedy shelter on the frontier, but many were comfortable and homey inside.

remained a scarce and expensive resource on the virtually treeless plains. Homesteaders still had to haul logs for many miles from railheads, or from isolated groves of hardwood trees.

Settlers that managed to acquire enough elm and cottonwood logs used them to build extremely practical and adaptable structures, which could be extended when necessary. The logs were notched at the corners to make rigid boxes, and "chinking" between the logs provided insulation. The chinking consisted of thin strips of wood which were pushed into the gaps between the logs and covered with a daub of earth and prairie grass. Cabin roofs were made from hand-split red oak or cedar shakes. Some of these log cabins were even whitewashed. But the continued scarcity of materials meant that most prairie cabins were much smaller than those in other areas. Typically, they measured just sixteen by eighteen feet,

Left: This cabin shows details of the corner joints, where the logs are neatly squared off, and the chinking used to fill any gaps between the logs. This home has an extra half-story, which was probably used for sleeping.

Right: Early settlers were known as sodbusters because they were the first to plow the virgin prairie turf. John Deere made his name by designing the first non-sticking steel plow in 1836, which turned the prairie sod into a fertile growing medium.

Below: This cabin is built from completely unshaped logs, but they fit together snugly.

and were built facing south, to catch the warmth of the sun.

The ongoing timber shortage ensured the popularity of the next building method introduced to the plains: framing. Frame homes used far less wood than log cabins, and were both sturdier and more weather proof. They were also simple

to build, as they required no foundations, and they proved to be extremely durable.

Plains homes representative of all three building methods survive today, and many have been preserved. Some of the early homes are still occupied, giving shelter to modern plainsmen and women.

Western Towns

Opposite page: Abilene, Kansas looked south from Third Street and Cedar. The photograph was taken in 1882.

The look and feel of Old Western towns is so completely familiar to us that we can easily imagine walking down the dusty boardwalk and through a pair of swing doors into the saloon. The classic frontier town looks flimsy, like an ephemeral movie set, and the insubstantial, flat-fronted buildings have a wonderful cinematic quality.

Real Western towns usually started as one-street settlements, with hitching rails in front of the buildings. In the early days, this main thoroughfare would be lined with archetypal Western institutions: saloons, trading posts, sheriffs' offices, livery stables, banks, gunsmiths, and telegraph offices. As the town became more established, a Wells Fargo office, Texas Rangers' office, newspaper office, barbershop, town jail, apothecary, dentist, photographer, or hotel might also open

Right: J. Mueller's shoe shop in Ellsworth, Kansas. Photographed in 1872.

Above: The church formed an important focus for early Western communities.

Previous pages: Wichita, Kansas in 1871. The town consisted of a street of false-fronted wooden buildings.

for business. Many towns also catered to the more spiritual side of life by establishing a church, and every town of the Old West required its own cemetery. Some of these were soon full.

Above: A more developed Western townscape, with brick and slate-roofed buildings, but cattle still wander unchecked.

Right: The commissary at Fort Smith, Arkansas. Judge Parker lodged here for some time.

Thousands of Western towns sprang up in the region as frontier life developed. They grew up at railheads, along cattle trails, near gold fields and silver mines, and around military forts. They were often isolated and surrounded by miles of empty, threatening wilderness. From the outset, Western civilization was completely different that than of the East. The landscape was bigger, and the towns were smaller.

The early establishment of law and order was crucial to the development of

Right: The St. James Saloon in Dodge City, Kansas. The interior is typical of Western bars of the period.

Above: St. Louis, Missouri became the center of the American beer industry when John Adam Lemp established his brewery there in 1840.

these townships into permanent settle-ments. Where this proved impossible, towns were often abandoned. Towns whose water or gold ran out, or those bypassed by the railroads or cattle trails, also died out, leaving very few traces.

Life on the frontier was extremely volatile, and new arrivals searched about restlessly, looking for land and opportunity. Many new towns were founded, and abandoned just a few years later.

The saloon was often the first business opened in a Western town, and might start out as just a tent or lean-to. When it became more permanent, it often doubled as a public meetinghouse. Brown's Hole, opened in 1822 near the Wyoming-

Above: The Bijou Saloon in Round Pond, Oklahoma, photographed in 1894.

Left: Every Western main street had its saloon.

Opposite page: A typical
parlor girl in a friendly pose.

Colorado-Utah border was the first drinking house that became known as a saloon. It catered to the region's fur trappers. In this male-dominated region, saloons were crucial to the early development of Western towns, which often had more than one. The prevalence of bars and drinking holes was often completely disproportionate to a town's population. Livingston, Montana, had a population of only three

Above: Crapper Jack's
Dance hall in Cripple Creek,
Colorado.

thousand people, but no fewer than thirty-three saloons. Saloons often served liquor (whiskey, bourbon, rye, and beer) twenty-four hours a day, and their clientele reflected a cross-section of the West's white male population. These men included cowboys, gunmen, lawmen, and gamblers. Women, Chinese, and African-Americans were unwelcome, and it was actually illegal for Indians to enter. Of course, the barring of women did not extend to the saloon girls who worked in the establishments, selling over-priced drinks to the customers and keeping them company. It is estimated that most towns provided at least one prostitute per hundred men.

Many proprietors of Western saloons were gunfighters on either side of the law. These included Wyatt Earp, Bob Ford (Jesse James's killer), Doc Holliday, and Wild Bill Hickok. Many of these men were also professional gamblers.

Left: The Western general store retailed a range of goods brought to the West by rail.

Opposite page: An elaborate whiskey decanter dating from the 1880s.

As the West became more sophisticated, saloons began to offer a variety of entertainment including fine dining, billiards, singing, dancing, and bowling. The Gold Rush meant that many more professional men (including doctors, attorneys, and precious metal specialists) whose tastes were more sophisticated, made their

Right: The cozy interior of a western general store with a range of goods for pioneer families.

way to the West. But the primary saloon pastimes continued to be drinking and gambling. Almost every saloon had a poker table, and many different card games were played. Of course, gaming often led to violence, and this regularly spilled out onto the street. A complex "bar etiquette," which governed the buying and accepting of drinks, prevailed in these drinking dens. Breeches of this unwritten code could also lead to serious trouble.

Above: Hotels reflected the increased mobility of Western life.

Equally important to every town was its general store, or trading post. Without it, it would be almost impossible for a town to get off the ground. It has often been remarked that some of the biggest fortunes made in the Old West were made not by miners or settlers, but by the tradesmen who supplied them. Depending on the location of the town, the store would stock farm supplies, mining equipment, or cowboy gear. They

Colt Lightning Storekeeper

Above: The gun was usually given a two-tone finish, but was sometimes nickel-plated.

This gun has a crisp-checkered hard rubber grip, but some examples had rosewood grips.

A shortened revolver of the kind which became popular during the later frontier period when clothing became more Easternized. The weapons could be more easily concealed in a coat pocket or a waistband. Some were carried in purpose-made shoulder holsters by companies like H.H.Heiser of Denver.This Storekeeper model was based on the 1877 Colt Lightning double-action revolver, which quickly became popular with lawmen and gunslingers alike. John Wesley Hardin was

carrying a .38 Colt Lightning revolver with a 2-inch barrel the day he was killed.

Although Colt's early attempts at double action were not flawless, the gun was quicker in getting off multiple shots –not having to be re-cocked between shots like its predecessor, the 1873 single-action.

The Colt Lightning double-action Storekeeper's model revolver came in .38 caliber, typically with a 2½-inch barrel, nickel or blued finish, and hardrubber

SPECIFICATIONS

Caliber: .38 inch

Length of barrel: 2½ inches

Cartridge capacity: Six

Finish: Blue or nickel

Grip: Hard Rubber

Action: Double action

Year of manufacture: 1878-1905

Manufacturer: Colt

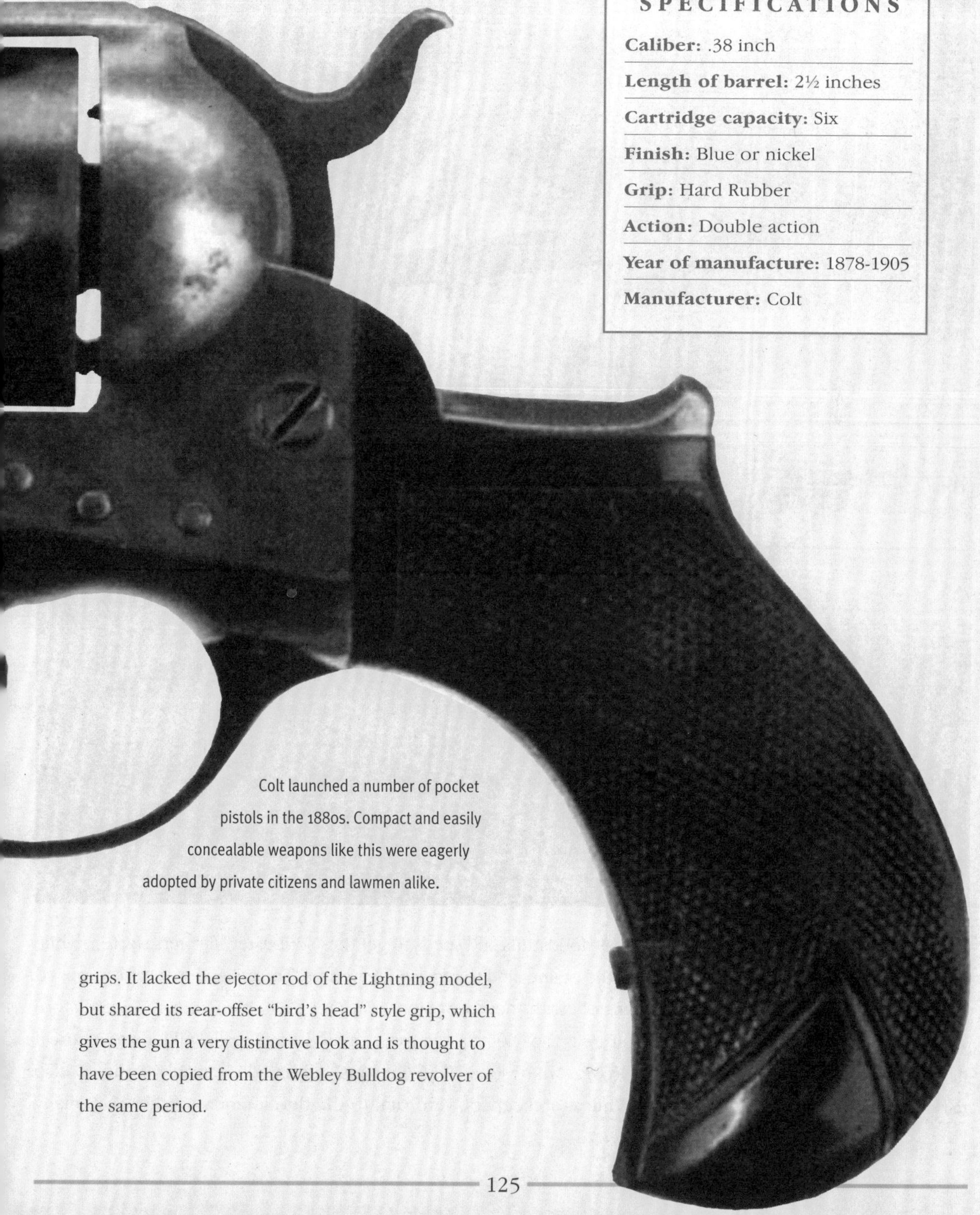

Colt launched a number of pocket pistols in the 1880s. Compact and easily concealable weapons like this were eagerly adopted by private citizens and lawmen alike.

grips. It lacked the ejector rod of the Lightning model, but shared its rear-offset "bird's head" style grip, which gives the gun a very distinctive look and is thought to have been copied from the Webley Bulldog revolver of the same period.

Above: Early Western towns were built entirely from lumber. In this sawmill, the water wheel is attached to the saw blade by a connecting rod known as a pitman arm.

also carried basic foodstuffs and seeds to get the "sodbuster" farmers started, while they prepared the prairie land to receive their crops. The general store also supplied the local townsfolk with their provisions. Perhaps the most famous Western store in popular culture is the Olesons' general store in Laura Ingalls Wilder's hometown of Walnut Grove, Minnesota. The Olesons' ambiguous social status is also interesting. While storekeepers were vital to the development of the West, many used their virtual monopolies to charge hyper-inflationary prices, and became very unpopular with their fellow townsfolk. On the other hand, many general stores and trading posts were great social centers, where news and gossip were exchanged.

As more "honest" women made their way west to join their men folk, frontier towns gradually developed the services that families needed, including medical care and education. Many well-educated young women came west to teach in the one-room schoolhouses of the region, braving loneliness and hardship to teach in very difficult conditions. Equally, many newly-qualified doctors moved west for adventure and experience, and stayed because they were so highly valued by the people of the frontier. Towns that adapted to this more "normalized" existence tended to survive, and develop a life of their own.

But after a few years of manic prosperity, many other Western towns simply disappeared from the map. The region is scattered with ghostly, abandoned settlements, whose eerie streets have not heard a footstep, or a hoofbeat, for many years.

Below and overleaf: Ghost towns and abandoned buildings litter the open spaces of the West.

Pony Express Riders

Opposite page: Frank E. Webner, the famous Pony Express rider.

Despite being one of the shortest-lived institutions of the Old West, the Pony Express has achieved a legendary status. This is undoubtedly due to the extraordinary caliber of the mail riders themselves. These men (or boys, as most of them were) have become synonymous with extreme courage, resilience, and toughness. Their spirit was the essence of the West itself. Not only did they have to counter the rigors of the trail and the dramatic weather conditions of the region, but also attacks from Indians and wild animals.

William H. Russell established the Pony Express in 1859, and set up a company with his partners William B. Waddell and Alexander Majors. His ambition was to deliver mail by an overland route from coast to coast in ten days or less, all year round. Before Russell's enterprise, mail from New York to the West travelled by steamship around South America, and this journey took at least thirty days. One of the stimuli behind the business was the start of the Civil War; Russell believed that the need for communication between the East and West was now critical. The first shipment of mail left Washington, DC by train on March 31, 1860. Three days later on April 3, a lone Pony Express rider left Pikes Peak Stables in St. Joseph, Missouri. Russell's Central Overland California and Pikes Peak Express Company used a carefully worked out route that ran for 1,966 miles between St. Joseph, Missouri, and Sacramento, California. The trail crossed plains, prairies, and deserts, and scaled mountain passes. To make the immense journey possible, Russell established stations at approximately ten-mile intervals, employing four hundred station hands, purchasing five hundred horses, and arranging for Iowan grain to be shipped to each station. He also advertised for express riders, specifying that he wanted "young, skinny, wiry fellows not over eighteen...expert riders, willing to risk death daily. Orphans preferred." He wasn't joking, but had soon gathered the two hundred candidates he needed. Most were younger than twenty years of age and weighed less than one-

Above: Although Pony Express ceased trading in 1866, Wells Fargo retained the famous logo until 1890.

PONY EXPRESS

St. JOSEPH, MISSOURI to CALIFORNIA
in 10 days or less.

☞ WANTED ☜

YOUNG, SKINNY, WIRY FELLOWS

not over eighteen. Must be expert
riders, willing to risk death daily.
Orphans preferred.
Wages $25 per week.

APPLY, **PONY EXPRESS STABLES**
St. JOSEPH, MISSOURI

hundred and twenty-five pounds. For their death-defying efforts, they were paid between $100 and $150 a month.

Before they could ride for the Pony Express, each rider had to take an oath of service, stating, "I agree not to use profane language, not to get drunk, not to gamble, not to treat animals cruelly, and not to do anything else that is incompatible with the conduct of a gentleman." Each rider covered between seventy-five and a hundred miles a day at the gallop, with an average speed of ten miles per hour. They changed their mounts for fresh ones at the stations Russell had established.

Above: the Pony Express route followed the Oregon, California, and Mormon Trails and the Central Nevada Route before crossing the Sierras into California.

According to legend, John Fry was the first westbound rider, and James Randall the first to set out eastbound. Many notable Westerners rode for the Pony Express in their youth, including Wild Bill Hickok, Buffalo Bill Cody, and Calamity Jane. The service attracted, and needed, tough characters. Bronco Bill Charlie was the youngest ever Pony Express rider, signed up at the age of eleven. The oldest recruit was forty. The riders soon became an important part of Western life, charting the course of history with the documents they carried. Robert "Pony Bob" Haslam, for example, made an epic ride to deliver the news of Lincoln's election. Despite being shot through the jaw and losing three teeth, Haslam continued on his way. The service also delivered a copy of Lincoln's March 1861 Inaugural Address to Congress in a record seven days and seven hours. Bill Cody himself made the longest non-stop ride in the history of the service, when he found his relief rider had been murdered at his post. He covered three hundred and twenty-two miles non-stop, using twenty-one fresh horses. Cody's regular route was the forty-five mile stretch west of Julesburg, Colorado.

Each Pony Express rider was equipped with a specially designed mailbag, or *mochila* (taken from the Spanish word for knapsack), complete with four locked leather compartments, or *cantinas*. Each rider used the bag to carry a maximum of twenty pounds in weight, which included his personal equipment. This consisted of a water sac, a bible (courtesy of Alexander Majors), a knife, a revolver, and a horn to alert the managers of the relay stages. To save weight and ensure that the riders carried as much mail as possible, their equipment was ultimately pared down to just the water and the revolver. Originally, Pony Express mail was charged at $5 per

Opposite page: William H. Russell's recruitment poster for young riders.

Left: An abandoned Pony Express mail station at Simpson Springs in Utah's West Desert. The location bears the name of Captain James H. Simpson, a topographical engineer from nearby Camp Floyd. Simpson stopped here while laying out an overland mail route between Salt Lake City and California, attracted by the abundant water supply. The first mail station was built here in 1858. Later, it was taken over by the Pony Express.

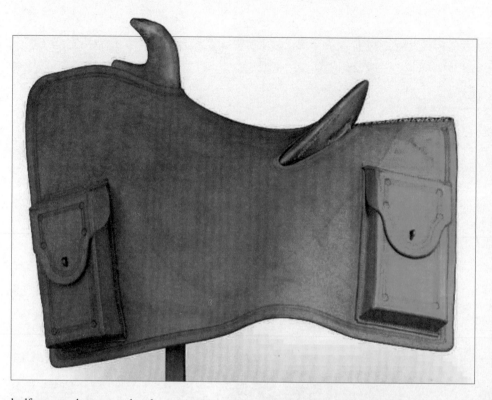

Right: This is a mochilla. These leather covers were thrown over the saddle, and were cut to fit over the saddle horn and cantle. The mail was carried in the mochilla's four leather cantinas, or compartments.

half-ounce, but to make the service more attractive, this was reduced to $2.50, and finally to $1.

Despite the high repute of the Pony Express, the company was never financially sound. Its money problems were compounded when it failed to win a one-million dollar mail contract from congress. But the final blow to the service was new technology: the telegraph. When the poles of the Creighton Telegraph Line reached Salt Lake City in October 1861, the mail service became obsolete overnight. It ceased operations two days later. The directors lost over $200,000 in the enterprise, the equivalent of millions of dollars today. Despite their entrepreneurship, two of the original Pony Express directors died in poverty. Only the God-fearing Majors made a successful new career, working for the Union Pacific Railroad. He survived until 1900.

In its short period of operation, the Pony Express riders covered over six hundred and fifty thousand miles and delivered nearly thirty-five thousand pieces of mail, with the loss of only one mailbag. A single rider had been lost, killed by an arrow shot by a Plains warrior. In 1866, the company's assets were sold to Wells Fargo Overland Mail Company for $1.5 million. Wells Fargo continued to use the Pony Express logo for its armored car service until 2001.

Despite its nineteen-month period of survival, the Pony Express had a huge impact on the West and has become an integral part of its romance. Perhaps its greatest achievement was psychological; the service broke the isolation of the Western settlers by bringing them news direct from the seat of government. It also helped keep the state of California and its gold on the side of the Union forces. Many believe that the Pony Express helped to preserve the Union itself by drawing East and West closer together, to forge one nation.

Russell's route between St. Joseph and Sacramento proved to have been very skillfully worked out, and was closely followed by the Union Pacific Railroad. The route is now shadowed by the US 36, which is known as The Pony Express Highway.

Russell's view of the West's future was also fulfilled. "The wilderness which lies between us will blossom as the rose, cities will spring into existence where the Indians and Buffalo now hold possession. Mountains will be tunneled, streams bridged and the iron monster which has become mankind's slave will ply between our confines and those far distant shores."

Below: A ruined Pony Express way station.

The Transcontinental Railway

Above: Theodore D. Judah was the chief engineer of the Central Pacific Railroad and mapped its route across the Sierra Nevada Mountains.

The building of a transcontinental railway to unite the nation was first proposed early in the nineteenth century. Ironically, the railroad became a reality just as the nation was being torn apart by civil war. Abraham Lincoln signed the Pacific Railroad Act in 1862, which set out both the route of the line and how the huge enterprise was to be financed. Lincoln firmly believed that the construction of the transcontinental line was critical to national unity. Theodore Dehone Judah, the chief engineer of the Central Pacific Railroad, had spent the summer of 1861 surveying the route the line would take. He explained the long and complicated route to the president using a ninety-foot long map. Back in 1856, Judah had written a thirteen-thousand-word proposal to build the railroad, and became a lobbyist for the Pacific Railroad Convention. He was to become one of the pivotal movers in the building of the transcontinental railroad.

The railroad was to have a huge impact on life in the West, opening it up to many more settlers. A dangerous trek that would have taken at least six months in the days of the wagon trains could now be accomplished in less than a week. But the railroad also sped up the decimation of the buffalo herds, and the annihilation of the traditional way of life of the Plains Indians.

The route of the transcontinental line followed the earlier trail routes and the Pony Express trails. It was to run between Sacramento, California, in the West and Council Bluffs, Iowa, in the East. It passed through Nevada, Utah, Wyoming, and Nebraska en route. The railway did not reach the Pacific until 1869, when a new stretch of line was opened up to Oakland Point in San Francisco Bay. The line was

integrated into the Eastern railway system until 1872, with the opening of the Union Pacific Missouri River Bridge. Its construction required tremendous engineering exploits to overcome the obstacles of the route. The line crossed several rivers (including the Platte in Nebraska), the Rockies (at the Great Divide Basin in Wyoming), and the Sierra Mountains. Spur lines were also built to service the two great cities of the Plains: Denver, Colorado, and Salt Lake City, Utah.

Above: Railway workers laid the track across the virgin land.

Right: A dramatic Currier and Ives print from 1870, entitled *Through to the Pacific*.

Opposite page: Steep-sided railway cuttings were blasted with dynamite. There were many accidents.

The Central Pacific broke ground in January 1863 on K Street in Sacramento, California, while the Union Pacific waited until December that year to start work in Omaha, Nebraska. The groundbreaking ceremonies began a monumental task that was to take six years and involve the construction of nearly two thousand miles of track. The route had to overcome many natural obstacles as the trains of the day were unable to turn around sharp curves or inclines of more than two percent. This meant that a range of innovative engineering solutions were required. This

Above: Chinese railway workers constructed most of the Central Pacific track. They lived in tent towns beside the line.

enormous challenge required a massive workforce of over a hundred thousand men, who came from a wide variety of backgrounds. The majority were Irish-American veterans from both sides of the Civil War, joined by Chinese immigrants, Mexicans, Englishmen, Germans, and ex-slaves from the Southern states. Brigham Young provided Mormon workers for the Utah sector of the line. These men were excellent, conscientious workers who ended each day of work with prayer and song rather than women and drink.

Above: Construction locomotives near Bear River, Wyoming.

The project also required a wide array of professional workers, including surveyors, engineers, carpenters, masons, teamsters, tracklayers, telegraphers, spikers, bolters, and cooks.

Railway construction could be very dangerous. The use of early explosives, including unstable nitroglycerin was particularly hazardous, and resulted in many deaths and injuries. The crews from the two railroad companies were under strong competitive pressure to complete as many miles of track as possible, and their work often became sub-standard. The railway companies were paid per mile of track, not

for the durability of their construction, so their priority was speed rather than quality. Slick track-laying teams laid as many as four rails per minute. Ultimately the Union Pacific was to build about two-thirds of the transcontinental track.

Anxious not to lose a minute of working time, the railroad companies housed thousands of workers in enormous work-trains. These had sleeping cars outfitted with three-tier bunk beds, kitchens, and eating cars. The life for these men was extremely hard, and the pay meager. There were several strikes, particularly among the less well-paid Chinese workers (who were also not given room and board). But

Below: Surveyors formed the first workforce along the line, and endured many hardships. They slept on the ground, and lived in constant fear of Indian attack.

the companies were ruthless employers. They cut the food supplies to the workers, and threatened anyone who stayed away from work with punitive fines.

The two ends of the Pacific line moved slowly together, further and further into the wilderness. The workforce was spread out over several miles and was accommodated in mobile tent towns that followed the route. The end-of-line boomtowns that were created were colorful and lawless. They included North Platte, Julesburg, Abilene, Bear River, Wichita, and Dodge City. The final tent town, Corinne, Utah, was founded in January 1869. Newspaper editor Samuel Bowles coined the term "Hell on Wheels" for these mobile construction towns. They were full of vice and criminality and were rough, bawdy, and brutal. He described their

inhabitants as the "vilest men and women... (a) congregation of scum and wickedness... by day disgusting, by night dangerous. Almost everybody dirty, many filthy, and with the marks of lowest vice; averaging a murder a day, gambling, drinking, hurdy-gurdy dancing, and the vilest of sexual commerce."

Above: Triple-decker railway cars used to house the construction workers.

In reality, the tent towns mainly consisted of saloons, gambling houses, dance halls, and brothels. Almost all the women living in these settlements were prostitutes. Murder, arson, and violent crime were common. Without any real law enforcement, frontier justice was the only control, and lynching was common. John Ford captured the decadent atmosphere of Hell on Wheels in his 1924 silent film, *The Iron Horse*. Ford's movie also showed the spirit of fervent nationalism that drove this massive project. Despite their inauspicious beginnings, many of these

Right: A banner celebrates
as the railroad reaches
Cozad, Nebraska. The town
was two-hundred and forty-
seven miles from Omaha.

tent towns became permanent settlements. Mark Twain described the end-of-the-line rail town at Sacramento as a "city of saloons," but it was soon to become the state capital of California.

The railroad companies also changed the racial make-up of America by encouraging immigration from both China and Europe. The Chinese population in particular grew exponentially, from less than a hundred people in 1870 to over one-hundred and forty thousand men and women by 1880.

The companies employed agents to scout for immigrants, who were paid per head. C. B. Schmidt was the champion of scouts, responsible for settling over sixty thousand German immigrants along the route of the Santa Fe Railroad.

Another intrinsic characteristic of this huge project would be corruption. The government legislated to award the constructors with six thousand four hundred acres of trackside land, and a tiered payment per mile of track: $16,000 per mile for level track, $32,000 per mile for plateau track, and $48,000 for the most demanding stages. Within two years, these rates had been doubled. Railroad investors ensured that as much track as possible was graded into the more expensive categories. Thomas Clark Durant was one of the worst offenders. In 1864, Durant established Credit Mobilier to build the First Transcontinental Railroad track, and awarded dummy contracts to his own company. He insisted that his engineers laid the Union Pacific track in large oxbows, and tinkered with the route to ensure that it ran through his own property. His behavior became notorious, and surveyor Peter Day said that "if the geography was a little larger, I think (Durant) would order a survey round the moon and a few of the fixed stars, to see if he could not get some depot grounds." In 1867, Durant was ousted, and Congressman Oakes Ames replaced him as the head

Above: Corinne, Utah was the final tent town along the construction route.

of the organization. Ultimately, the company was revealed as fraudulent, having taken contracts worth $72 million dollars to build a railway worth only $53 million. But as railroad executive Charles Francis said, "It is very easy to speak of these men as thieves and speculators. But there was no human being, when the Union Pacific railroad was proposed, who regarded it as other than a wild-cat venture."

Union Pacific's corrupt investors became synonymous with the worst excesses of the so-called "Gilded Age." The term was coined by Mark Twain to describe the post-Civil War extravaganza of industrial-scale corruption, when massive fortunes were made and lost equally quickly. The huge volume of investment capital required to build the railroads made them especially vulnerable to speculation and sharp practice. Many railway investors were cheated and bankrupted. Oliver Jensen described these years as "the roughest age in the history of American capitalism." Many of the most magnificent San Francisco mansions were built with railroad money. The railroads were huge employers, and also provided a massive stimulus to the general economy.

On May 10, 1869, the Central Pacific and Union Pacific tracks finally met at Promontory Summit, Utah. Leland Stanford, the Governor of California and one of the "big four" investors in the Central Pacific, used a silver hammer to drive home

Below: Union Pacific director Thomas Clark "Doc" Durant stands on the advancing track in Nebraska, 1866.

the final, golden spike that joined the two lines. This was one of the world's first global media events, as both hammer and spike were wired to the telegraph line, and Stanford's ringing blows were simultaneously broadcast to the East and West Coasts of America. A signal of "Done" was sent across the country from Staten Island to the Golden Gate, and ignited a unprecedented national celebration. The dream of Manifest Destiny had finally been achieved.

The line had a great impact on the whole country, but its effects were most directly felt in the West. It proved to be a major stimulus to both immigration and trade. Charles Nordhoff described its fundamental importance: "On the plains and in the mountains, the railroad is the one great fact." Soon, other railroads crisscrossed the Plains, including the Kansas Pacific, North Pacific, Denver Pacific, Texas and Pacific, Burlington and Missouri River, Denver and Rio Grande, Atchison, Topeka, and Santa Fe railroads. By 1876 it was possible to travel between New York and San Francisco in three-and-a-half days. For most people, though, the reality of rail travel was basic and uncomfortable. In 1879, Robert Louis Stevenson described his Union Pacific train carriage as being "like a flat-roofed Noah's Ark, with a stove and a convenience, one at either end, a passage down the middle, and transverse benches upon either hand."

Settlement of the prairie led to a massive increase in American farming. The two million working farms that existed in 1860 had grown to six million by the end of the century. Westward migration corresponded with a huge influx of settlers into the United States itself; immigration from overseas doubled to over five million in the 1880's.

For the Native Americans, the coming of the

railroad was a disaster of epic proportions. The colossal increase in white settlement was one great source of anger. The other was the decimation of the American bison. This animal was unique to the Plains, and before the railroad it was estimated that as many as sixty million roamed the prairie in massive herds. The buffalo was crucial to the existence of the Plains Indians and had a special spiritual significance to them. "Everything the Kiowas had had come from the buffalo," said tribe member Old Lady Horse. "Their tepees were made of buffalo hides, so were their clothes and moccasins. They ate buffalo meat." The other Plains tribes, including the Cheyenne, Lakota, and Apache, were equally dependant on the buffalo.

But the railroad companies saw the ancient bison herds as a dangerous nuisance, useful only for the feeding of their workforce. They hired a generation of buffalo hunters to wipe them out. The most famous of these was Buffalo Bill, who worked for the Kansas Pacific Railroad. Mounted on his horse, Buckskin, and armed with his gun, Lucretia, Buffalo Bill shot over four thousand animals in less than eighteen months. He also

Above: Cecil B. DeMille's 1939 movie *Union Pacific* starred Barbara Stanwyck. It focused on the national unity engendered by the railroad.

Left: An emigrant ticket from Chicago to San Francisco.

Opposite page: This 1869 poster celebrates the grand opening of the railroad from the Atlantic to the Pacific.

Opposite page: Buffalo Bill worked as a buffalo hunter for the Kansas Pacific Railroad.

organized many hunting expeditions. Buffalo hunting became so popular that the railway companies encouraged their passengers to shoot buffalo from specially adapted railcars. Elisabeth Custer described how "the wild rush to the windows, and the reckless discharge of rifles and pistols put every passenger's life in jeopardy." The trend became so widespread that the Kansas Pacific Railroad ran its

Above: This dramatic Currier and Ives print shows bison swarming along the route of the railroad.

own taxidermy service to mount trophies for their customers. The result of this dreadful slaughter was that, by the end of the end of the nineteenth century, only a thousand bison survived from the majestic herds that had dominated Plains life for centuries. As Sitting Bull bitterly commented, "What is this? Is it robbery? You call us savages. What are *they*?"

Seeing their way of life being destroyed before their eyes, some of the more warlike Plains Indian tribes began to organize scouting parties to vandalize trains and attack surveyors and other railway workers. This gave the rail companies the

Left: Shooting buffalo from trains became so popular that the Kansas Pacific Railway Company established its own taxidermist to mount the passengers' trophies.

Below: Union Pacific locomotive 82 and its crew. The train was photographed in 1872 on the line between Echo, Utah and Evanston, Wyoming.

excuse they needed to strike back. According to General Grenville Mellen Dodge, the chief engineer of the Union Pacific, "We've got to clean the damn Indians out, or give up building the Union Pacific Railroad." The Sand Creek Massacre of November 1864 was one of the most appalling incidents that took place, when men of the Colorado Territory militia destroyed a village of Cheyenne and Arapaho, killing over two hundred elderly men, women, and children. Although the massacre was widely condemned, no one was brought to justice. Sand Creek led to a series of revenge killings in the Platte Valley, and over two hundred innocent white settlers were murdered. The increasing spiral of violence made it progressively more difficult for an accommodation to be found between the Plains natives and the railroad companies. The U.S. Cavalry was deployed to protect the security of the trains. Dodge ordered the Powder Ridge Expedition of 1865, in which his forces rode against the Lakota, Cheyenne, and Arapaho tribes. Although this was partly successful, hostilities soon escalated into the Red Clouds War, fought against the Lakota tribe in 1866. The Lakota braves inflicted heavy casualties in the conflict, and it was the worst defeat that the U.S. Cavalry was to suffer until Little Bighorn, ten years later.

Their resistance to the railroad led to the Plains tribes being confined in reservations, where they were powerless to protect their ancestral hunting groundsor the buffalo.

Above: The Central Pacific and Union Pacific tracks met on May 10, 1869.

Despite the mixed heritage of the Transcontinental Railroad, its completion was an extraordinary achievement that was celebrated as an icon of Western culture. The railroad is familiar from any number of Westerns that show the great iron horses crossing the monumental Plains landscape. In 1936, Cecil B. DeMille released *Union Pacific*, which explored the corruption that surrounded the building of the line. *How the West Was Won*, John Ford's epic movie of 1962, also dealt with the dramatic construction of the Union Pacific line. The film unequivocally blames the railroad bosses for enraging the Arapaho tribe at the expense of their workers' lives.

The Transcontinental Railroad left a permanent mark on American life in both the East and West of the country. The sound of the train whistle became a haunting and romantic sound across the prairies. The line itself has been renewed many times, but much of it is still laid on the original, hand-prepared grade. In several places, where later routes have bypassed the original line, it is still possible to see the obsolete track, abandoned in the wilderness.

Remington Double Derringer

The derringer was a popular choice of defensive weapon for frontier people, especially women. A derringer is defined as the smallest usable handgun of a given caliber. Derringers appealed to women because they could be easily concealed in a purse or dress pocket, or tucked into a garter. Guns that were specifically designed for female use were called "muff pistols," but Derringers were also marketed to men.

The weapon was named for Henry Deringer, a Philadelphia gunsmith who developed a range of compact, high-caliber pocket pistols that, despite their size, had reasonable stopping power. Deringer's guns were so successful that his name became synonymous with all weapons of the type. The press report of Abraham Lincoln's assassination wrongly spelt the name of John Wilkes Booth's weapon as "Derringer." This version of the gun's name fell into common usage.

Early derringers were not repeating firearms. Repeating mechanisms such as those used in semi-auto-

SPECIFICATIONS

Caliber: .41 inch Rim fire Cartridge

Length of barrel: 3 inches

Barrel shape: Round/ribbed

Finish: Blue steel

Grips: Hard Rubber

Action: Breech loading double barrel

Year of manufacture: 1870

Manufacturer: Remington Arms Company, Ilion, New York

Below: Even the fixing screw for the handgrip was delicately designed.

matic handguns or revolvers would have added significant bulk and weight to the gun, defeating the purpose of these highly concealable weapons. The original cartridge derringers held only a single round. These guns were usually chambered for either single pinfire or rimfire .40 caliber cartridges. The barrel pivoted sideways on the frame to allow access to the breech for reloading. The famous Remington derringer doubled the firing capacity of the early models, while maintaining their compact size. This was achieved by adding a second barrel on top of the first. The barrels pivoted upwards to reload. Each barrel held one round, a .41 rimfire bullet, and a cam on the hammer alternated between the top and bottom barrels. Travelling at only four-hundred and twenty-five feet per second, the derringer's bullets moved slowly enough to be seen by the naked eye, but at close quarters they could be fatal. Remington sold the gun between 1866 and 1935.

Wells Fargo

Below: The Wells Fargo
offices in San Francisco.

Wells Fargo was one of the great institutions of the West, and was a positive force for the civilizing of the wild frontier. Its very name conjures a thrilling image of a six-horse stagecoach loaded with gold, thundering across the romantic landscape of the Plains. The business activities of Wells Fargo became part of the fabric of the West, serving people of every background and profession. The company also sought to control lawlessness in the region, especially along the stage routes.

Henry Wells and William Fargo founded the company in 1852, and set up their first office at 420 Montgomery Street in downtown San Francisco. This location was in the heart of the '49ers' tent city. The new company offered financial services, and also traded in gold. Even more importantly, they also offered express, secure carriage for all kinds of cargo, especially gold dust and bullion from the area's newly sunk mines. Right from the beginning, there was a thread of altruism and impartiality in the company culture. Wells Fargo offered their services to all "men, women, or children, rich or poor, white or black." Indeed, they ran their business for all the settlers and frontier people of the West. Henry Wells was also a proponent of sexual equality, founding Wells College for Women in New York with the slogan, "Give her the opportunity!" By the 1880's, several women were Wells Fargo agents, sometimes taking over from their husbands as company employees when they were widowed. Veterans of the U.S. Army have now worked for the company for over a hundred and fifty years.

Opposite page: N.C.
Wyeth's 1909 painting, *The
Pay Stage*. Wells Fargo
stagecoaches were usually
protected by an outrider
armed with a shotgun.

Integrity was a great factor in the success of the business and Wells Fargo agents often became highly esteemed figures in the new towns of the West. New agents were recruited from well-respected members of the community, including storekeepers and attorneys. Each was given a certificate of appointment by the company. As well as the express service, the agents also offered basic banking and financial services.

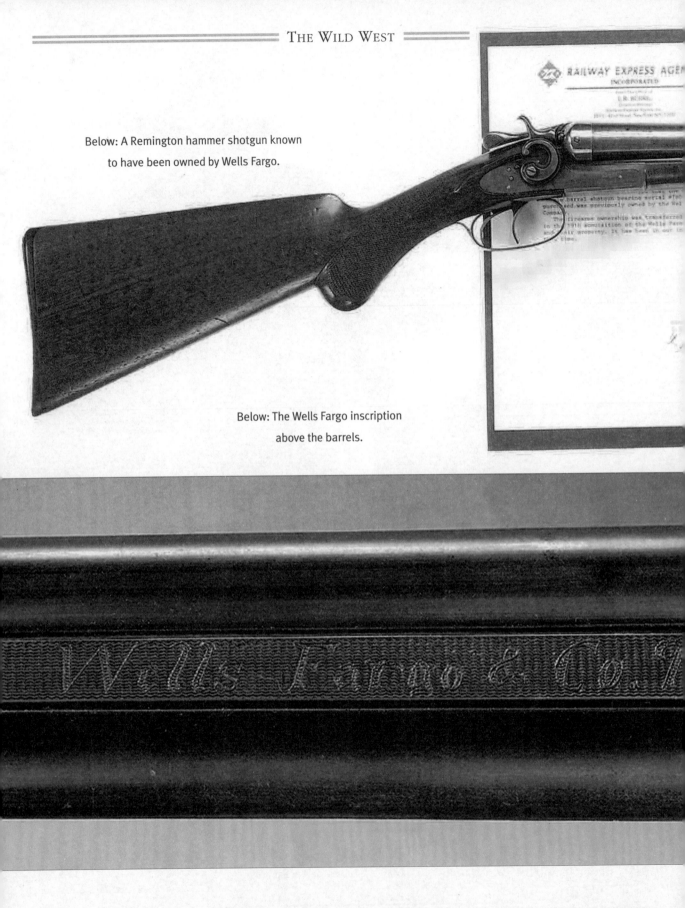

Below: A Remington hammer shotgun known to have been owned by Wells Fargo.

RAILWAY EXPRESS AGE
INCORPORATED

Below: The Wells Fargo inscription above the barrels.

Left: Wells Fargo issued their operatives with recognizable badges. Their logo became a symbol of civilization coming to the West.

The company started their overland stagecoach line in the 1860's. Wells Fargo had had shares in the Butterfield Overland Mail Company established in 1858. Ultimately, Wells Fargo took the company over and used this for the basis of their mail business. The company sent the mail by the fastest means possible; stagecoach, steamship, railroad, pony rider, or telegraph. Their operatives often brought the mail through at dreadful personal risk, and it was said that the mail was delivered "by God and Wells Fargo." Wells Fargo also employed detectives to investigate fraud and any other illegal practices in connection with their

Above: The Wells Fargo stage waits for passengers outside a commercial hotel.

Opposite page: A modern-day recreation of the Wells Fargo stagecoach rattling into town.

business, and employed armed escorts and shotgun riders to discourage theft and hold ups. They were reputed to carry cut-down shotguns, which were easy to conceal under the seat of a wagon and lethal at close range. This modus operandi daunted many less serious villains, but the company did fall victim to several serious offenders. Black Bart was one of the most irksome stage robbers to victimize the company, beginning his campaign of robbery in 1875. They hired James B. Hume as their chief detective to try and stop the holdups, and he remained with the company for thirty-two years, becoming one of the most famous detectives in the country. Hume finally caught up with Black Bart after twenty-eight stage robberies. He assigned an armed guard to ride in every express car that carried mail as well as

Above: A Wells Fargo's padlock, manufactured by Ayers, Climax, and Romer. Opposite page: Madison Larkin was a Wells Fargo messenger and shotgun guard. He was photographed in Phoenix, Arizona in 1877.

Wells Fargo valuables, and posted a standing reward of $300 for information about any crimes committed against the company. Wells Fargo also became the victim of train robberies. The first big one happened in 1870 when the Central Pacific out of Oakland was held up near Truckee. Seven masked men stole $42,000 in gold.

By 1866, Wells Fargo was operating all the major overland stagecoach lines west of the Missouri, and soon drove on to Salt Lake City. Gradually, Wells Fargo took over the routes of the Pony Express. Their stages eventually rolled over three thousand miles of territory. They used stagecoaches constructed by carriage builder

A gold panning pan embossed with the Wells Fargo logo. The pan is twelve inches across.

J. Stephens Abbot and master wheelwright Lewis Downing, constructed in their Concord, New Hampshire, factory. The unique feature of the Wells Fargo coach was its suspension, which rested on bull hide leather "thorough braces." This gave the coaches a rolling gait rather than a jarring

Above: A small Wells Fargo coach, drawn by a single horse.

motion. Mark Twain accurately characterized the Wells Fargo coach as "an imposing cradle on wheels." The coaches weighed in at around two-and-a-half thousand pounds and were decked out with damask cloth interiors, which cost a substantial $1,100.

Trains became an increasingly vital part of the Wells Fargo network. By 1888, the railroad enabled Wells Fargo to offer an "Ocean-to-Ocean Service" through twenty-five different states. The company was now divided into three departments, "P" Pacific, "C" Central, and "A" Atlantic.

Wells Fargo continued to run its express business, delivering valuable cargoes of every kind, up until 1918, when it was taken over as part of the government war effort.

Introduction to the Gunfighters

Of all the wild characters of the Western frontier, the gunfighter was the most feared and flamboyant. They were not simply violent, for in a violent age, this was hardly unique. As the editor of the *Kansas City Journal* remarked in 1881, "The gentleman who has 'killed his man' is by no means a *rara avis*… He is met daily on Main Street." The gunfighters whose reputations have survived all had some defining characteristic that has kept their image alive: high morals, depravity, good looks, courage, mystery, vicious temper, sadism, marksmanship, or dandyism.

In fact the term "gunfighter" did not come into popular use until the 1870s. Bat Masterson was one of the first to popularize the word in his newspaper column, with his firsthand accounts of the luminaries of the West. But he generally preferred the term "mankiller."

The earlier terms used to describe a man who lived by his gun were either "man-killer" or "shootist" (as bad man Clay Allison described himself). They were an integral part of the West, and a direct result of the conditions there. Whereas the law governed disputes in the East, the gun was the Western arbiter of choice. Gunfighters worked on both sides of the legal divide, both as lawmen ("civilizers") and criminal outlaws. Many swapped sides when it suited them. Most were motivated by money, and were only loyal to their own interests.

The more specific idiom of "gunslinger" is thought to date from much later, first appearing in J. Gordon Edwards' Western movie *Drag Harlan*, of 1920. The word subsequently became popular in Western fiction, often appearing in the work of Zane Grey.

Gunfighters themselves came from a wide sweep of backgrounds: they ranged from men available as "guns for hire" in range wars or for specific contract killings, through to lawmen whose ultimate aim was to civilize the West.

The term "gunfighter" was also used to cover men who fought in gunfights, but these were far less frequent than might be supposed from western films and dime novels. To add to the confusion, "gunfight" itself was also a loose term. It could apply to a shoot-out or gun battle where several men were involved (like the 1881 incident at the O.K. Corral). But it could also refer to a duel fought with guns between just two men, where the participants squared off to each other in the

Above: Bat Masterson in later life, looking highly respectable.

Opposite page: Wild Bill Hickok, Texas Jack Omohundro, and Buffalo Bill Cody. A trio of great Westerners.

Above: Famous Western novelist Zane Grey (1872–1939).

Opposite page: N.C. Wyeth's graphic painting, "The Gunfight," captures the ferocious violence of a saloon showdown.

classic side-on stance. A good example of this would be Bill Hickok and Dave Tutt's classic gunfight fought in the square at Springfield, Missouri, in 1865.

"Gunslinging" was far more popular in Western movies than it ever was in real life. In countless Western movies, the "gunslinger" twirls his pistols around, does trick sharp shooting, and generally shows off his prowess with his weapons. This almost never happened in real life. Once drawn, it was imperative to discharge your gun as soon as possible, to avoid being shot to death. Gunslinging would have been a highly dangerous diversion from the main business of the gunfighter – staying alive.

In real life, gunmen almost never squared off to each other in the shootouts that are so popular in Western films and literature. Gunfighters had far too much respect for each other's skills to risk it, knowing that a real gunfight would be fatal for at least one of the duelists, if not both.

Indeed, well-known gunfighters were held in such general fear that they were very rarely challenged by anyone who knew their reputations. Equally, gunfighters on the wrong side of the law feared the best of the gunmen law enforcers, and sought to avoid them at all costs. (Early Western townsfolk were fully aware of this and were willing to pay large sums to high-profile gunmen to protect them, and establish law and order.) First-rate gunfighters who died violently were mostly ambushed and killed by second-rate gunmen who were far too afraid to face them openly. Several famous gunfighters were killed in this underhand way, having fallen victim to their own fearsome reputations. These fatalities included Billy the Kid, John Wesley Hardin, and Wild Bill Hickok. Others, like Jesse James, were betrayed and murdered by their own treacherous followers, caught off-guard for a few fatal moments.

In fact, reputation was often a tool of the gunfighter's trade, and he would groom it like he would hone his shooting skills. Many men of the type quite deliberately exaggerated their kill tally, including Wyatt Earp and Wild Bill Hickok. Earp was reputed to have been involved in over a hundred gunfights, but only five of these can be confirmed. Hickok's fearsome reputation netted him $150 a month to keep the peace in Abilene, but his actual kill rate was quite modest.

Despite appearances, the avowed intention of most gunfighters was to live long, and die in their beds. Some who were lucky enough to achieve this include Wyatt Earp and Luke Short. Others, like Bat Masterson, moved into other, less risky professions, and successfully outlived the violent era of the western gunfighter.

Robert Clay Allison, 'The Shootist'

Below: Robert Clay Allison is twenty-six in the conventional studio portrait.

Robert Clay Allison was no gentleman gunfighter. Clay was a moody and vicious man who bred fear in everyone who knew him. He was born on September 2, 1840, in Tennessee, the fourth of nine children born to his parents, Jeremiah Scotland Allison and Mariah R. Allison. He was born disfigured with a club foot. His father was a Presbyterian minister who made his living in the sheep and cattle business. Sadly, Jeremiah died when Clay was just five. Clay worked on the family farm at Waynesboro, Tennessee, until the age of twenty-one, but always had a reputation for having a vile temper and terrible mood swings.

On October 15, 1861, Clay joined the Tennessee Light Artillery Division of the Confederate Army. But on January 15, 1862, he was medically discharged due to "personality problems." His discharge papers described him as "incapable of performing the duties of a soldier because of a blow received many years ago. Emotional of physical excitement produces paroxysmals *[sic.]* of a mixed character, partly epileptic and partly maniacal." His brother Monroe was reported as a deserter in the same year. Despite his mental health problems, Clay rejoined the Confederate army in September 1862, as part of the 9th Tennessee Cavalry, serving under the famous rebel General Nathan Bedford Forrest. On May 4, 1865, Clay's company surrendered at Gainesville, Alabama. He was held as a prisoner of war for a few days, convicted of spying and sentenced to be shot. The night before his execution was scheduled, he killed his guard and made his escape. The Civil War had bred feelings of hatred for black people in Allison, and upon leaving the army he joined the embryonic Ku Klux Klan. Trudging back to the family farm, Clay encountered a Union officer who was trying to seize the property; legend has it that Clay snatched a gun from the house and shot the officer dead. Forced to keep out of view, Clay worked as a cattle hand after leaving the army, and moved to the Texan Brazos River Territory in 1865. He was accompanied by his brothers Monroe and John, his sister Mary, and her future husband, Lewis Coleman.

During this time, Clay worked as a ranch hand and trail boss, driving cattle to New Mexico. He may have been among the eighteen herders who blazed the Goodnight-Loving Trail in 1866. Things obviously went well for him, as by 1870 he had acquired his own ranch in Colfax County, New Mexico. But local newspapers were already reporting that he had dispatched as many as fifteen

Above: In this far more famous photograph, Allison is shown with his leg in plaster, having discharged his own gun into his foot.

local men, and he had a grim reputation for violence, especially when he was drunk. His first truly notorious – and grotesque – killing happened in late 1870. Allison was drinking in a saloon when a hysterical woman approached him. She told him that her husband had gone mad and killed a number of his own ranch hands at their cabin, along with their infant daughter. Allison rounded up a posse, but they found no bodies at the ranch. However, a few days later, bones were discovered on the property, and the ranch owner was arrested and imprisoned. Enraged by the man's behavior, Allison broke him out of jail, lynched him, and cut off his head, riding twenty-nine miles to Cimarron with this gruesome trophy on a pole before displaying it in a local saloon. This kind of behavior did nothing to endear people to Allison, who was clearly mad. In the spring of 1871, a prank he was involved in seriously backfired. Famously, Allison shot himself in the foot while encouraging General Gordon Granger's army mules to stampede. A famous photograph of Clay was taken at this time, complete with bandaged foot and crutch.

Allison's presence in New Mexico also attracted other killers to the area, who wanted to enhance their own reputations by adding him to their list of kills. In 1874, Chunk Colbert, for one, coolly invited Allison out to dinner before trying to shoot him under the table. Many years before, on his way across the Brazos River, Allison had severely beaten the ferryman, who happened to be Colbert's uncle, accusing

Above: A classic Bowie knife, complete with an eight-inch blade and "clip" point.

the man of cheating him. Unfortunately, Allison beat Colbert to the draw, and killed his dining companion just as coffee was served. When he was asked why he had accepted a dinner invitation from a man he knew wanted to kill him, Allison responded that he "didn't want to send a man to hell on an empty stomach."

In October of the following year (1875) Clay lynched Mexican Cruz Vega from a telegraph pole, seemingly for being involved in the killing of a Methodist circuit rider. When Vega's friend Pancho Griego attempted to revenge him, Clay shot him dead in the St. James Hotel in Cimarron. In December 1876, Clay and his brother John became involved in a saloon brawl in Las Animas, Colorado, and ended up shooting and killing the local sheriff, Charles Faber. Allison was charged for the crime, but acquitted on grounds of self-defense.

In 1876 Allison is reputed to have been involved in the murder of three black soldiers, but was never held accountable for these murders either.

In 1877, Allison had a brush with a gunman of a completely different caliber than himself: Wyatt Earp, in Dodge City, Kansas. Clay was angry about the way that cowboys were treated in the notorious town. But the two posturing gunfighters kept their fight verbal, and went on their way intact.

As time went on, Clay's behavior became increasingly deranged. He was a heavy drinker, and this must have exacerbated his problems. When a dental appointment to cure a raging toothache went awry and the nervous dentist began to drill the wrong tooth, Allison furiously bundled the dentist into his own chair and ripped off half the man's lip in trying to extract one of the dentist's own teeth.

Another event that demonstrates Allison's bizarre view of the world was the so-called Bowie knife grave affair. He had fallen into a water dispute with a neighboring rancher, and suggested that they should settle their differences by digging a grave big enough to hold them both. They should then climb into the pit, each armed only with a Bowie knife, and see which one of them survived to climb out. The victor would arrange a tombstone for the vanquished. Given the bizarre violence Allison displayed, it is very surprising that he never spent a day in jail. In the end events overtook him, and the "grave" encounter never took place.

In 1878 Allison sold his New Mexico ranch to his brother John for $700, and moved to Hemphill County, Texas, with the rest of his family. He was planning to ranch, and registered a brand for his cattle.

On February 15, 1881, Clay married Dora McCullough in Mobeetie, Wheeler County, Texas. The couple were to have two daughters. Despite his reputation, Allison served as a juror in Mobeetie, although he was also reputed to have ridden naked and drunk along the main street there. Locally, he was known as the "Wolf of the Washita."

In 1883 Allison bought a ranch in Pecos, Texas, and became involved in local politics. For some years he seemed to lead a fairly regular life, but this was cut short by an unfortunate accident. Driving supplies from Pecos back to his ranch, Allison was thrown from his wagon. One of the rear wheels of the heavily-loaded wagon ran over his neck, killing him instantly. It was July 1887, and Allison was forty-seven years of age. The following day he was buried at Pecos Cemetery. His gun was inscribed, "Gentleman gun fighter." A second marker was added sometime later with the highly unlikely description, "He never killed a man that did not need killing."

Clay's ignominious end was highly unusual for a "shootist" at this time. (Clay himself had coined this term to describe a man who lived by the gun.) Men of Allison's vicious and violent type generally expired in a hail of bullets or dancing at the end of a rope.

Billy the Kid

Below: Full-length portrait of Billy the Kid. For many years, he was thought to be left-handed because the photograph had been mistakenly reversed.

Billy the Kid, the teenage outlaw, was one of the most colorful figures and gunmen of the Old West. He was a controversial figure in both life and death. He is considered by some observers to be a cold-blooded, psychopathic killer, while others see him as a boy who "loved his mother devotedly" and was led to a life of criminality by neglectful adults. Either way, he is credited with at least six killings, and his ballad boasts that "he'd a notch on his pistol for twenty-one men."

Billy was born to Irish parents in New York City in November 1859. His birth name was William Henry McCarty Jr., but he was called Henry by his mother, Catherine. His father died when he and his brother, Joseph, were very young, and his mother died in 1874, just a year after remarrying. By this time, Billy's family was living in Silver City, New Mexico, where they had gone to seek a cure for their mother's tuberculosis. Billy's stepfather didn't want the two boys, so he put them into foster homes where The Kid, who was now fourteen, washed dishes to earn his keep. Billy's juvenile life of crime started at this time. He stole some cheese from a rancher, and was then found to be in possession of stolen clothing and firearms. Unfortunately, being locked up for this minor misdemeanor scared him so much that he decided to escape by climbing the chimney. For the next couple of years, he tramped around working as a ranch hand and gambler, trying to avoid brushes with the law. But everything went downhill rapidly after he shot and killed a bully who was teasing him. Unable to get honest work, he reluctantly joined a gang of rustlers known as The Boys. These were led by the Scotsman John R. Mackie. In 1877 an altercation with a bullying blacksmith, Frank Cahill resulted in Cahill being shot to death. Billy fled to the Arizona territory and joined the Evans Gang, a band of cattle rustlers. The gang reputedly stole animals belonging to cattle magnate John Chisum. It was during this period that McCarty was attacked by Apaches, who stole his horse and left him to wander alone in the desert. He painfully made his way to the nearest settlement, which was owned by the Jones family. They took him, and "The Kid" decided to try legitimate work, assuming a new name: William H. Bonney. He was soon working for the English rancher John Tunstall. Turnstall and Billy developed a close relationship, and many believe that Billy looked upon his employer as the father he had never had. Unfortunately, Tunstall was murdered by members of the Murphy-Dolan gang in the Lincoln County War. Knowing Tunstall's affection for his horses, the gang then shot his favorite horse and put his

hat on the dead animal's head. Distraught, Bonney joined the feud on the side of the regulators. When Lew Wallace became the governor of New Mexico in 1878, Bonney wrote to him asking for immunity in return for his testimony against Tunstall's killers. He met up with the governor, armed with a pistol and a Winchester rifle. Despite helping Wallace to convict the notorious John Dolan, Billy was kept a prisoner and was forced to make his own escape.

Above: Tintype photograph of Billy the Kid.

By now Bonney was a celebrity, and the newspapers coined the sobriquet "Billy the Kid" because of his smooth skin and youthful looks. The Kid was reputedly fed up with having every murder in the West attributed to him, and moaned that "I don't know as anyone would believe anything good of me." He managed to avoid capture for two years, but when he was framed for the murder of Deputy James Carlyle, Pat Garrett was charged with bringing him to justice. Garrett finally caught up with The Kid on December 23, 1880, in a cabin in Stinking Springs. After a brief standoff, Billy surrendered. He was charged and sentenced for the murder of Sheriff Brady during the Lincoln County War, and was taken back to Lincoln to await hanging. The Kid was fully aware that there could now be no reprieve, so he made his final escape, killing guard J.W. Bell. He also took time out to gun down Robert Olinger with his own weapon. Olinger had teased him during his prison stay. Later, The Kid said that he wouldn't have shot Bell if he hadn't tried to run away, but he offered no apology for Olinger's dispatch.

Public opinion now swung against Billy, and Pat Garrett was charged once again with bringing him to justice. It took him three months to catch up with Billy in Fort Sumter. At the very moment that Garrett was pumping rooming house owner Pete Maxwell for intelligence about the Kid's movements, Billy walked in to get a steak for dinner. Garrett felled the youngster with two bullets from his .45 caliber single-action Colt, one of which lodged in Billy's heart. The Kid spoke fluent Spanish, and his rather pathetic final words were, *"Quien es? Quien es?"* - "Who is it? Who is it?"

Fair Mexican maidens play guitars and sing
A song about Billy, their boy bandit king

Billy's brief but colorful career as a gunman and outlaw was over. He was reputed to have gambled with Doc Holliday, dined with Jesse James, and shot targets with Bat Masterson.

His advice to those that would follow in his footsteps was simple: "Advise persons never to engage in killing." Many of his friends and acquaintances mourned

Opposite page: This damaged photograph portrays the tall Bob Ollinger, shot by Billy the Kid in 1881. Ruthless businessman James Dolan is seated.

Above: Pat Garrett, who hunted Billy the Kid with John W. Poe and James Brent.

his passing very sincerely, praising his sense of humor, his loyalty to his friends, his extreme bravery, and the kindness he showed to his horses. Billy looks a little simple in his portrait, but contemporaries spoke of his intelligence and cunning. Many also spoke derisively of Pat Garrett's self-interest. Garrett gained the office of sheriff of Lincoln County for his work in killing The Kid, and wrote the best-selling biography, *The Authentic Life of Billy the Kid: The Noted Desperado of the Southwest.*

But Billy was no "good bad man." By the time of his death, he was pretty well bad through and through, and many believed he was a cold-hearted murderer. But the teenage outlaw of the Southwest has left probably the biggest legend of any gun-slinging wrongdoer of the West.

I'll sing you a true song of Billy the Kid
I'll sing of the desperate deeds that he did
Way out in New Mexico long, long ago
When a man's only chance was
his own forty-four.

When Billy the Kid was a very young lad
In the old Silver City he went to the bad
Way out in the West with a gun in his hand
At the age of twelve years he first killed his man

Now this is how Billy the Kid met his fate
The bright moon was shining,
the hour was late
Shot down by Pat Garrett,
who once was his friend,
The young outlaw's life had now
come to its end.

Left: Pete Maxwell's house. It was here during the night of July 14, 1881 that Pat Garrett sat in Pete's bedroom and shot the Kid.

Colt Lightning

Above: The Colt Lightning with the standard barrel length of 4½ inches and the ejector rod.

This was the first Colt model to feature the distinctive bird's head-shaped grip that was thought to have been influenced by the Webley Bulldog , a popular English revolver of the frontier period.

Henry McCarty, alias Antrim, alias William H. Bonney, but better known to us as Billy the Kid, was in and out of scrapes for all of his short life. Starting in the Lincoln County Wars, he was credited with killing twenty-one men, one for each year of his life. His actual total was thought to be nearer to six.

In his line of work, a rapid-fire revolver would have been a valuable asset, and the aptly named Colt Lightning is on record as being Billy's favorite weapon, in .38 inch caliber. Indeed, there was strong demand for a double-action weapon, and the early models of 1877 strongly resembled the Colt Single-Action or Peacemaker on which they were based. Double action was achieved by adding a strut, which connected the trigger movement to the hammer. This allowed the trigger to slip past the strut at the top of the cycle, thus releasing the hammer. It could also be cocked manually and fired like a single-action. This did have its disadvantages. The trigger pull was necessarily stronger and there were more parts to wear out. But this did not seem to deter Billy, or indeed any of the other 165,999 purchasers of the gun. It was a popular weapon in the final years of the frontier.

SPECIFICATIONS

Caliber: 0.38

Length of barrel: 2½, 3½, and
4½ inches

Barrel shape: Round

Finish: gray with traces of
original blue

Grips: Hard Rubber

Action: Double

Year of manufacture: 1877-1909

Manufacturer: Samuel Colt,
Hartford, Connecticut

Above: Above: The Storekeeper
version of the Lightning had no ejector
rod. Instead, the arbor spindle had a
knobbed end to enable it to be easily
unscrewed to allow the cylinder to be
removed for reloading. This one has
the 2½ inch barrel.

Black Bart

Above: An early tintype of Black Bart, one of the most notorious goldfield robbers. His respectable appearance belies his true profession.

Opposite page: Gold mining was extremely labor-intensive, and only one miner in ten made any money from the goldfields.

Charles E. Bowles, Boles, or Bolton – AKA Black Bart, T.Z. Spalding, and Po8 – was one of the most notorious highwaymen of the post-Gold Rush era. He was a gentleman thief who dressed like a dandy and left doggerel poems at the scenes of his crimes. His strange sense of humor and polite manners made a strange contrast to his prolific thieving. Wells Fargo & Co. was to become Bowles's chief victim, and his nemesis.

Bowles was born in Norfolk, England, in 1829. His parents were John and Maria Bowles, who went on to have ten children. The family immigrated to the United States when Charley was two and settled on a hundred-acre farmstead in Jefferson County, in upstate New York. Strong and fit, Charley was lucky enough to survive a bout of infantile smallpox, usually fatal at the time.

In 1849, he and his brother David set up to make their fortunes in the western goldfields. After a tough winter in Missouri, the pair moved on to Sacramento, California, in 1850. But despite several attempts to strike it lucky in the Gold Rush, which resulted in the deaths of both his brothers from camp diseases, Charley was left pretty much empty-handed. In 1854 Bowles found himself back in Illinois, and married a woman named May Elizabeth Johnson. They had four children together. But Charley never liked ordinary farm life, and was quick to volunteer for the Union Army when the Civil War broke out. He enlisted with the 116th Regiment of the Illinois Infantry on August 13, 1862. He was quickly promoted to First Sergeant in Company B. During his time in the army, he took part in several major actions, including Sherman's Yazoo Expedition (December 1862 to January 1863), the assault on Fort Hindman, the siege of Vicksburg, and the Battle of Resaca. In 1864 he was severely wounded in the side and was extremely lucky to survive his injury. Despite this setback, he returned to his unit, fought in the Battle of Atlanta (featured in *Gone with the Wind*), and took part in Sherman's March to the Sea and his Campaign of the Carolinas. He finally left his regiment in June 1865. But Bowles

found life on the family farm in New Oregon, Iowa, completely stultifying and he was soon back in the goldfields. His failure there – and the reasons for it – were to have a great and malignant influence on his future. Charley had started to work a small Montana gold mine by himself using a process of running water through a series of troughs. Agents of Wells Fargo approached Charley to buy the mine, but he refused, so they cut off his water supply and ended his venture. Forced to abandon his dig, Bowles wrote to his wife about the injustice of the situation, threatening to "take steps." He wrote a final letter to Mary from Silver Bow, Montana, on August 25, 1871. Continuing his tramp around the gold regions, he lost contact with his family, and they assumed that he had died in the Western wilds.

But for eight years, between 1875 and 1883, a well-dressed and polite highwayman committed twenty-eight robberies on Wells Fargo stagecoaches across the Gold Country and California. Wearing a flour sack as a mask and garnished with a jaunty derby hat, "Black Bart," as Bowles styled himself, never fired the shotgun he carried and – terrified of horses – committed his crimes on foot. This trail of lawlessness began on July 26, 1875, when Bowles robbed the Wells Fargo Sonora-to-Milton stagecoach. He politely addressed the stage driver, John Shine, asking him to "please throw down your treasure box, sir?" His poetic signature first came to light after his 1877 robbery of the Sonoma County Point Arena-to-Duncan's Mill stagecoach. A poem, written on a waybill, was left on a tree stump under a stone:

> *I've labored long and hard for bread*
> *For honor and for riches*
> *But on my corns too long you've tred*
> *You fine-haired sons of bitches*
> *Black Bart*
> *The Po8*
> *Driver, give my respects to our friend, the other driver;*
> *But I really had a notion to hang my old disguise hat on his weather eye.*
> *Respectfully, B.B.*

On July 25, 1878, "B.B." left another poem after stealing a $200 diamond ring and $379 in cash:

> *Here I lay me down to sleep*
> *To wait the coming morrow*
> *Perhaps success, perhaps defeat*
> *And everlasting Sorrow*

Let come what will I'll try it on
My condition can't be worse
And if theres money in that box
Tis munny in my purse

Black Bart
The Po8

Over the course of his career, Charley often chatted politely with his victims. "No, don't get out," he said to a woman passenger while robbing the La Porte-to-Oroville stage in 1878. "I never bother the passengers." In 1879, he quipped to the driver of the same stage, "Sure hope you have a lot of gold in that strongbox, I'm nearly out of money." In 1881 the driver of the Yreka-to-Redding coach asked him, "How much did you make?" "Not very much for the chances I take," Bart answered. In fact, he had been stealing around $6,000 a year and living a fairly luxurious lifestyle. He preserved this modus operandi for twenty-eight holdups, most of which took place in Southern Oregon and California.

His luck finally ran out in November 1883, when he attempted to rob the Sonora-to-Milton stagecoach. Bart was shot by Jimmy Rolleri, a young man who was riding shotgun for the driver, Reason E. McConnell. Having jumped down from the driver's box to look for game, he returned to see Bart trying to hatchet open the strongbox. Jimmy managed to wing Black Bart, and even though he managed to escape with thestolen gold, he left his derby and equipment behind a nearby rock. These things proved to be his undoing. The Calaveras County sheriff found a woman who had sold Bart his provisions, but the clue that located this gentleman bandit was a laundry mark on the handkerchief he had dropped at the scene of the crime. This led Wells Fargo detective agents James Hume and Henry Nicholson Morse to his door, at 37 2nd Street, San Francisco, where he was living as Charles E. Bolton, a respectable mine

Above: Black Bart in old age. He asserted that he "never robbed a passenger, or ill-treated a human being."

engineer. Hume described him as "a person of great endurance. Exhibited genuine wit under most trying circumstances. Extremely proper and polite in behavior, eschews profanity."

Convicted of a selection of hold-ups, partly because he openly confessed to crimes perpetrated before 1879 (believing the statute of limitations had expired on these), Bart was convicted to a six-year prison sentence in San Quentin. But in 1888 he was released for good behavior after serving just four years. His health and eyesight had been affected by his time in prison, but he declined to return to his family, though he struck up a correspondence with his wife, Mary. He told her that he was sick of being shadowed by Wells Fargo, but finally gave Agent Hume the slip in February 1888.

In November that same year, a stagecoach was robbed by a masked highwayman who left a poem behind:

> *So here I've stood while wind and rain*
> *Have set the trees a-sobbin,*
> *And risked my life for that damned box*
> *That wasn't worth the robbin'.*

Hume declared that the holdup had been a copycat crime, and there are no further confirmed sightings of Charley Bowles. Rumors persisted that he had been killed at an unsuccessful hold-up, or moved to New York, Montana, or Nevada. Some people even assumed that Wells Fargo had paid Black Bart off. Whatever the truth, this gentleman of the road somehow managed to disappear like the dust on the trails he had haunted during his illustrious career.

Butch Cassidy

"*As technology thrusts us relentlessly into the future, I find myself, perversely, more interested in the past. We seem to have lost something – something vital, something of individuality and passion. That may be why we tend to view the Western outlaw, rightly or not, as a romantic figure.*"

– Robert Redford

"*The best way to hurt them is through their pocket book. They will holler louder than if you cut off both legs. I steal their money just to hear them holler. Then I pass it out among those who really need it.*"

– Butch Cassidy

Of all the Western gunmen and outlaws, none were more fondly remembered and celebrated in folklore than Butch Cassidy. Leader of the Wild Bunch Gang, Cassidy was known as the Robin Hood of the West. Of all the Western bandits, he and his Wild Bunch had the longest and most lucrative criminal careers. Later on, Butch

Below: An early view of Salt Lake City, complete with wagons.

Right: Robert Leroy
Parker, alias Butch
Cassidy, photographed
in the Wyoming
Penitentiary. Despite his
reputation, Cassidy was
not a killer.

and his partner, the Sundance Kid, were to continue with this successful formula, right into the twentieth century. If rumor is to be believed, he was also one of the few Western gunmen to survive into old age.

Butch was born in Beaver, Utah, on April 15, 1866. His real name was Robert LeRoy Parker. His parents were Mormons. Butch's grandfather, Robert Parker, was one of the original Mormon pioneers who set out on the long trek west to Salt Lake City. Unfortunately, he froze to death one night and was buried along the trail by his wife and oldest son, Butch's father, Maximillian. The surviving Parkers continued on to Salt Lake City and established the family in the West. As an adult, Maxi Parker helped other Mormons make their way to Utah and married Ann Campbell Gillies. The couple bought a ranch near Circleville, Utah, and raised their family there. Butch was the eldest of their thirteen children. Despite this ultra-respectable family background, once the young Butch left home, he soon fell under the influence of a local horse thief and cattle rustler, Mike Cassidy. Butch followed the venerable Western tradition of pursuing ranch work. While working at the Eugene Amaretti ranch in Wind River, Wyoming, he was described as a "crack shot, and the best there with a rope. He could ride around a tree at full speed and empty a six-gun into the tree, putting every shot within a three-inch circle." Cassidy also had a brief stint as a butcher in Otto Schnauber's Meat Market at Rock Springs, Wyoming, and this is where he acquired the sobriquet of "Butch." He adopted Cassidy as his last name in veneration of his first criminal mentor. Effectively, he had reinvented himself. In his new identity, Butch seemed free to adopt a completely different way of life than that of his parents. His first offence was trivial, shoplifting some jeans and a pie from a closed shop. At least he had the decency to leave an IOU. But although he was acquitted of this misdemeanor, it seems as though Butch continued to lead a life on the edge of criminality, trading stolen horses and rustling cattle. In 1887, Cassidy met Matthew Warner. Originally, the relationship seemed legitimate. Warner owned a racehorse, which the pair raced in Telluride and in Brown's Park on the Utah-Colorado border. They were highly successful, and divided the winnings between them. But in June 1889, Cassidy, Warner, and two associates robbed the San Miguel bank in Telluride, Colorado.

The raid netted the gang $21,000. They succeeded thanks to excellent forward planning, casing the joint thoroughly in advance of the robbery. Butch used his share of the spoils to buy a ranch near Dubois, Wyoming, and tried to make a living there. Unfortunately, he failed, and returned to his previous career of horse stealing. Cassidy was also suspected of being involved in a protection racket. Butch was

Above: The Wild Bunch. Butch Cassidy is the smiling figure at the right, Sundance is on the left.

arrested in Lander, Wyoming, and on July 15, 1894, he was sentenced to two years hard labor in the Wyoming penitentiary. His prison description portrays him as being five feet nine inches tall, with a light complexion, dark hair, and blue eyes. He was noted to be unmarried, of unknown parentage, no religion, and intemperate habits. Butch had certainly moved a very long way from his Mormon background. Released early by Governor William Alford Richards, Cassidy promised that he would not commit any further offenses in Wyoming. The "gentleman outlaw" was as good as his word, pursuing his criminal career in other states for the majority of his career. It was not until 1900 that he robbed a Union Pacific train near Tipton, Wyoming.

Over the following five years, Butch Cassidy put together a gang of skilled outlaws and masterminded a series of highly successful bank and train robberies in Idaho, Utah, New Mexico, Nevada, Texas, and Montana. Cassidy was one of the first criminals to use the so-called Outlaw Trail, a meandering path that began in Mexico, ran through Utah, and ended in Montana. The trail linked a series of hideouts and ranches that were sympathetic to outlaw cowboys.

By 1896, the gang was well-known throughout the west as the Wild Bunch and had netted over $270,000 in spoils. Cassidy himself was known as The King of the Wild Bunch. The gang included such criminal luminaries as Harry Longabaugh (the Sundance Kid, originally from Pennsylvania), Harvey Logan (Kid Curry), Bill Carver, Ben Kilpatrick (the Tall Texan), Harry Tracy, Henry Wilbur Meeks (another Mormon from Utah), and Butch's closest friend, Elzy Lay. Butch described the "Bunch" in this way to his family "There were a lot of good friends, but Elzy Lay was the best, always dependable and level-headed. Sundance and I got along fine, but he liked his liquor too much and was too quick on the trigger."

The gang was responsible for the most lucrative series of crimes in the history of the Old West, but was not considered particularly violent. It was even celebrated for fighting for settlers' rights "against the old time cattle baron." But in fact, several gang members were guilty of a number of murders, including those of Sheriff Joe Hazen, Sheriff Edward Farr, and posse man Henry Love. Ironically, it was Elzy Lay who was convicted of the murders of Farr and Love, and was sentenced to life imprisonment in the New Mexico State Penitentiary. Butch himself swore to his father that he had never killed a man, but added that "some of my boys had itchy fingers. I tried to control 'em." The gang was also famous for its wry humor. In 1901, the Wild Bunch sat for a group portrait photograph. In the resulting image, known as the Fort Worth Five photograph, the men look uncannily like the Dodge City Peace Commission with their smart suits, derby hats, and watch chains. The Pinkerton Detective Agency obtained a copy of the photograph, and used it on their wanted posters for the gang.

As railroads crossed the West and communications got better, it got harder and harder for criminals to escape the burgeoning law machine. In 1900, several Wild Bunch members were involved in shootouts with various lawmen, and Kid Curry's brothers George and Lonny were killed.

Butch and Sundance realized that their days as Western gunmen were over. Their carefully-planned strategy of using secret hideouts was becoming less and less secure. They could feel the tightening of the net as state law officials and the

Above: Formal portrait of Sundance and Etta Place, taken at De Young's studio in New York.

Pinks closed in on them. The Wild Bunch disbanded, and the pair fled east to New York City in 1901, accompanied by Sundance's girlfriend, Etta Place. From there, they set sail for Buenos Aires on the British steamship *Herminius*. Butch and Sundance bought a huge fifteen-thousand-acre ranch in Cholilo, Chubut Province, Argentina, complete with a four-room log cabin. They stocked it with thirteen hundred sheep, five hundred cattle, and thirty-five horses. But after three years of trying to live honestly, the pair became short of money again and started a campaign of robbing Argentinean banks of money and gold. They escaped with a substantial sum of money and sold the Cholila ranch. They then caught the steamship *Condor* into Chile, but were to make a further foray back into Argentina in December 1905, robbing the Banco de la Nacion in Villa Mercedes of 12,000 pesos.

In 1906 the trio split when Etta Place decided she wanted to return to America. Despite the risk, Sundance escorted her back to San Francisco. Butch got work guarding the company payroll at the Concordia Tin Mine in Bolivia, and Sundance joined him on his return. But the pair was irrevocably drawn to the easy life, and in 1908 they attacked a silver mine courier near San Vicente, Bolivia, and stole 15,000 pesos from him. A pair of bandits was subsequently tracked to a small lodging house in the town, which was soon surrounded by a posse of armed lawmen, soldiers, and the local mayor. When the Bolivians opened fire, the bandit pair returned it. A hellish fire fight opened up, and the bandits expired in a hail of

bullets. It was speculated that one of them had fatally shot his partner in crime in the head, to put him out of his misery. It was assumed that the dead men were Butch and Sundance, and the pair did nothing to disabuse this assumption.

In her 1975 book, *Butch Cassidy, My Brother*, Lula Parker Betenson claimed that her brother Butch Cassidy returned to the United States in 1908, using the alias William Thadeus Phillips. Phillips settled in Morenci, Michigan, where he married Gertrude Livesay. They then moved to Arizona. They adopted their son William Richard Phillips in 1919. According to Betenson, her brother unsuccessfully tried gold mining in Alaska before establishing the Phillips Manufacturing Company in Spokane, Washington, in 1912. He sold adding machines, farm machinery parts, automatic garage-door openers, and automobile gas mileage indicators. Lula says that in 1925, Butch attended a family reunion in Circleville, Utah, which was attended by their father Maxi, their brother Mark, and Lula herself. She maintained that Butch had told their father that he had tried to quit his life of crime on many occasions, but explained that "when a man gets down, they won't let him get up. He never quits paying his price."

In 1930 William Phillips's business failed in the depression, and Lula's book tells how Butch tried in vain to locate caches of money he had hidden during his bandit career. In 1934, he wrote his own life story, *The Bandit Invincible, the Story of Butch Cassidy*, but failed to find a publisher. Phillips died of cancer on July 20, 1937, at the age of seventy-one. He was cremated, and his ashes were scattered over the Little Spokane River.

Above: Pinkerton agents acted as Union spies during the Civil War and helped to break up the unions. The term "private eye" was inspired by their symbol.

Colt Dragoon

Below: Detail of the Cylinder showing the honest patina of age. Originally, many of these weapons had intricate engravings of combat scenes on the cylinders.

In the late 1840s, Texas became the focus of weapons activity on the Western frontier. The Alamo massacre of 1836, and the subsequent wWar of Texan Independence, resulted in a heavy demand for advanced weapons with which to defend the newly established republic. Demand for Colts was stimulated by the notable success of the Texas Paterson Colt revolvers at Hays's Big Fight. Captain Jack Hays and a detachment of fifteen Texas Rangers defeated over eighty Comanche using the weapon. The Indians had rushed the small force of Texans after their first volley of

SPECIFICATIONS

Caliber: 0.44

Length of barrel: 8 inches

Barrel shape: Round

Finish: Gray with traces of blue

Grips: Walnut

Action: Single action 6 shot repeating revolver

Year of manufacture: 1848

Manufacturer: Samuel Colt, New York City

The Colt Dragoon is one of the first models in what is regarded as the classic Colt shape. Its massive proportions and heavy brass fittings gave it an unfortunate handicap in the weight department.

shots, thinking that the Rangers had paused to reload. But the repeating handguns continued to fire, with devastating effect.

When the war with Mexico began, The Rangers were enlisted into the U.S. Cavalry and became Dragoons. This honorable name was given to the new Colt pistol, patented in 1848. The Colt Dragoon was available in .44-inch caliber, which made it a particularly potent weapon with good stopping power. The six-shot cylinder gave it remarkable flexibility for the time, and it acquitted itself well in use against Indians and Mexicans alike. Its introduction was also well timed for use in the 1849 Gold Rush, when the demand for weapons of self-defense rose alarmingly.

Nobody was going to jump your claim staring down the barrel of a .44 Dragoon. However, the gun did have its drawbacks. Weighing in at a considerable four pounds, two ounces, it was the second-largest Colt revolver ever made. (The Colt Walker was 6 ounces heavier). This weight meant that the gun was supplied with a pommel holster rather than a belt type. Later models also had a shoulder stock, enabling them to be fired like carbines. Many examples were factory-engraved with Texas Ranger and Indian fight scenes, in honor of the gun's pedigree. Despite later advances in pistols, the Dragoon was carried for many years on the frontier. Over 20,000 examples were made.

The Dalton Gang

Opposite page: After the failure of the Coffeyville bank raids, the corpses of Bob and Grat Dalton are held up for the photographer.

Below: Bob Dalton and his sweetheart, Eugenia Moore.

" *The Daltons died without taking their boots off.*"

– Sign placed next to the Daltons' graves

Lewis and Adeline Dalton had a large family of fifteen children; ten boys and five girls. Most of the Dalton offspring were born in Cass County, Michigan, where Lewis owned a saloon, but the family later settled on a farm outside of Coffeyville, Kansas. With no hint of what was to come, the Daltons' eldest son, Frank, became a Deputy U.S. Marshal, working for Judge Isaac Parker in Oklahoma's dangerous Indian Territory. His younger brothers revered him and the whole family were devastated when he was cruelly murdered by outlaw Will Towerly. Already wounded by the horse thief Dave Smith, Frank begged Towerly not to shoot him, saying that he was already dying, but it was no use. He was buried in Coffeyville Cemetery.

Frank's younger brothers, Emmett, Gratton, and Bob followed him into the service, but were soon disillusioned. Emmett described the work that was expected of them: "Grafting – as we of today know the term – was a mild, soothing description of what occurred." There was also some disagreement over unpaid expenses, and the brothers quit. They subsequently became involved in a little cattle rustling and became outlaws, working on the wrong side of the law. This is a pattern that Western gunmen often followed, starting on one side of the law and ending on the other. Having once been identified as wrong-doers, the penalties for law-breaking were so draconian that petty criminals were almost obliged to continue in a life of crime. This is what happened to the Daltons. Bob and the other brothers formed an eight-man gang, recruiting five other criminals to join them: Bill Power, Dick Broadwell, George Newcomb, Charley Pierce, and Charlie Bryant. The gang then began a brief but flamboyant career of train robberies and holdups, ultimately planning to break all records by pulling off a double bank heist in their hometown of Coffeyville. It was Bob Dalton's ambition to "beat anything Jesse James ever did – rob two banks at once, in broad daylight." Targeting their home town was their first mistake.

Above: The Condon Bank at Coffeyville, photographed at the time of the raid.

They rode into town, armed with pearl-handled Colt .45s, disguised as a U.S. Marshal and his posse. Despite wearing false beards, the three Dalton brothers were almost instantly recognized by a passerby, who alerted the marshal and townsfolk. They had planned to rob the First National Bank first, and then go on to the C.M. Condon & Company Bank. Their first raid went off successfully, but as they left the Condon Bank they were met by a hail of bullets from a group of armed citizens led by Marshal Charles T. Connelly. A massive gun battle ensued in which Connelly and three townspeople were killed. After Connelly's demise, liveryman John J. Kloehr took over the attack, and four members of the Dalton gang fell, shot in what is now known as Death Alley. The four gang members killed were Bob and

Grat Dalton, Bill Powers, and Dick Broadwell. Emmett Dalton was very seriously injured, collecting twenty-three gunshot wounds, but – miraculously – he survived.

The bodies of the dead gang members were treated with scant regard, photographed like trophies, and publicly displayed. For years, the two dead Dalton brothers lay in a grave unmarked except for a rusty piece of iron pipe, to which the gang had tethered their horses. Some years later, Emmett erected a headstone for them. He had been sentenced to life imprisonment after the disastrous Coffeyville raids, but was released after serving fourteen years in the Kansas State Penitentiary in Lansing. Emmett went on to lead a blameless life. He moved to California and became a real estate agent, author, and movie actor. In 1909, he was

Above: Bill Powers, Bob and Grat Dalton, and Dick Broadwell lie dead and handcuffed outside Coffeyville Jail on October 5, 1892.

Above: Emmett Dalton survived his incarceration, and appeared in a Hollywood movie about the Dalton brothers.

employed as a consultant on a film about the Dalton gang's last stand, and wrote several books condemning criminality. In 1918, he played himself in the film version of his book *Beyond the Law*. In 1931, Emmett published *When the Daltons Rode*, which was later made into a movie about the gang's brief career. He died six years later in 1937.

The Dodge City Peace Commission

The Dodge City War must be one of the most famous bloodless conflicts in history, and a consequently a strange interlude in the history of Western gunfighters. From its beginnings, Dodge City, Kansas, was known as The Wickedest City in America, and was a hub of gambling, carousing, the whiskey trade, and prostitution. *The Hays Sentinel* said that the town was "full of prostitutes, and every house is a brothel." The so-called Dodge City Gang ran the town on the simple principle that any activity that made money was a good thing. The local merchants and saloonkeepers ran the town for the pleasure of thousands of cowboys that drifted through, and took as much money from them as they could. *The Yates Center News* described the town as "a den of thieves and cutthroats, the whole town in league to rob the unwary stranger." Local saloon keeper James H. Kelley – mayor of Dodge City from 1877 until 1881 – was the leader of the gang, and the Masterson brothers, Charlie Bassett, and Wyatt Earp were his most prominent associates. But in 1881, Mayor B. Webster was elected on a reform ticket to clean up the town. Many townsfolk were sick of the constant brawling, gun fighting, and vice that afflicted Dodge City, and were looking for a more peaceful way of life. Ironically, although Webster had opened a dry goods store in the town in 1872, by the time he was elected mayor he also owned two saloons. His cleanup campaign was really a way of cornering the town's lucrative rackets for himself and his friends. He soon started to substitute prominent Gang members with his own people, replacing city marshal Jim Masterson with one of his bartenders, Fred Singer. Webster then went on to post a series of moral ordinances throughout the town reading, "All thieves, thugs, confidence men, and persons without visible means of support will take notice that the ordinance enacted for their special benefit will be rigorously enforced on and after tomorrow." In reality, Webster used the fines he collected to fund his appointed lawmen and retain his grip on Dodge. He levied fines of $5 to $100 on prostitutes, brothel keepers, vagrants, or those involved in "any unlawful calling whatever," so this was a lucrative source of income.

Luke Short arrived in the town in 1882. Bat Masterson described his five-foot six-inch frame as a "small package, but one of great dynamic force." Short was a well-known gambler, dandy, and man killer, celebrated as the "Undertaker's Friend." He had shot Charlie Storms dead inside the notorious Oriental Saloon in Tombstone. He was also a close friend of Wyatt Earp and Bat Masterson. Short

Above: Timberline, a noted Dodge city prostitute, still displays some of the good looks she had before debauchery, drink, and disease ruined her and many other "soiled doves."

Left: Dodge City advises would-be troublemakers to refrain from carrying firearms in the city limits. Prickly Ash Bitters was a popular alcoholic drink brewed from this aromatic and bitter shrub. It was a favorite "gunfight lubricant."

Right: The Dodge City
Peace Commission of 1883,
photographed by C.S. Fly.
Back row: (left to right)
Harris, Short, Masterson,
W.F. Petillon (Petillon added
himself to the original
photograph). Front row:
C.E. Bassett, Wyatt Earp,
M.F. Mclain, and Neil
Brown. The Commission
assembled to support
fellow gunslinger Luke
Short.

subsequently bought a half share in Dodge's Long Branch Saloon, but Mayor Webster longed to get this loose cannon out of town and drive him out of business. As far as Webster was concerned, Short was a dangerous business rival with undesirable friends and acquaintances. Supposedly as part of Webster's "cleanup" of the town, Sheriff Louis C. Hartman arrested three "singers" at the Long Branch. Furious, Short tried to spring the women from jail, but ended up in a shootout with Hartman. A few days later, Short was captured by Marshal Jack Bridges, charged with assault, fined $2,000, and deported from the town as an undesirable. He caught a train east to Kansas City, from where he wired his friends to come to his aid. Bat Masterson suggested that Short should go to Topeka to discuss his predicament with Governor George Washington Glick. Glick was an anti-prohibitionist, and was immediately sympathetic to Short's tale of "political differences and business rivalry." When Glick summoned the county clerk of Ford County, W.F. Petillon, to give evidence, he confirmed Short's version of events. On May 15, the *Kansas City Evening Star* published a list of the men who were assembling to facilitate Short's return to Dodge City "and protect him from molestation". They included Wyatt Earp, Doc Holliday, Shotgun Collins, Rowdy Joe Lowe, Bat Masterson, and Charlie Bassett. Dodge's thoroughly intimidated Sheriff Hinkle started to meet all incoming trains from Kansas City with a posse in tow.

Wyatt Earp arrived in Dodge City on May 31, 1883, accompanied by Dan Tipton, Johnny Green, Texas Jack Vermillion, and Johnny Millsap. Bat Masterson's friend and part-time lawman "Prairie Dog" Dave Morrow met the group from the train. Earp persuaded Morrow to swear him and his companions in as deputies so that they could legally wear their guns in town. Morrow obliged. Several more "Peace Commissioners" subsequently arrived to

Above: Luke Short was the proprietor of the famous Elephant Saloon in Fort Worth, Texas, which became the haunt of the most accomplished Western cardsharps.

support their friends, including Charlie Bassett, Frank McLain, and Shotgun Collins. Terrified, Sheriff Hinkle wired Governor Glick, asking him to send militiamen to keep the peace. Glick declined, and Webster now knew that he was in a hopeless position. He summoned Wyatt Earp, who was well known for his reasonableness and even temper, to cut a deal and prevent an all-out gun war in the town. Short reappeared in Dodge on June 4, conspicuously armed with at least three guns, one on each hip and a shotgun in his hand. By now, around fifty men were gathered in the Long Branch Saloon ready to support Luke Short's right to return to Dodge City.

By the time Governor Glick's Adjutant General, Thomas Moonlight, arrived in the town a couple of days later, he thought that the trouble had been greatly exaggerated. By this time, the two sides had reached an amicable accommodation. Gambling and prostitution would continue, but the worst elements would be weeded out. Luke Short would be able to return to his business undisturbed. Bat Masterson arrived in town on June 9, and agreed with Moonlight's assessment of the situation. "If at any time they did 'don the war paint,' it was completely washed off before I reached here."

The bloodless Dodge City War was over without a shot having been fired. Moonlight established "Glick's Guards," a group of men selected from both town factions to keep the future peace in Dodge. But the most lasting souvenir of the occasion was the famous photograph of Short and seven of his most notorious friends, taken by C.S. Fly in June 1883. This gang of eight gunfighters, gamblers, lawmen, and saloon keepers became known as the "Dodge City Peace Commission." Sitting in the front of the picture are Charlie Bassett, Wyatt Earp, Frank McLain, and Neal Brown. Standing at the back are W.H. Harris, Luke Short,

Bat Masterson, and W.F. Petillon. After the picture was taken, the "Commission" dispersed around the country, never to be seen together again.

Unabashed by having been the cause of so much trouble, Luke Short sold his share of the Long Branch saloon in November that year, and moved on to Fort Worth, Texas, where he bought another saloon. Short threatened to sue Dodge City for having forced him to leave the town in 1883, and was awarded an out-of-court settlement by the town. He put the money to good use, became a successful and wealthy professional gambler, and moved into Fort Worth's high society. But he never lost his impetuous streak, and killed the well-known gunfighter Jim Courtright in a February 1887 shootout. But it was illness, not violence, that was to bring about Short's demise just six years later. In 1893, he died of "dropsy" at the Gueda Springs mineral spa, at the ripe old age of thirty-nine. Not even his body was returned to Dodge City, and his wife buried him at Fort Worth.

The Doolin-Dalton Gang

Below: The Rose of Cimarron. A well-known prostitute, she was associated with the Doolin-Dalton Gang.

In 1893, Bill Doolin was to form what was to become one of the most violent and disreputable gangs of the Old West. Of all the bands of robbers and shootists that roamed the West, the Doolin-Dalton gang (also known as the Wild Bunch, the Oklahombres, and the Oklahoma Long Riders after their long duster coats), was to meet the most comprehensively violent end. Between 1892 and 1904, all eleven gang members died from gun wounds administered by lawmen or their agents.

William M. "Bill" Doolin was born in Johnson County, Arkansas in 1858. He was the son of a farmer, but rode west in 1881, working odd jobs until he arrived in Oklahoma Territory. He ended up working as a ranch hand at the H-X ranch on the Cimarron River. Doolin became a skilled cow poke and was equally handy with his six-shooter. It was here that Bill hitched up with the Dalton brothers (who had also worked at the H-X). The men formed an alliance that was to evolve into the Wild Bunch. Doolin had his first serious brush with the law in 1891, while he was working at the Bar X Ranch. He and several other cowhands rode into Coffeyville, Kansas, to celebrate Independence Day with a glass of beer. Unfortunately, as Kansas was a dry state, the local law soon became involved in the party. A shootout broke out when the lawmen tried to confiscate the liquor, and two fell wounded. It was the fulcrum of Doolin's life. Implicated in the shootings, he was a wanted man who lived outside the law for the rest of his life.

Two months after this affray, Bill was already riding with the Dalton brothers, participating with them in numerous train robberies in Indian and Oklahoma Territories, including those at Leliaetta, Red Rock, and Adair. Doolin did not flinch at any kind of violence, and shot a doctor dead during one of these raids. Fortunately for him, Bill did not accompany the Daltons on their ill-fated Coffeyville banks raids of October 5, 1892. Many reasons have been proposed for his omission from the gang that day: Bob Dalton was jealous of his popularity, or thought he was too wild, or Doolin's horse went lame. Whatever the true reason for his absence, the Dalton gang was decimated by the Coffeyville debacle. Bob and Grat Dalton, Bill Powers, and Dick Broadwell were all shot to death, and Emmett Dalton was seriously wounded and captured. Despite this, the remnant of the gang, including Bill Doolin, Bill Dalton, George Newcomb, and Charlie Pierce, immediately continued their campaign of robbery and violence, with a train robbery at Caney, Kansas, just a week later.

The gang immediately started to recruit new members to replace the dead and injured, trawling the area for suitable men. Doolin enlisted Dan Clifton, George Waightman, Roy Daugherty, Alf Sohn, Ol' Yantis, Tulsa Jack Blake, and Bob Grounds to form one of the most prolific bands of outlaws in the West. For three years the gang terrorized the area, robbing from banks, trains, and stagecoaches. On November 1, 1892, the gang raided the Ford County Bank at Spearville, Kansas. This resulted in the first death of the re-formed gang. Ol' Yantis was cornered at his sister's farm in Oklahoma Territory and gunned down by a posse of lawmen. On June 11 the following year, the seeds of Doolin's own destruction were sown when the gang held up the California-New Mexico express just west of Cimarron, Kansas. The raid was successful, netting around $1,000 in silver, but Doolin was shot in the right foot. The wound was to cause him trouble for the rest of his life, and ultimately impeded his final escape.

Above: Bill Doolin, one of the West's most notorious bad men.

But for the moment, the gang became more and more daring, and Doolin got married on March 14, 1893. His bride was Edith Ellsworth of Ingalls, Oklahoma Territory, a preacher's daughter. Whether Edith knew of Bill's colorful career is unknown, but she was to stick with him for the rest of his life, keeping their relationship secret. Bill's romance led him to spend a considerable time in Ingalls, and the gang became popular in the town, using George Ransom's saloon as their headquarters. Gang member George Newcomb also found love in the town with Rose Dunn. Rose was to go down in western legend as the Rose of Cimarron. But the gang's domestic comfort was disturbed on September 1, 1893, when they were cornered in the town by a posse of thirteen men. These enforcers included five U.S. marshals, who had entered the town in two wagons. The marshals were led by Deputy Marshal John Hixon. A fierce gun battle that was to become known as the Battle of Ingalls broke out in which three of the marshals were shot. Deputy Dick

Speed was shot dead instantly, while Deputies Tom Hueston and Lafe Shadley (shot by Bill Dalton) died from their wounds the following day. George Newcomb was also wounded, and pinned down by the firefight. Rose braved the bullets to run Newcomb from the Pierce Hotel, bringing him two ammunition belts and a Winchester rifle. She was also reputed to have fired at the marshals to cover her lover's escape from the town. Several bystanders, including local man Frank Briggs, were also killed, and several more were wounded in the firefight. The marshals called out to Doolin to surrender, but his only reply was to tell them to "go to hell!" A single gang member, Roy Daugherty (also known as Arkansas Tom Jones), was captured and sentenced to fifty years in Guthrie Prison, but the rest of the Wild Bunch escaped unscathed. Dalton and Doolin left town riding a single horse, as Dalton had lost his mount in the battle.

But despite this narrow escape from justice, the gang continued with their thieving. Two more men joined the Wild Bunch in early 1894: William F. Raidler and Little Dick West. On January 3, 1894, the gang began the year with a raid on the post office at Clarkson, Oklahoma Territory. They followed this by robbing the Farmers Citizens Bank at Pawnee and the Santa Fe station at Woodward.

By this time, U.S. Marshal Evett Dumas Nix of Oklahoma Territory was sick and tired of the Wild Bunch's activities and assembled the legendary Three Guardsmen to bring the gang to justice. The famous trio, first brought together in 1889, consisted of Deputy U.S. Marshals Bill Tilghman, Chris Madsen, and Heck Thomas.

Nix's written orders of March 20, 1894 were clear: "I have selected you to do this work, placing explicit confidence in your abilities to cope with those desperados and bring them in – alive if possible, dead if necessary." But even as The Guardsmen started to track the gang down, chasing them across five states, the Wild Bunch continued to cut a swath of mayhem throughout the area. In April, they attempted to rob retired U.S. Deputy Marshal W.H. Carr's store at Sacred Heart, Indian Territory. Carr was shot in the stomach during the raid, but managed to shoot George Newcomb in the shoulder. The gang fled empty-handed. But in May 1894, the gang successfully robbed the bank at Southwest City, Missouri, of $4,000. By this time, Bill Dalton had left the Wild Bunch to start his own gang. He recruited Jim Wallace, Big Asa Knight, Jim Knight, and George Bennett to join him. On May 23, they celebrated with a raid on the First National Bank in Longview, Texas. It was disastrous. On June 8, 1894, the local law successfully trailed the gang to their hideout near Ardmore, Texas. Bill Dalton and two others were shot dead, while the fourth man spent the rest of his life in jail.

The net was also tightening around Bill Doolin and his cohorts. On March 3, 1895, a posse tracked the gang to Rose Dunn's family farm, just outside Ingalls. The Dunn family had never been members of the Wild Bunch, but had harbored them from time to time and fenced stolen goods on their behalf. To encourage their quarry to give themselves up, the deputies threw in a stick of dynamite. The Wild Bunch had an extremely narrow escape, having left the previous day.

Above: An unusual panoramic view of Coffeyville, Kansas. The photograph was taken after the Daltons' infamous bank raids made the town notorious.

On April 3, 1895, the gang pulled off their final raid. It was on the Rock Island train. By an amazing stroke of bad fortune, they were unable to open the train safe, which contained an army payroll of over $50,000. They were reduced to robbing the unfortunate passengers instead. Guardsman Chris Madsen picked up the gang's trail on the following day and found the Wild Bunch camping near Ames, Oklahoma Territory. Tulsa Jack was shot and killed in the ensuing gun fight, but the gang itself was shattered by these events and never reunited.

Under the leadership of Nix, the marshals now resorted to more subtle tactics, posting rewards for the killing or capture of gang members and for information leading to their whereabouts. The strategy worked, and when George Newcomb and Charlie Pierce returned to their refuge at Dunn farm, the Dunn brothers shot and killed both men as they lay asleep in their beds. The fact that George Newcomb was their sister's lover didn't save him. Shattered by this betrayal, Bill Doolin tried to cut a deal with Nix for a light prison sentence for robbery, but Nix refused. Bill was forced to hide out in New Mexico with Little Dick West. But Bill missed Edith and their young son, and returned to Oklahoma to collect his family. The trio then made their way to Kansas. But Marshal Bill Tilghman tracked Edith to their refuge in Eureka Springs, Oklahoma, and after a fist fight in a bathhouse, managed to capture Doolin himself. Taken to Guthrie, Oklahoma, to stand trial, Doolin made good his promise that he

Left: Christopher Madsen was born in Denmark and served in the Danish army before immigrating to the United States. He joined the Fitch Cavalry before becoming a Western lawman.

would never spend time behind bars by organizing a mass break-out for himself and thirty-seven other prisoners on July 5, 1896. He fled to Mexico and hid at writer Eugene Manlove Rhode's ranch. With Doolin out of the way, the surviving gang members scattered far and wide.

Despite Doolin's violent and criminal nature, it was his love for his wife and child that were to be his nemesis. Lonely for their company, he left the relative safety of Mexico to collect Edith from her family's home at Lawson, Oklahoma

Opposite page: Henry Andrew Thomas, known as "Heck." Thomas was one of the famous Three Guardsmen, with Bill Tilghman and Chris Madsen. Together, they helped to establish the rule of law in early Oklahoma.

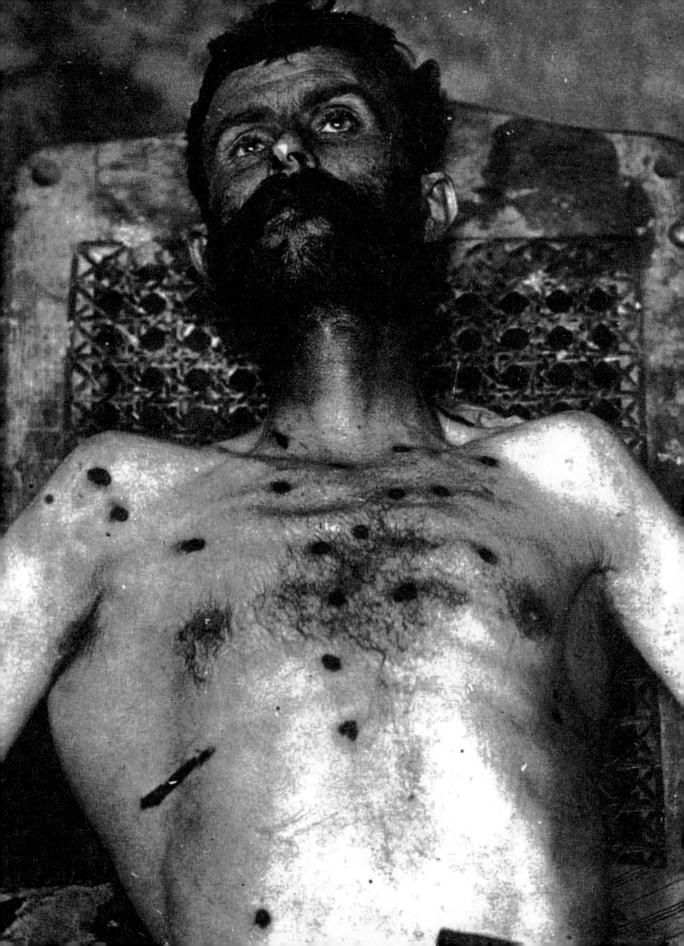

Territory. As he approached the farmhouse on foot, quietly leading his horse, Marshall Heck Thomas and his posse ambushed him. Heck called on Doolin to surrender. Doolin's response was to raise his rifle, and the posse shot it from his hands. Doolin then pulled a six-gun. It was to be his last violent action. Deputies Bill Dunn and Heck Thomas brought him down with a rain of bullets and shotgun fire. It was August 24, 1896. For a man of his chosen profession, Doolin had almost made it to old age.

Even in death, the famous outlaw was allowed no dignity; his corpse was put on show, undressed to the waist to show his fatal injuries. It was really true, the man who had organized a spree of robbery and murder that had terrorized the West had met his own ignominious end.

By the time of Doolin's death, only two other Wild Bunch members were still alive and free: Dynamite Dick Clifton and Little Dick West. Briefly, the pair joined up with the Jennings Gang, but left after a short time with them. Clifton survived until 1897, when he was shot and killed by a posse led by Guardsman Chris Madsen near Checotah, Indian Territory. The following year, Chris Madsen's Marshals also accounted for Little Dick West, in Logan County, Oklahoma Territory, on April 8, 1898. Little Bill Raidler was the final member of the Wild Bunch to meet his maker. Captured by Bill Tilghman, Raidler had been in jail since September 1895. He was paroled for ill health in 1903, but his freedom proved short lived. He died in 1904, from wounds received at the time of his capture.

The ignominious end of the Doolin-Dalton gang was largely the work of U.S. Marshall Nix, who had made their capture and dispersal his top priority. He knew that the West could not accommodate men of this kind and hope to become civilized. As well as his high-profile appointment of the Three Guardsmen, it is estimated that as many as a hundred marshals worked on their capture under Nix's direction. In addition to bringing about the end of a veritable tide of lawless behavior, the destruction of the Wild Bunch sent out a strong message that the age of the criminal gunman's supremacy was drawing to a close in the West.

Opposite page: Bill Doolin lies dead on a mortuary slab, riddled with bullets. He was killed by a posse in Lawson, Oklahoma in 1896.

Colt Buntline Special

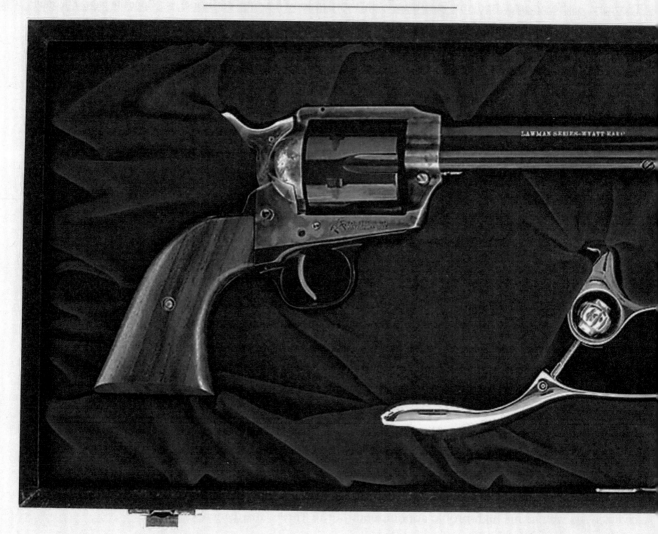

An exciting version of the Colt Single Action appeared at the Philadelphia Centennial Exhibition of 1876, when the weapon was offered with a sixteen-inch barrel and a skeleton shoulder stock. Only thirty examples were originally offered. The gun acquired its legendary association with Wyatt Earp when (it was claimed) dime novelist Ned Buntline (Edward Judson) ordered five Colt Special .45 revolvers to equip the Dodge City Peace Commission, of whom Earp was one. This is how the guns got their name,

the Buntline Specials. It is not known if Earp actually carried his Special, but Buckskin Frank Leslie, a Tombstone gambler and bartender, ordered a ten-inch version in 1881. This was the year of the Earp brothers' famous gunfight at the O.K. Corral.

Clearly these experimental modifications would have turned the Colt Single Action into a very useful weapon. Fired down a sixteen-inch barrel, the .45 cartridges would have been extremely accurate and have had great stopping power at range. The nickel-plated skeleton stock

meant that the shootist could hold the gun extremely steady, and take careful aim before squeezing the trigger. The gun could also be fired without the stock, and the extra length and weight of the barrel would have ironed out any tendency to kick. The gun went on to be manufactured for many years after 1876, and is still available in presentation cases like the one shown.

SPECIFICATIONS

Caliber: 0.45

Length of barrel: 16 inches

Barrel shape: Round

Finish: Blue/casehardened

Grips: Walnut

Action: Single Action Revolver

Year of manufacture: 1876

Manufacturer: Colt

Above: A modern reproduction of this legendary arm, complete with skeleton stock and silk lined presentation case. Such weapons are highly prized by collectors.

Wyatt Earp

Below: The Colt Buntline
Special, said to have been
carried by Wyatt Earp.

Wyatt Earp was born in Monmouth, Illinois, and grew up on a farm in Iowa. He became one of the most complex and interesting of the gunfighter frontiersmen of the West. In 1864, Wyatt and his brothers moved to Colton, California, with their parents, which was near San Bernadino. Like many frontier men, Wyatt worked in a succession of "Western" jobs: shotgun messenger for Wells Fargo, railway worker, and buffalo hunter. He also joined several of his contemporaries in law enforcement, including Bat Masterson and Bill Hickok. Wyatt served as a deputy marshal in Wichita, Kansas, and in Dodge City itself. He was reputed to have carried a Colt handgun, either an Army or a Peacemaker. Less reliably, legend has it that he also used a Colt "Buntline Special," with a

detachable stock. This particular weapon may just have been a presentation piece, given to him in the 1920s by an adoring fan. Ned Buntline presented the original Buntlines to various members of the Doge City Peace Commission, but not all of the recipients considered the weapons practical. Personally, Earp was noted as a tough and decisive man, but was also considered by many to be self-contained, a "cold fish." Despite this, he was a lifelong friend of both Bat Masterson and Doc Holliday, who he originally met while working in Kansas. Like many Western gunmen, Wyatt also gained a reputation as a talented professional gambler.

Earp had gone East and married in 1870, but his new wife died suddenly. He remarried and left Dodge City in 1878, setting up home with his brothers and their wives in Tombstone, Arizona. Tombstone was then a boom silver mining town, originally founded in 1877. Known as "the town too tough to die," it seemed an ideal location for the family. In dress and manner, the Earp brothers exemplified the gentlemen gunmen of their era; they were hard as nails but poised and stylish. Wyatt subsequently acquired the gambling concession in the town's Oriental Saloon, and his brother Virgil became Town Marshal. Brother Morgan worked for

Left: Wyatt Earp fought in the most famous shootout of all time, the O.K. Corral.

the local police department. Earp's second marriage failed, and he met his third wife, Josephine Marcus, in Tombstone. But everything in town wasn't rosy. A feud developed between the Earp brothers and Ike Clanton's Gang that culminated on October 26, 1881, with the most famous gunfight of them all, just outside the O.K. Corral, where the Earp brothers "swapped lead" with the Clanton-McLaury Gang. Although three men died at the O.K. Corral, the Earp brothers survived the shootout. But in the following year, Morgan Earp was gunned down by an unknown assassin. Predictably, his death was avenged by the surviving Earp brothers, and Wyatt was obliged to skip town to Colorado to avoid being tried for murder. Despite this, Wyatt remained in law enforcement. In 1893, he became a member of the so-called Dodge City Peace Commission (together with Bat Masterson and Charlie Bassett, among others), which convened to support fellow gunslinger and saloon owner Luke Short. The city fathers of Dodge City wanted

Right: Bader &
Laubner's saloon at
Dodge City in the
1880s, complete with a
polished wood bar and
huge plate glass
mirrors.

to clean up the town and make it more attractive to settlers, so they tried to evict undesirable elements like Short and his ilk. They soon backed down when Luke's friends turned up.

Wyatt and Josie spent the next few years tramping around the booming mining towns of the frontier, gambling and investing in real estate and saloons as they passed through. In 1897 they operated a saloon in Alaska at the peak of the gold rush there, and made a fortune estimated at around $80,000. They then headed for Tonopah, Nevada, cashing in on that town's gold strike.

Earp ultimately took up prospecting himself and staked many claims in the Mojave Desert, including several just outside Death Valley. At one stage, he was reputed to have sold a worked-out silver mine for $30,000. In 1906, Earp struck seams of both gold and copper, and spent the final winters of his life working these veins. In the summers he and Josie lived (in some style) in Los Angeles, mixing with the Hollywood glitterati of the time.

Wyatt died in Los Angeles in 1929, at the ripe old age of eighty. He was one of the very few gunslingers to make it into old age, and was perhaps unique in that he was able to enjoy his own burgeoning reputation. He was an intensely paradoxical man, one who had both upheld and manipulated the law: a speculator and gambler, who was also an able businessman and investor who knew the value of hard work. He was a loyal friend and partner who inspired great devotion from his friends, but was also noted for his cool demeanor and lack of personal warmth.

Like all the old gunslingers, he had his own tricks of the trade. Earp claimed that he only ever loaded five bullets into a six-shooter to "ensure against accidental discharge."

Robert Ford

Robert or "Bob" Ford has the unenviable distinction among Western gunfighters of being defined for posterity by the man he murdered; the far more celebrated Jesse James.

Best known as "the dirty little coward," Robert Newton Ford was born in 1861 in Ray County, Missouri. From childhood, Robert hero-worshiped Jesse James, reading the nickel novels he inspired. Bob finally got to meet James in 1880. He and his older brother Charles began to hang around on the outer circle of the remnant of the James-Younger Gang. By this time, several members had been gunned down and captured, so Jesse was probably glad to have the two Fords. Charles was one of six gang members that perpetrated the James-Younger Gang's final train robbery at Blue Cut, where they took around $3,000 in cash and jewelry from the passengers. Robert did not take part in any specific crimes, but was happy to mind the gang's horses and stand-by to help. At this time, the Fords were living with the James family in St. Joseph, Missouri, passing themselves off as Jesse's cousins. Jesse then invited the Ford brothers to join him in what was to be his final crime. He planned to raid the Platte City Bank, and set himself up as a gentleman farmer.

Above: Bob Ford poses paradoxically with a Colt Peacemaker. The gun he is most famous for was the one he used to gun down Jesse James – a nickel-plated Smith & Wesson New Model No.3.

But things began to take a terrible turn in January 1882 when two wanted James Gang members took refuge in the farmhouse home of the Ford brothers' sister, Martha Bolton. This pair of bandits, Wood Hite and Dick Liddel, fell into a quarrel about Martha's favors and drew their weapons. Robert Ford was friendly with Liddel and promptly shot Hite (a cousin of the James brothers') in the head. Missouri's newly elected Governor, Thomas T. Crittenden, brought Ford in to answer for the murder. Fearful of being hanged, and mindful that the governor

Above: Dick Liddell plotted to kill Jesse James. He is armed with a Whitney Navy pistol.

had offered a huge reward for the capture of Jesse James, Ford told Kansas City police commissioner Henry Craig that he could deliver the outlaw to him, alive or dead. Craig was sick of the James brothers' criminality and was determined to eradicate them. On January 13, 1882, Ford cut a deal with the governor for a pardon for the murder of Wood Hite and the reward of $10,000 to capture or assassinate Jesse James. No doubt he also hoped to make a name for himself as the man who brought Jesse James to justice.

In the 2007 movie *The Assassination of Jesse James by the Coward Robert Ford*, Jesse James is portrayed as being anxious and depressed at this time, aware that his luck is running out fast. He feels completely surrounded by federal agents, Pinkerton men, and the sheriffs and marshals of the West. Bizarrely, he seems to cultivate a friendship with Robert Ford, even though he is fully aware that Ford can't be trusted. By this stage, he may also have a suspicion that Ford had killed his cousin, Wood Hite. As the men discussed the upcoming raid on the Platte City Bank, in the James family home, Jesse uncharacteristically put down his gun belt on a

Below: The South East Plaza, Las Vegas, New Mexico, in 1881. Cattle roamed freely between the saloons and gambling dens.

Colt Peacemaker

Below: The model shown was manufactured in 1896 and has the 4¾-inch barrel option, and its own original buscadero-style holster.

No weapons appraisal of the gunfighters could be considered complete without the Colt Peacemaker, or Single Action Army Revolver as it was more properly called. Along with the Winchester 1873, the Colt Peacemaker became famous as "the gun that won the West." Both models were deliberately marketed to use the same ammunition, namely .44-40. This version was marketed as the Colt Frontier Six Shooter. This meant that it was only necessary to carry one type of shell, a self-contained center-fire cartridge. The two guns presented the all-around flexibility of a repeating rifle for long-range work, with the quick-shot revolver for use at short range. Both had outstanding stopping power, provided by the large caliber ammunition.

But the Colt was tremendously expensive at $17 (around $700 today). Back in 1874, this would have been about a month's wages for the average cowhand. Despite its high price, the gun would have been a good investment for a professional outlaw, gunfighter, or lawman.

Interestingly, the Peacemaker was not Samuel Colt's own design, as he died in 1862. This was well before the advent of the center-fire ammunition that made the 1873 revolver so effective. However, it can certainly be argued that Colt's powerful vision for revolving firearms continued to influence his company for many years after his death. After all, as the popular saying went, "God made man, but Colonel Colt made them equal."

The featured example was the property of the Sheriff of Magdalena, New Mexico. It has its original handmade single-loop buscadero holster, decorated with brass tacks and braided rawhide edging. Many guns of this type have been handed down in families for generations.

SPECIFICATIONS

Caliber: 44-40 and .45 Colt

Length of barrel: 3, 4¾, 5 ½, and 7½ inches

Barrel shape: Round

Finish: Blue or Nickel plate

Grips: Hard Rubber

Action: Single

Year of manufacture: 1873 to the present (with a gap from 1941-55)

Manufacturer: Colt's PT.F.A MFG. CO., Hartford, Connecticut

chair to straighten a crooked picture. Robert Ford took this opportunity to shoot the unarmed outlaw in the back of the head. The brothers then ran into town to telegraph the good news to Governor Crittenden and claim their reward. It was at this point that everything started to go horribly wrong for the brothers. They were immediately arrested, tried, and sentenced for murder for James's death, before Crittenden pardoned them. Shaken, they were grateful to be given just a small portion of the massive reward they had been promised.

The Ford brothers' life became completely nightmarish. Forced to act out their betrayal of James nightly in a touring stage show, Charles Ford fell ill with tuberculosis and became addicted to morphine. Worn down by remorse and self-loathing, he committed suicide on May 4, 1884. Bob Ford was reduced to making a living by posing for photographs as the "man who killed Jesse James" in dime museums. Later in 1884, Ford and Dick Liddel opened a saloon in Las Vegas, New Mexico, but Ford was forced to leave the town as he became the target for every would-be assassin in town. He was obliged to wander around the West, trying to stay alive. He survived another murder attempt in Kansas City and moved on to Walsenberg, Colorado, where he opened another saloon. When prospectors discovered silver in Creede, Colorado, Bob moved his business there. He opened Ford's Exchange on May 29, 1892. Six days later it was burned to the ground (supposedly by the Soapy Smith Gang), so the resilient Ford opened a tent saloon in the town until he could rebuild. But just three days later, on June 8, 1892, Edward O'Kelley strolled into his business with a sawn-off shotgun. "Hello, Bob" he called out to Ford, who turned around to see who it was. Kelley discharged both barrels into Ford, killing him instantly. O'Kelley himself became notorious as the "man who killed the man who killed Jesse James." He was pardoned for Ford's murder, but was to meet a similar fate himself. In January 1904, he was gunned down in a shootout with an officer of the law.

Patrick 'Pat' Garrett

Like Bob Ford, Pat Garrett's historical reputation largely rests on the identity of one of his "kills." In his case, it was the July 14, 1881, shooting of Billy the Kid. But in every other respect – background, intelligence, and caliber – the two men were completely different.

Patrick Floyd Jarvis Garrett was born in Cusseta Chambers County, Alabama, on June 5, 1850. He was one of seven children born to John and Elizabeth Garrett. When he was three years old his father bought a plantation in Louisiana, near

Below: The dapper Pat Garrett was elected sheriff and ordered to hunt down Billy the Kid. He shot the twenty-one-year-old dead in a darkened bedroom on the night of July 14, 1881.

Above: Like many famous Westerners, Pat Garrett worked as a buffalo hunter for a few years.

Haynesville and the Arkansas state line, and Pat and his siblings were brought up there. Garrett grew up to be strikingly tall, with a spare frame and an intelligent face. He was nicknamed "Long John," or "Juan Largo." Pat left home in 1869 to work as a Texas cowpuncher on the LS ranch in Dallas County. Part of his job was to control cattle rustling, and so he soon became adept at handling firearms. But Garrett soon tired of life on the range, and left the LS to join his partner W. Skelton Glenn as a buffalo hunter. Unfortunately, the hot-tempered Garrett fell into a quarrel with a fellow hunter over some hides. The man came at him with a hatchet, and Garrett ended up by shooting him. Legend has it that, as he lay dying, the hunter asked Garrett to forgive him, and brought his killer to tears. Forced to lay low for a while, Pat drifted to New Mexico in 1878 and got work as a cowhand on

Peter Maxwell's ranch. Although the ranch was to play an important part in Garrett's future, he once more tired of the cowboy life and left it to work as a bartender at Beaver Smith's Saloon in Fort Sumner. It was while he was working at the saloon that he met the three people who were to be the greatest influences in his life. In 1879, he met and married a local girl, Juanita Gutierrez, but she sickened and died within a year of their marriage. The following year, 1880, he married Juanita's sister, Apolonaria. This union was far more successful, and the couple went on to have nine children together. The third person Garrett met at the saloon was Billy the Kid. The two men struck up a close saloon friendship, gambling together so often that they became known as "Big Casino" and "Little Casino."

This cozy relationship was to come to a crashing end. In November 1880 Garrett was appointed Sheriff of Lincoln County. The area had only just recovered from the infamous Lincoln County wars, but was still plagued with violent rival gangs. Garrett was charged with bringing law and order to the area, and one of the first tasks he was given was to capture jail escapee Henry McCarty, better known to Garrett as his friend "Little Casino." Governor Lew Wallace saw Billy as a menace to the peace and personally offered a reward of $500 for his capture. The relentless Garrett confronted Billy's gang just a few weeks after his appointment, as they rode into Fort Sumner. He shot and killed gang member Tom O'Folliard, but the rest of the gang escaped, including Billy. Garrett tracked them down again less than a week later at Stinking Springs, New Mexico. A second gang member, Charlie Bowdre, was killed in an exchange of gunfire, and Billy himself was captured. Convicted for his many crimes, Billy was incarcerated in the Lincoln County jail, but in April 1881, he managed to escape by killing two guards, J.W. Bell and Bob Olinger. Three months later, Garrett had tracked him down again, this time to the ranch of his old friend Peter Maxwell.

Garrett's version of the events around Billy's subsequent demise was that the Kid came into the room where he was talking to Maxwell, asking *"Quien es? Quien es?"* Garrett immediately discharged two shots, one of which lodged just above the

Below: Billy the Kid's friend Tom O'Folliard. He was killed in a gunfight with Garrett's posse.

Colt Frontier

Above: The owner's name, J. H. Ward, is emblazoned on the back strap. Ward was the Sheriff of Vinta, Colorado.

The Colt Frontier was launched in 1878 at the height of the action in the West. Popular calibers were .44–40 and .45-inch, with the barrel available in various lengths. Shorter barrels were more easily concealed and were therefore of interest to plainclothes lawmen and criminals alike. The gun was a double-action revolver allowing for rapid fire. It was an improved version of the Colt Lightning, on which it was based, with a larger frame and sturdier components. The gun is instantly recognizable by the disc on the side of the frame, just behind the cylinder. It was popular with a number of Western

SPECIFICATIONS

Caliber: 0.44-40

Length of barrel: 4¾ inches

Barrel shape: Round

Finish: Blue/gray mixed with surface rust

Grips: Hard Rubber

Action: Double

Year of manufacture: 1878-1905

Manufacturer: Colt

The design of the Frontier really set the pace for Colt revolvers for the next 100 years.

characters, including Pawnee Bill Lilly who taught his wife May to become a crack shot using the gun. Rose Dunn, "The Rose of Cimarron," who was involved with the Doolin Gang, also favored the Frontier. She is cradling the gun lovingly in her most famous portrait.

The featured weapon is a .44–40-inch caliber version of the model and is engraved "J.H. Ward. Sheriff, Vinta CO." on the back strap. Ward was Sheriff of the town from 1886 to 1912, and was responsible for capturing and bringing in Butch Cassidy. Significantly, he was also a party to Cassidy's parole.

Above: Pat Garrett, John W. Poe, and James Brent. They were the sheriffs of Lincoln County between 1877 and 1881.

Kid's heart. Another, much less credible version of the killing, in which Garrett tied up Paulita Maxwell in her bedroom, lured Billy into the room, and killed him with a single blast from his Colt Frontier, was also widely circulated.

Although most people were delighted to see the back of Billy, the manner of his dispatch did not enhance Garrett's reputation. Shooting an unarmed friend, without warning, was not considered true to the code of the Western gunman. Although Sheriff Garrett was the hero of the hour, most people saw his treatment of Billy as cowardly. He lost his re-election campaign for sheriff and never received Governor Wallace's reward.

Disgusted by this lack of gratitude, Pat turned to ranching and collaborated with his friend Ash Upson on a book about Billy entitled *The Authentic Life of Billy the Kid, the Noted Desperado of the Southwest*. As eight other books had already been published on McCarty, Garrett's book sold badly.

Over the next few years, Garrett tried and failed to re-enter law enforcement and public life in several different roles: as Sheriff of Grant County, New Mexico, state senator, and Sheriff of Chaves County. He briefly joined the Texas Rangers, but left the service after only a few weeks.

It was 1896 when Garrett was finally appointed as a sheriff once more, in Dona Ana County. He was confirmed in the position with an election in January the following year. This was largely because the governor felt that his help was required to solve the case of the disappearance and probable murder of Colonel Fountain and his eight-year-old son, Henry. The main suspects were local lawmen William McNew, James Gilliland, and Oliver M. Lee. Although Garrett's posse finally caught up with Lee and Gilliland in July 1898, he was unable to capture them and one of his deputies was killed in a shootout with the accused men. Later, Lee and Gilliland surrendered and were tried for the murder of the two Fountains. But in the absence of the bodies, they were acquitted.

In 1901, Garrett's luck turned again. President Theodore Roosevelt was fascinated by stories of the gunfighters of the Old West, and became friendly with several famous Westerners, including Pat Garrett. In December that year, he appointed Garrett as his customs collector in El Paso, Texas. Garrett retained the post until 1905, but at that point, Roosevelt refused to reappoint him to the job. Garrett's close friendship with a man called Tom Powers, who was reputed to have beaten his own father into a coma, had damaged his reputation. Despite a face-to-face meeting with the President, Garrett failed to change Roosevelt's mind.

Bitterly, he returned to his ranch in the San Andres Mountains of New Mexico, but new problems started to pile in on him. He owed substantial taxes and was being held responsible for a defaulted loan that he had co-signed for his friend. Debts began to pile up and he owed money to many people in the local area.

Realizing that he needed to do something drastic, Garrett decided to sell his ranch. After some difficult negotiations with local rancher Carl Adamson, the pair cut a deal for Garrett's property. Unfortunately, Garrett's misfortunes didn't end there. He had leased part of his land to goat farmer Jesse Wayne Brazel, who now

Right: Pat's son, Jarvis Garrett, marked the location of his father's shooting death.

held him to ransom for his cooperation in allowing the deal with Adamson to go through. After a heated discussion between the three men in Las Cruces, Garrett and Adamson were riding back along the San Augustin Pass when the irate Brazel caught up with them on horseback. In court Brazel maintained that, in the ensuing argument, Garrett leaned forward to pick up his double-barreled shotgun, so he shot him first in "self-defense," fatally wounding the lawman in the head and stomach. Adamson verified his story and Brazel was acquitted. This was a typical end for a man with a gunslinging reputation; they inspired so much fear that their adversaries were minded to shoot first, rather than take their chances in a fair fight.

Garrett's remains were laid out in the undertaker's parlor, and dozens came to see the mortal remains of the man who had gunned down Billy the Kid. His body was too tall for any pre-made coffin, so an especially long one had to be shipped in from El Paso.

Garrett's funeral service was held on March 5, 1908, and he was buried next to his daughter Ida (who had died eight years earlier) in the Masonic Cemetery in Las Cruces. His son, Jarvis Garrett, marked the location of his father's shooting in the 1930s, and the site is now protected by an organization known as the Friends of Pat Garrett.

John Wesley Hardin

" *The man who does not exercise the first law of nature – that of self preservation – is not worthy of living and breathing the breath of life.* "

"I had no mercy on men whom I knew only wanted to get my body to torture and kill." – John Wesley Hardin

Oh I'm a good ol' rebel, now that's just what I am
For this fair land of Freedom, I do not give a damn,
I'm glad I fit against it, I only wish we'd won,
And I don't want no pardon for anything I've done.
– Confederate Civil War song

Unlike almost all Western gunmen, John Wesley ("Wes") Hardin was largely a professional manslayer. His nicknames and epithets are proof enough of the fear that he inspired. He was known as "the meanest man in Texas," "the dark angel of Texas," and "a homicidal desperado."

In common with several other Western bad men, John's father, James G. Hardin, was a preacher who named his son after the founder of the Methodist faith. Hardin was born on May 26, 1853, in Bonham, Texas. His mother was Mary Elizabeth Dixon Hardin. In his autobiography, her son described her as being "blond, highly cultured… charity predominated in her disposition." The family did not have a settled home; they were Texas wayfarers who drifted from the home of one relative to another. Despite this, the Hardin parents were highly respected in the various communities in which they lived. But from a very early age it was obvious that John had an extremely violent temper and vengeful nature. He was almost expelled from his father's own school for attacking another boy, John Sloter, with a knife when he was fourteen. By the age of just fifteen he had made his first kill. His victim was a black ex-slave known as Mage. In later life, Hardin justified his flight from justice by saying that "To be tried at that time for the killing of a Negro meant certain death at the hands of a court backed by Northern bayonets." It is alleged that he killed three Texas Rangers as they tried to bring him in. This was to

Above: John Wesley Hardin became the most feared gunfighter in Texas. He claimed to have gunned down forty-four men, but his tally was more likely to have been twenty.

Above: Abilene in 1879. The town was a mixture of brick-built and false-fronted wooden buildings.

Opposite page: A tintype
of John Wesley Hardin,
made at Abilene in 1871.

set up a pattern, and Wes Hardin was to kill several more black men over his "career." It is very likely that he saw freed slaves as the embodiment of the ignominious defeat of the South. By the age of seventeen Hardin had become a professional gambler, duelist, sometime follower of the Klu Klux Klan, and all round bad man. Gambling was to influence the balance of his life, and he reveled in his sobriquet "Young Seven-up," that referred to one of his favorite card games. Wes had also evolved an unusual way of carrying his pistols which he believed gave his draw the edge of speed. His holsters were sewn into his vest, with the butts pointed inwards, across his chest. This meant that he crossed his arms to draw, and he practiced this maneuver every day. The tide of killings in which he was involved continued. Among others, he shot gambler Jim Bradley to death in 1869; a man who tried to rob him in Kosse, Texas; Waco City Marshal L.J. Hoffman; and Jim Smally of the Texas police.

During this time, when he was constantly on the run for some murder or other, Wes worked as a cowboy on the cattle drives, including the Chisholm Trail. In 1871, he met Wild Bill Hickok in Abilene, Texas, where Hickok was Town Marshal. In his autobiography, Hardin wrote "I have seen many fast towns but I think Abilene beat them all." The two gunmen became friends of a sort; Hardin was delighted to be seen in the company of the celebrated gunfighter and Hickok treated the younger man as a protégé. But after Hardin shot and killed a stranger in the adjacent hotel room for snoring, Hickok realized that his friend was deranged, and vowed to punish him. Hardin knew that Hickok would show him no quarter and fled the town. "If Wild Bill found me in a defenseless condition, he would… kill me to add to his reputation."

Soon after this ignominious departure, Hardin was reunited with the Clements branch of his family. But trouble seemed to follow him around. In 1872, he was shot by Phil Sublett during a poker game and seriously injured. He temporarily surrendered himself to Sheriff Dick Reagan, but thought better of it and escaped from Gonzales jail. This short brush with the justice system did not subdue Hardin's violent temper. In 1873 he shot Dewitt County Sheriff Jack Helm, and on May 26, 1874, he celebrated his twenty-first birthday by shooting Texas Deputy Sheriff Charles Webb of Brown County. It was for this crime that Hardin was finally brought to justice, and his killing of Webb also had a devastating effect on his family. The outraged citizens of Brown County formed a lynch mob to take their revenge on anyone associated with Webb's killer. Hardin's parents, wife, brother Joseph, and two male cousins, Tom and Bud Dixon, were taken into protective

custody in the local jail. But this did not save them. The mob broke in and hung Joseph Hardin and the two Dixon brothers. It was said that the posse cut the hanging ropes deliberately long so that the men died a slow and agonizing death of strangulation.

A price of $4,000 was put on Hardin's head for the murder of Webb. Undercover Texas Ranger Jack Duncan finally caught up with Hardin, who was living under an assumed name of James W. Swain, on a train in Pensacola, Florida. For once in his life, Hardin's draw failed, as his pistols got caught in his suspenders. He was finally arrested in 1877. Convicted of Webb's murder, Wes was sentenced to twenty-five years in Huntsville prison in Texas. He served nearly seventeen years in jail, during which time he battled with ill health and was bed-ridden for two years. But he also took his enforced seclusion as an opportunity to study theology and law.

Hardin's wife, Jane Bowen Hardin, had died during his time in prison, on November 6, 1892. So when he received an early pardon from Governor Hogg in 1894, he was released as a forty-one-year-old widower with three grown-up children. Pardoned in 1895, Hardin passed his law exams and obtained a license to practice. The following year he married the fifteen-year-old "Callie" Lewis, but the marriage was soon over.

In 1895, Hardin moved to El Paso, and worked as a lawyer while writing his autobiography, *The Life of John Wesley Hardin as Written by Himself.* On March 30 of that year, the *El Paso Herald* announced that "John Wesley Hardin, at one time one of the most noted characters in Texas, is in the town."

But Hardin's personality had not improved during his time in jail. He committed his final murder, of an innocent Mexican man in El Paso, for a $5 bet. He was also gambling again. In May 1985, he took back $95 he had lost in a dice game at gunpoint, and was subsequently fined $25 for "unlawfully carrying a pistol."

Hardin's return to his old ways of squabbling and disputatious behavior was to be his undoing. Hardin started an affair with one of his married women clients and unwisely boasted that he had hired two local lawmen, Jeff Milton and George Scarborough, to kill her husband, Martin McRose. Mrs. McRose herself was then arrested by El Paso lawman John Selman Jr. for "brandishing a gun in public." Hardin became involved in a verbal brawl with Selman and his father John Selman Sr. on the afternoon of August 19, 1895. Later that day, Hardin visited the town's Acme Saloon Bar and began shooting dice with local furniture dealer Henry Brown. Selman Sr. came in, saw Hardin, and shot him in the head. Although this bullet killed Hardin instantly, Selman pumped a further three shots into his lifeless body, as though he could hardly believe that the notorious man killer lay dead on the floor. Legend has it that Hardin's last words were, "Four sixes to beat, Henry."

The most deadly gunfighter in American history was shot down like a dog at the age of forty-two. Selman was acquitted of the crime. When he died, Hardin was carrying a .38 caliber, two-and-a-half inch barrel Colt Model 1877 Lightning revolver with mother-of-pearl grips (serial number 84304). The gun had been presented to him by a grateful client and was shipped from the Colt factory in 1891. Unfortunately for him, Wes Hardin never got a chance to draw it from its tooled leather holster, bought in El Paso. His previous gun had also been a Colt revolver; an 1877 .41 caliber Thunderer. He had used this gun to hold up and rob the Gem Saloon.

Over his short and violent career, Hardin claimed to have killed at least forty men, although he always maintained that he didn't kill anyone who didn't need killing. This certainly wasn't the case. Even by the standards of his type, Hardin was a violent and capricious murderer who killed men for little or nothing; maybe just because he had made a bet to do so, or because he hated the color of their skin. In the end, his death can only be viewed as poetic justice.

Hardin's unfinished autobiography was published in 1896, the year after his death.

Winchester Model 1887 Lever Action Shotgun

The 1887 Shotgun was hardly the most elegant of the company's weapons.

In the final years of the Frontier, many weapons evolved into more deadly versions of earlier arms. Gone was the primitive percussion system, which took time to load, and muzzle-loaders that suffered from variable powder charges and poor gas sealing. Center-fire brass cartridges and double action had made the revolver a much more serious weapon. Outlaws like Billy the Kid quickly caught on to the latest models, such as the Colt Lightning and Frontier-type revolvers. Rifles with reliable repeating mechanisms were also available. Similarly, shotgun design had to move with the times.

In gunfights, a shotgun was often needed to pin down opposing forces of overwhelming strength. Shotguns also appeared in the role of protecting jails or bullion shipments, where their close-range devastation would deter potential hold-ups. But they suffered from the serious drawback of having only a two-shot capacity in double-barrel form. Colt had developed an early version of a revolving shotgun, but this never really took off. It was left to Winchester to develop a lever-action shotgun to reflect their successful rifles. Designed by John Browning, the 1887 shotgun was chunky and aggressive-looking, just right for a weapon designed to intimidate. It had a five-shot magazine in a tube positioned under the barrel, and was available in 10 and 12-gauge. The barrel lengths of the gun ranged from thirty-two inches to a "sawn-off" twenty inches for crowd control (or criminal) purposes.

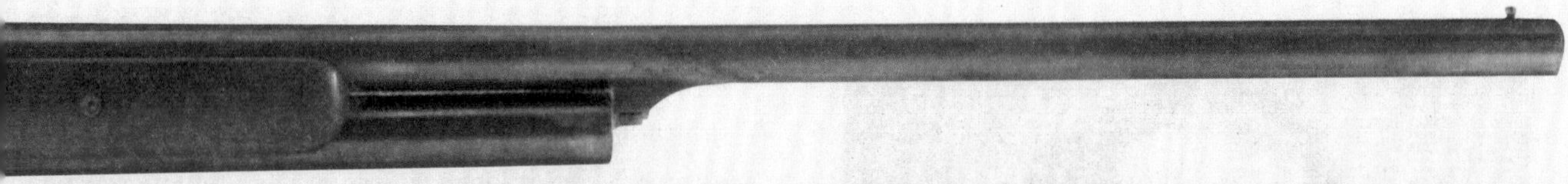

The gun was a favorite weapon with the Texas Rangers, and it continued in production until 1920. A weapon of this kind was used by Texan lawman George W. Scarborough, who killed the assassin of John Wesley Hardin, John Selman, in an alley. Scarborough died following a shootout in Deming, New Mexico, in 1900. These were violent times indeed.

Above: Close-up of the familiar Winchester underlever action and 5-shot magazine tube slung under the barrel.

SPECIFICATIONS

Caliber: 12-Gauge

Length of barrel: 28 inches

Barrel shape: Round

Finish: blue/casehardened

Grips: Walnut

Action: 5 shot lever action

Year of manufacture: 1887

Manufacturer: Winchester Repeating Arms Co., New Haven, Connecticut

Wild Bill Hickok

Above: Wild Bill Hickok was a lifelong dandy. Here, he wears his trademark black frock coat and silk neckerchief. On the opposite page, he is dressed for his appearance with Buffalo Bill Cody's theatrical troupe in 1873.

To this day, the reputation of Wild Bill Hickok epitomizes that of the gun-fighting lawman; he was a "genuine lover of law and order," as well as a great showman and latter day duellist.

Hickok was born in Troy Grove, Illinois in 1837. In 1855 Bill joined General Jim Lane's "Free State Army," where he first met the young William Cody. His prominent nose and upper lip earned him the nickname "Duck Bill," but he referred to himself as "Wild Bill" and it stuck. In 1858 Bill became one of the first four constables of Monticello Township, Kansas. Having been seriously injured by a bear, Bill was sent to Rock Creek Station, Nebraska to recuperate. It was here in 1861 that the twenty-four-year-old Bill shot and killed David McCanles in a shootout. He was tried for murder, but was judged to have acted in self defense.

When the Civil War broke out, Hickok joined the Union army as a teamster and had risen to being a wagon master by the time he was discharged in 1862. Reputedly, he went on to spy and scout for the army. After the war he returned to the law. But on July 21, 1865 all that nearly came to an end when he shot and killed Davis Tutt Jr. in a "quick draw" shootout in Springfield, Missouri. The pair had quarrelled over a gold watch. This famous gunfight was the first recorded prototype of what was to become the classic gunfight of western legend. Again, Hickok was brought to justice, but acquitted on the basis that he had shot Tutt in self defense in a "fair fight." Many disagreed.

In 1866 he became Marshal of Fort Riley, Kansas. This was the time of the Indian Wars, and in 1867 Bill was attacked by a large group of Indians while scouting on the Great Plains. He killed two of the braves, and the others retreated and let him pass. In the following year, Bill took off to Niagara Falls to try his hand at acting in the revue *The Daring Buffalo Chases of the Plains.* Unfortunately, Bill proved to be a terrible actor, and in 1868, he returned to the law as Marshal of Hays, Kansas, sometimes working alongside Bill Cody as a scout. After an eventful time in Hays,

Above: Two dead cavalrymen, gunned down by Bill Hickok at Hays City in 1870.

Hickok was invited to become Town Marshal of Abilene, Texas, in 1871. Most of his predecessors in the job now lay in Boot Hill cemetery. They included the previous incumbent, pacifist Marshal Tom "Bear River" Smith, who had been murdered by an axe-wielding homesteader in November 1870. Not unreasonably, the weary citizens felt that a "noted" and feared individual like Hickok would stand a better chance of keeping the peace, particularly during the annual spring cattle drives. These generally resulted in the town being completely torn up by lawless cowboys. In fact, Hickok's reputation wasn't entirely deserved. He was a tremendous self-publicist who actively propagated the fiction that he had killed over a hundred white men. His real lifetime tally was actually closer to forty. Once installed as town marshal, he proceeded to clean up the town, running Abilene from a card table in the Long Branch Saloon, and earning a massive $150 a month for his services. One cowboy described him as looking like a "mad old bull," and he made every attempt to look as intimidating as possible. His habitual costume consisted of a black frock coat, a low-brimmed black hat, and two ivory-butted and silver-mounted pistols thrust behind a red silk sash. He wore the pistol handles reversed, "cavalry-style," to speed his draw. His favourite weapons were two silver-plated Colt 1851 .36 Navy pistols, engraved "J.B. Hickok-1869," and he carried these weapons until his death.

Hickok's larger-than-life presence in Abilene succeeded in keeping a lid on much of the town violence. He was also surprisingly successful in bringing gun control to the town, disarming even reluctant Texans. He posted a notice that disarmament would be vigorously enforced, and the *Abilene Chronicle* reported this. Their editorial comment ran: "There's no bravery in carrying revolvers in a civilized community. Such a practice is well enough and perhaps necessary when among Indians or other barbarians, but among white people it ought to be discountenanced."

Above: Wild Bill Hickok, photographed at Rolla, Missouri, in 1864 or 1865. At the time, he was a contract scout for the Union.

As marshal, Hickok was also responsible for street cleaning, and kept the town roads clear of dead dogs and horses. He was paid a bonus of fifty cents for every stray dog he shot. On one occasion, he was called upon to dispatch a mad Texas longhorn that was rampaging through the town. Hickok greatly enjoyed his time in Abilene, rooming with a succession of prostitutes, gambling, and drinking heavily. The famous painter N.C. Wyeth painted a wonderfully atmospheric portrait of a dandified Hickok unmasking a card cheat in typical form. But his tenure in the cow town came to a disastrous end when he accidentally shot and killed his deputy,

Mike Williams, during a gunfight with gambler Phil Coe. Hickok was devastated by Williams's death, weeping copiously as he laid the body on a snooker table in the saloon. Hickok paid for the deputy's funeral. After eight months of Hickok's cleanup Abilene Town Council decided not to renew his expensive contract, and decided to ban the cattle drives instead.

Jobless, Hickok drifted east. In 1873 he joined Buffalo Bill Cody and Texas Jack Omohundro in their *"Scouts of the Plains"* revue. But Bill hated the work and was hopeless in his starring role. By this time he was an unsteady drunk and had a surprisingly high, girlish voice that left him open to ridicule. Drink had also left him ill-tempered, and he often threatened to shoot the stagehands. He left the show, and in March 1876 he married fifty-year-old circus proprietor Agnes Thatcher Lake. A few months later he joined his friend Charlie Utter in a trek to the goldfields of South Dakota. They arrived in Deadwood, Dakota Territory, in July 1876. Hickok seems to have had a premonition that he would meet his end in the town and wrote to his wife, "Agnes darling, if such should be we never meet again, while firing my last shot, I will gently breathe the name of my wife – Agnes – and with wishes even for my enemies I will make the plunge and try to swim to the other shore."

The end arrived on August 2, 1876, as Hickok played poker in Nuttal & Mann's Saloon. Unable to take his usual seat with its back to the wall, Hickok twice asked fellow player Charles Rich to swap with him, but to no avail. By this stage in his life Hickok's eyesight was failing, due to trachoma, so he was particularly concerned for his safety. As he played, a cowardly ex-buffalo hunter, Jack McCall, walked within a few feet of Hickok, shouted "Take that!" and shot the ageing gunfighter in the back of the head. As he fell, his hand of cards scattered on the table; the ace of spades, ace of clubs, eight of clubs, eight of spades, and queen or jack of diamonds. The hand is known to this day as the "Dead man's hand."

Hickok's contemporary obituary in the *Cheyenne Daily Leader* was scathing. It implied that he was an obsolete figure from the "lawless times" of the past, who had degenerated into a "tame and worthless loafer," his constitution ruined by "wine and women." But his Deadwood grave is visited to this day, and his legend is undiminished. Any gunman would have done well to listen to his professional advice, given in an interview of 1865, "Take time. I've known many a feller slip up for shootin' in a hurry." He maintained that he valued accuracy rather than speed, but then he was one of the fastest draws ever known in the West.

Hickok's friend Charlie Utter placed a death notice for his friend in the *Black Hills Pioneer,* "Died in Deadwood, Black Hills, August 2, 1876, from the effects of a

pistol shot, J.B. Hickock [sic] (Wild Bill) formerly of Cheyenne, Wyoming. Funeral services will be held at Charlie Utter's Camp, on Thursday afternoon, August 3, 1876." Almost the entire town attended the funeral. Hickok's grave in Deadwood's Ingleside Cemetery was identified with a wooden marker, on which was written "Pard, we will meet in the happy hunting ground to part no more. Good bye, Colorado Charlie, C. H. Utter."

Perhaps of all of the Western gunfighters, Hickok was the closest to the stereotype: a ruthless and prolific killer, dueller, law man, and gambler who never had a quiet day in his life.

Above: A photograph of the cast of Cody's 1873 show, *"The Scouts of the Plains"*. Hickok is second from the left, seated next to Texas Jack.

Left: N.C. Wyeth's moody portrait of Wild Bill Hickok unmasking a chard cheat. Wyeth enjoyed painting the mercurial Hickok.

Below: Hickok's tombstone bears Charley Utter's moving epitaph. Sadly, his name is misspelled.

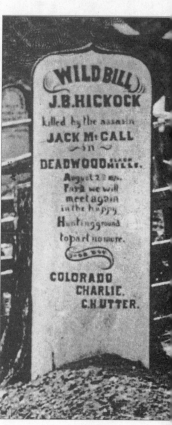

Doc Holliday

Opposite page: Holliday
was diagnosed with
terminal tuberculosis as a
student. He hastened his
end with alcohol abuse.

John "Doc" Holliday was unusual amongst the gunfighters, good and bad, in that he came from a well-to-do background. He was born on August 14, 1851, in Griffin, Georgia, to Henry Burroughs Holliday and Alice Jane Holliday. He was their eldest surviving child. Henry Holliday was a Confederate major in the Civil War, and was later elected Major of Valdosa, Georgia. But misfortune came early in his life. John was intensely close to his mother, Alice, but she died in 1866. To compound his loss, his father remarried within an indecently hasty three months.

Equally atypical for a Western gunman, Holliday studied for a university degree. He qualified as a doctor in dental surgery in Philadelphia. But a second major blow

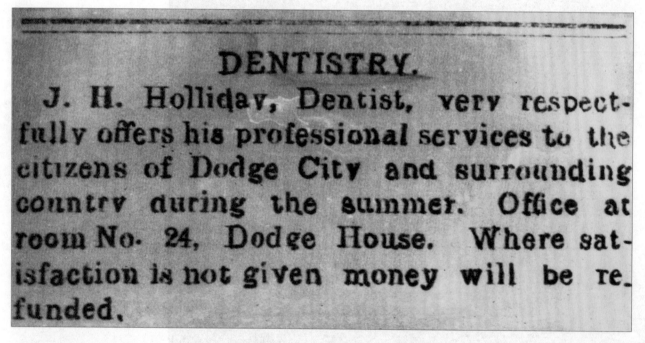

DENTISTRY.

J. H. Holliday, Dentist, very respectfully offers his professional services to the citizens of Dodge City and surrounding country during the summer. Office at room No. 24, Dodge House. Where satisfaction is not given money will be refunded.

Above: Holliday began his professional life as a dentist, but decided to pursue an alternative career as a gambler and gunman.

was to befall him soon after his graduation, when he was diagnosed with tuberculosis. Effectively, he spent the balance of his life on borrowed time, and this may have accounted for the extremely cavalier way he led it.

Holliday began to practice dentistry in various Western boomtowns, including Dodge City, but his illness necessitated a move west to a hotter, drier climate. By now he was too ill to follow his profession, so he headed west to Dallas and, like so many men of his type, he became a professional gambler. Fellow gunman and sometimes friend Bat Masterson described Doc as being of a "mean disposition and an

Above: A gunfighter's Heiser shoulder holster.

ungovernable temper, and under the influence of liquor (he) was a most dangerous man." His unpleasant temper and vagabond lifestyle was to descend into a corrosive cocktail of violence and murder. Holliday went about armed with a gun in a shoulder holster, a gun on his hip and a long, wicked knife. His long list of killings started with the murder of a local gambler in Dallas, and a pattern of "kill and run" established itself. Doc was never again to feel safe in one place for too long. The most foolish murder he committed was that of a soldier from Fort Richardson, which brought him to the attention of the United States Government. Doc escaped,

Above: Big Nose Kate had a volatile relationship with Doc Holliday.

but now had a price on his head and was wanted by the law. He moved to Denver, and managed to remain anonymous until his violent temper resurfaced. He slashed a gambler, Bud Ryan, with his long knife, and almost killed him. At this time, he also became involved with the only woman that stayed in his life for any length of time, the infamously named "Big Nose" Kate. Big Nose was a well-known madam and prostitute, reputed to practice these professions through choice. She was also one of the most famous of the gunwomen of the West, and an excellent shot. Although she and Doc attempted to live together respectably, the bright saloon lights were her natural habitat and she returned to them time after time. Their relationship lasted, on and off, for many years, but it was always highly volatile. On one occasion, Big Nose sprang Doc from jail in Fort Griffin, but when their relationship soured, she just as quickly turned him in. The pattern of Doc's life was now set. Effectively, he was a professional killer. He rode with Wyatt Earp for some time, using the opportunity to add to his murder tally. One of Holliday's few redeeming features was his deep sense of loyalty to his friends and to Earp in particular. Earp described him as a "most skilful gambler, and the nerviest, fastest, deadliest man with a six-gun I ever saw." But although Wyatt valued Holliday, he was also embarrassed by his terrible, violent behavior.

Although Doc claimed he had escaped nine attempts on his life (five ambushes and four hangings), he finally died in bed in Glenwood Springs, Colorado. His failing health had led him to this health resort, to try the sulphur spring water. He was just thirty-six years old, but contemporary accounts described his body as being so ravaged by drink and illness that he looked like a man of eighty. At the end, he took to his bed for fifty-seven days, and was delirious for fourteen of them. Considering his style of life, this was a very strange way for him to die. His final words probably referred to this: "This is funny," he said.

Jesse James

Jesse James was born in Clay County, Missouri, on September 5, 1847. He was four years younger than his brother Frank James, but Jesse was to dominate Frank throughout his life. Jesse fought notionally on the Confederate side during the Civil War, but was actually embroiled in a parallel guerrilla campaign waged by various sets of bushwhackers, including the Quantrill gang. Their activities mainly consisted of raiding, stealing, and murdering civilians. Jesse's commanding officer noted

Below: An early photograph of Jesse Woodson James. His gang invented the bank robbery and initiated a sixteen-year-long murder spree.

that he was the "keenest...fighter in the command." Frank James was a member of the secessionist Drew Lobbs Army, whose violent activities led to the family being expelled from Clay County. This period in Jesse's life formed his outlook for life. His father, Robert James (a Baptist minister), had been murdered by Kansas raiders, and his formidable mother, Zerelda James Samuel, was imprisoned for spying against the Union. He himself had been badly wounded in the chest during a shootout with a party of Union cavalry. This all led to an enduring hatred of everything that reminded him of the "oppressive" North, including banks and trains.

When he returned home from the war, Jesse formed a family gang of outlaws together with his brother Frank and four younger half-brothers. At first, as they confined their attacks to the aforementioned banks and trains, the James gang had some public support. They are also credited with having perpetrated the first armed bank robbery in United States history, raiding the Clay County Savings Association in Liberty, Missouri, in February 1866. Unfortunately, an innocent schoolboy was killed as they made their escape. Despite this, John Newman Edwards, the famous Missouri editor, referred to Jesse as "America's Robin Hood" who had a "chivalry of crime." Perhaps James's most enduring claim to fame is that he and his gang invented the bank robbery and staged the first large-scale train hold-up in the country's history.

Left: N.C. Wyeth's shadowy portrait of the James gang in hiding conveys a sense of weary watchfulness and high tension. Jesse has the haunted look of a wanted man.

Merwin Hulbert Revolvers

Merwin Hulbert and Co. were New York dealers, promoters, and marketers of firearms. They made no weapons themselves but instead contracted with other manufacturers to supply them with guns, usually under their own brand. This 1880s range of neat, compact center-fire revolvers was made for them by Hopkins and Allen, and came in a number of styles. All used an unusual loading

One of these guns is known to have been owned by Jesse James in 1882, the year he was murdered.

SPECIFICATIONS

Type: six-shot single-action revolver

Origin: Hopkins and Allen, Norwich, Connecticut

Caliber: .44-40

Barrel Length: 3¼in-7 inches

mechanism, where the barrel and cylinder assembly were twisted sideways then pulled forward to allow the cartridge cases to drop out and new rounds to be inserted. One of the early Hulbert/ Hopkins and Allen pocket (First and Second models), the single-action weapon

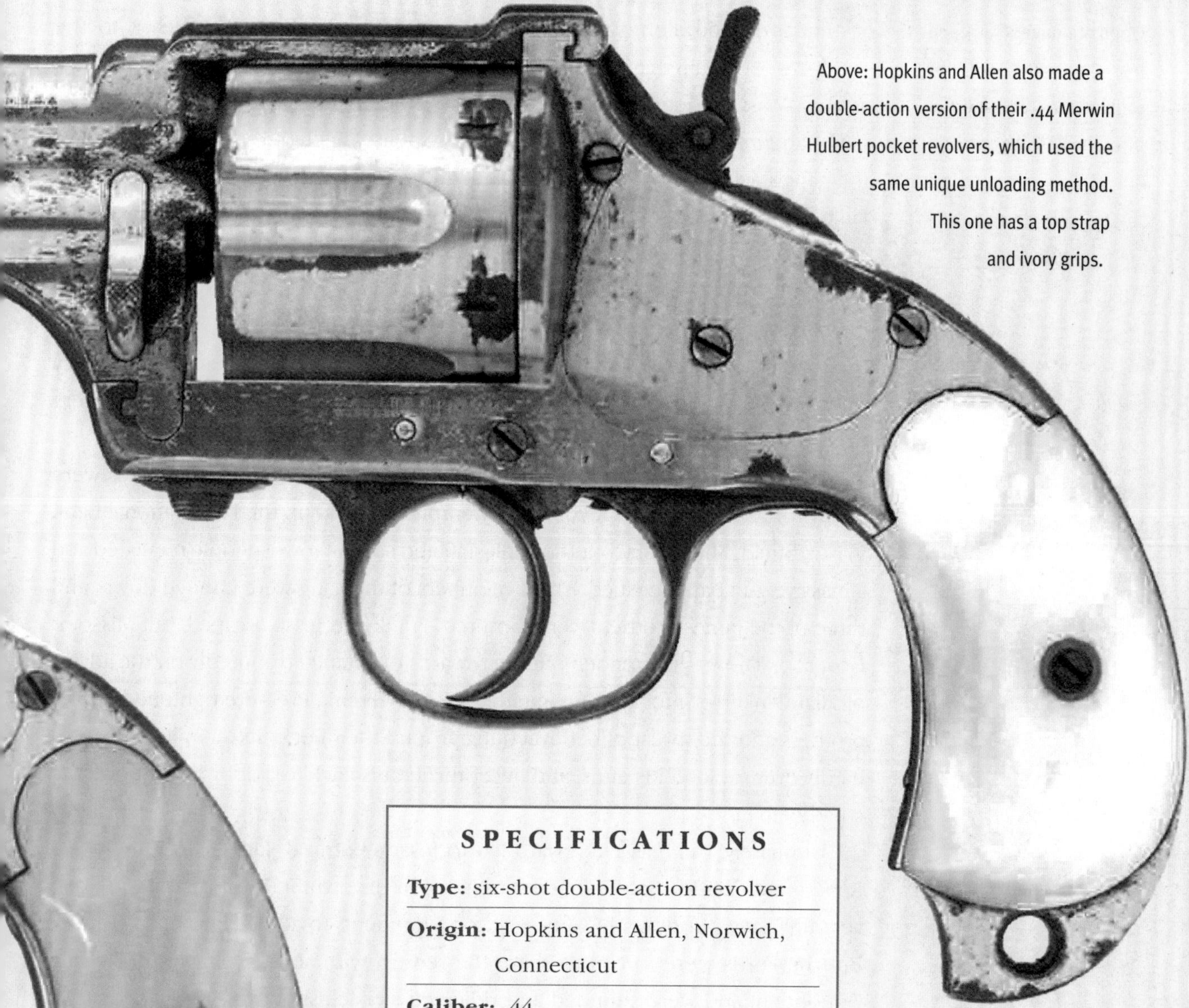

Above: Hopkins and Allen also made a double-action version of their .44 Merwin Hulbert pocket revolvers, which used the same unique unloading method. This one has a top strap and ivory grips.

SPECIFICATIONS

Type: six-shot double-action revolver

Origin: Hopkins and Allen, Norwich, Connecticut

Caliber: .44

Barrel Length: 3½in

shown here has an open frame with no top strap, nickel-plated finish, ivory grips, and "scallop-style" cylinder flutes. It fires the .44-40 cartridge, although it was also made in .44 "Russian" and .44 Merwin Hulbert calibers. The later Third model had a top strap and more conventional flutes.

Opposite page: Frank and Jesse James pose with the tools of the trade shortly after the Civil War.

James played along with his press image, handing a press release to the conductor of a train that the gang had just raided. It helpfully described their attack as the "Most Daring Robbery on Record." He considerately left blanks for the newspapers to fill in with the value of their spoils. Finally, the banks grew tired of the gang's activities and brought in the Pinkerton Detective Agency. Despite the Pinks' famous motto, "We Never Sleep," the gang successfully gunned down several agents who tried to infiltrate their home territory. Frustration finally led the Agency to mount a grenade attack on the James family home in 1875. This backfired disastrously. Frank and Jesse's nine-year-old half-brother was killed in the raid and their mother's arm was so badly shattered that it had to be amputated. The Agency was roundly condemned for this barbaric behavior, and the James Gang were very nearly awarded an amnesty.

The gang continued their spree of thieving and murder until the tables were finally turned on them in 1876. They attempted to hold up the First National Bank in Northfield, Minnesota, but the bank staff and several townspeople retaliated and a massive gun battle ensued. Three members of the gang were gunned down, and three of the James brothers were captured. Frank and Jesse escaped, but Missouri Governor Thomas Crittenden offered rewards of $10,000 (reputedly on the advice of Allan Pinkerton) for turning in either Jesse or Frank. Pressure tightened on the brothers and the threat of betrayal hung around their necks like a millstone. Jesse hardly ever took off his guns, and never turned his back to a door or window if he could help it.

Ultimately, the massive reward led to Jesse's betrayal. James Gang members Robert and Charley Ford gunned him down in his own St. Joseph home. He had very unwisely put down his gun, just for a moment, to adjust a crooked picture. But the Fords were forced to share the reward with several officials, including Crittenden, and were shunned and ridiculed as back-shooting cowards. Charley couldn't stand this treatment and committed suicide. Robert was condemned to the even worse fate of re-enacting the shooting every night in a stage show, where he was often booed off stage. He was finally shot to death in a tent saloon in Creede, Colorado.

Jesse's ruthless campaign of murder and pillage, which had lasted for sixteen years, was finally over. His death concluded one of the most serious crime waves ever to hit the West. Jesse's rather bizarre and fiercely protective mother insisted he be buried in the yard of the family home, where she charged visitors twenty-five cents each to see his tombstone, which read:

Right: A collection of
weaponry and equipment
owned by The Outlaws.

Jesse W James
Died 3 April 1882
Aged 34 years, 6 months, 28 days
Murdered by a traitor and a coward
whose name is not worthy
to appear here.

Frank James couldn't take any more of the claustrophobic outlaw life without his brother to boss him around.

He turned himself in, saying, "I am tired of this life of taut nerves, of night-riding, and day-hiding... tired of seeing Judas on the face of every friend I know." N.C. Wyeth brought this paranoiac tension to life in his portrait of the James gang in hiding: anxiety is etched into each face; each man nervously clutches his gun. A strangely sympathetic Missouri jury refused to convict Frank, and he gave up his life of crime, spending the remainder of his life in various humdrum jobs.

Even during their lifetime, the James gang were the subject of many dime novels, but their personality cult really took off after Jesse's death. There were many postmortem sightings of him, just as there would be for Elvis in the twentieth century. But his death also signalled the fact that the "era of the bad man" was drawing to a close. Better methods of law enforcement meant that outlaws felt more and more exposed and were forced to hide in more and more remote regions to escape detection.

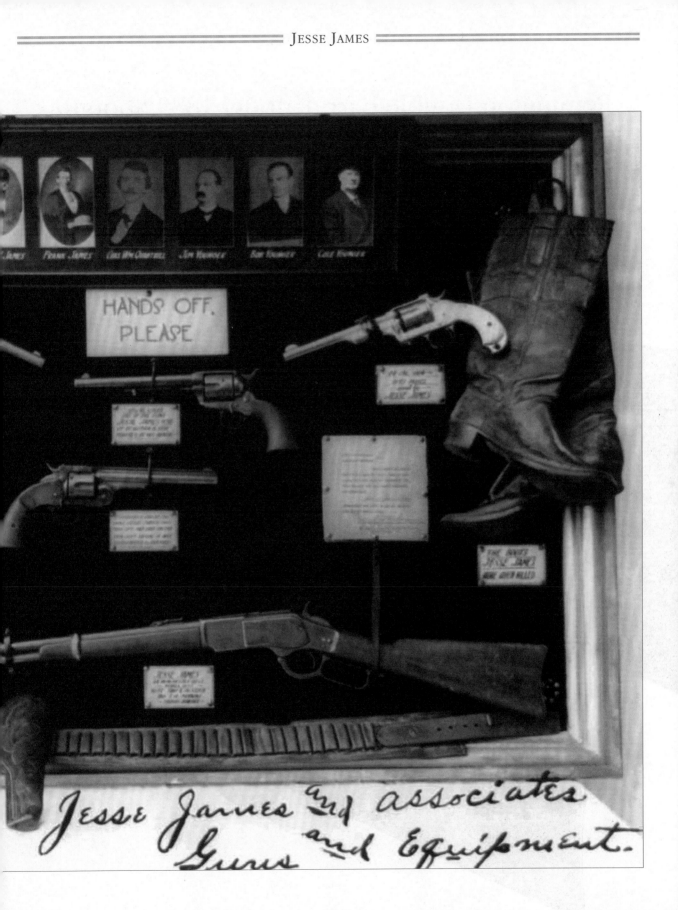

Remington Double Barrel Model 1889 Shotgun

By the 1880s we start to see a new character on the scene. His respectable dress sets him apart from the cowhands. These were professional men like the famous Doc Holliday, a qualified dentist. As a respected member of the community, Holliday became a member of Wyatt Earp's Dodge City Peace Commission. His weapon of choice was usually a shotgun, and Earp described him as "the nerviest, fastest, deadliest man with a six-gun I ever saw." He was also a professional gambler and killer, a sinister and surprising combination in a medical man. I am sure we would find the Doc in a Dodge City alleyway holding several bad guys "backed against the wall," courtesy of his shotgun.

Above: Close-up of the checkered pistol grip and double triggers show that the gun has been well-used.

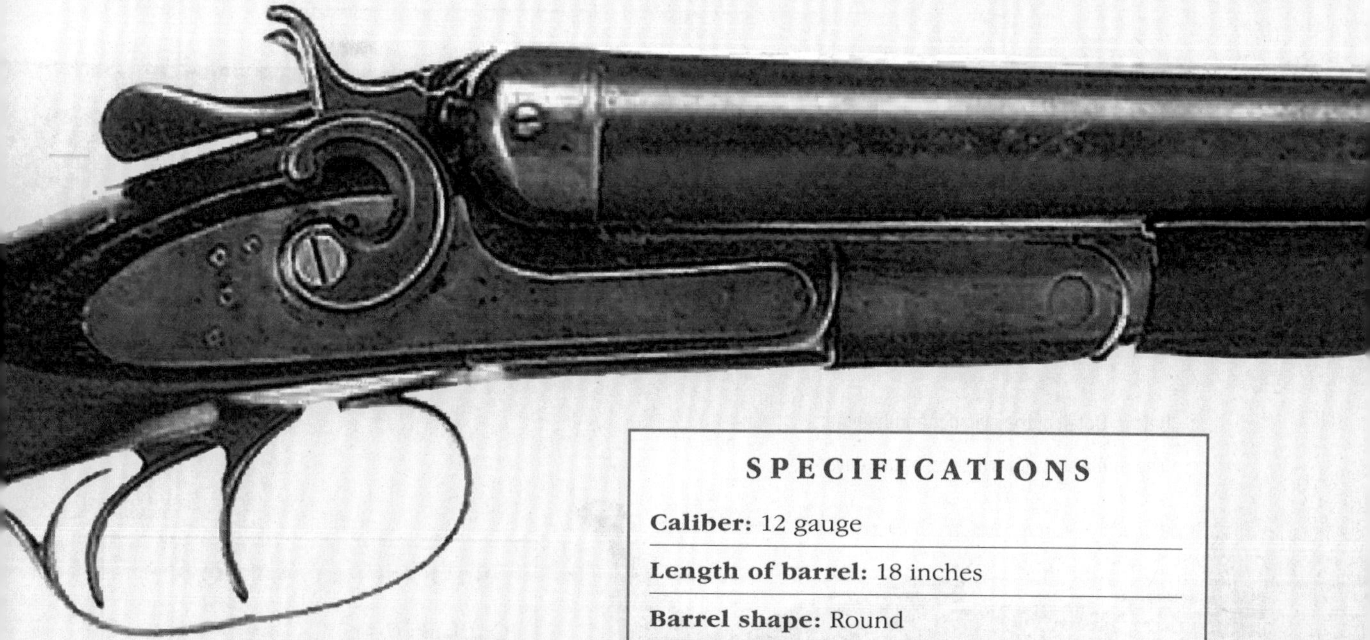

Below: The barrels have
been shortened to give a
devastating blast at close range.

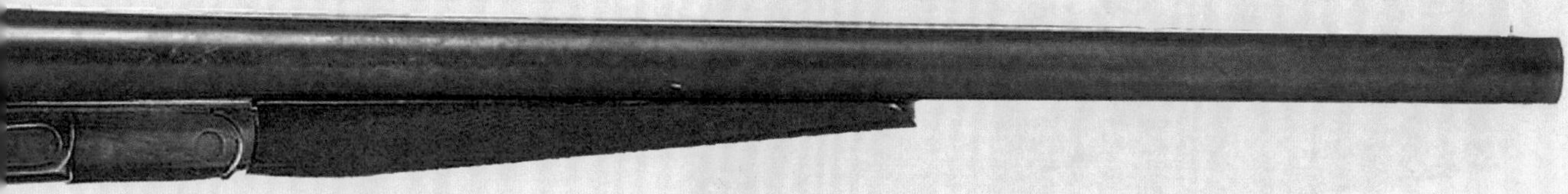

SPECIFICATIONS

Caliber: 12 gauge

Length of barrel: 18 inches

Barrel shape: Round

Finish: Browned steel

Grips: Walnut, checkered with pistol grip

Action: Breech loading double barrel

Year of manufacture: 1889

Manufacturer: Remington Arms Company,
Ilion, New York

Western Shotguns were specially designed to create respect in close quarter fights. They had shortened barrels to allow for maneuverability and a widespread shot pattern. To this day, criminals saw off gun barrels to achieve the same effect. At close range, a twitch in the Doc's fingers would send the bad guys "all to hell in pieces." The Remington shown here has a pistol grip stock to allow the gun to be fired from the hip and external hammers for quick cocking. This type of gun was particularly popular with law enforcement agents and stagecoach guards.

Colt Model 1860 Army Revolver

Below: Detail of the cylinder and hammer.
The frame screws have seen better days!

SPECIFICATIONS

Caliber: 0.44

Length of barrel: 8 inches

Barrel shape: Round

Finish: Gray patina

Grips: Walnut

Action: Single

Year of manufacture: 1860

Manufacturer: Samuel Colt,
    Hartford, Connecticut

When the Civil War began, Samuel Colt was anxious to support the Union forces despite having made pre-war sales worth around three million dollars to the South. His plans for his own special division, Colts Rifles, which would have operated outside state control, were thwarted. But it was recognized that his ability to produce some of the finest firearms then available was a major asset to the Union cause.

Left: In many ways, a nicer-looking gun than its tremendously successful replacement, the Peacemaker.

Above: The rounded barrel section and cutaway in front of the cylinder distinguish this gun from its sister arm – the Navy.

When Colt replaced the Dragoon model in 1860, he was determined to correct one of that model's major disadvantages, its weight. The earlier gun weighed a full four pounds, two ounces, whilst his later version weighed in at a more manageable two pounds, ten ounces. The new gun was produced between 1860 and 1873, when it was finally replaced by the Peacemaker. Over 200,000 examples were manufactured. The Union government purchased 120,000 of these to supply their troops during the Civil War. The result was that many of these weapons were still in circulation on the frontier in the 1870's. In fact, it is likely that vaunted lawman Wyatt Earp carried one of these weapons, rather than the Buntline Special that legend has

decreed. The gun itself is probably one of the most familiar-looking Colts ever made, and has rather elegant proportions. A streamlined cylinder and a long, slim barrel make it less chunky-looking than the Single Action model that replaced it.

Our featured weapon is a composite model, meaning that it has different serial numbers on the frame, barrel, wedge, and cylinder, showing that these parts have been interchanged at some time in its history. Presumably, this was during its military life. The original factory die-rolled scene of a Mexican War naval engagement is clearly visible on the cylinder.

Bat Masterson

Above: William Barclay Masterson, a leading member of the Dodge City Gang. He was always sartorially elegant.

Bat Masterson was undoubtedly one of the most colorful characters of the Old West. "Gentleman Lawman," dandy, gunfighter, and notorious gambler, his profile is archetypal of the Western gunman.

Bat was born Bartholomew Masterson in November 1853 (sometime between the 23rd and 26th) in Quebec, Canada, the son of a prairie farmer. He would later change his name to William Barclay Masterson, but became known at "Bat" after the "batting" walking cane he would carry later in his life. He was one of five notorious brothers born to Thomas and Catherine Masterson, who farmed in both Canada and the United States. The brothers (George, Thomas, Edward J., Bat, and James) went on to become famous in the area of law enforcement, and especially for bringing the infamous Dodge City under the rule of law. The family moved to Sedgwick County, Kansas, in 1871, where several of the Masterson brothers drifted away from the life of the farm to try their hand at buffalo hunting. Neither Bat nor his brother Ed were very interested in pursuing an education, so they took jobs as railroad graders for the Atchison, Topeka, and Santa Fe Railroad. The job took the brothers to Dodge City for the first time, working for contractor Raymond Ritter. But when Ritter skipped town owing the brothers $300, Bat and Ed moved on to a more glamorous life as buffalo hunters, supplying meat to the railroad crews they had worked with. In 1872, Bat first came into contact with Wyatt Earp while both young men were hunting buffalo on the Salt Fork of the Arkansas, and a lifelong friendship began.

Based in the panhandle town of Adobe Walls, Texas, Bat was soon to come into contact with Quanah Parker's Comanche and Cheyenne braves when the disgruntled Indians attacked the town on June 27, 1874. Effectively, the Plains tribes were being starved out of their traditional way of life by the decimation of the buffalo by professional hunters like the Masterson brothers. The white hunters, armed with their "Big Fifty" Sharps rifles, were gradually pushing the vast plains herds to the verge of extinction. At the age of twenty, Bat was the town's youngest defender at the "Battle of Adobe Walls." This was his first taste of real fighting. Five hundred Indians attacked around thirty-five settlers, but luckily the town consisted mostly of sod houses, which were impervious to the Indians' arrows. After an attack that lasted several hours, in which four settlers were killed and around thirty Indians fell, the tribes withdrew. The United States Army then deployed men from Fort Leavenworth to relieve the beleaguered defenders of Adobe Walls, fighting under the command of General Nelson A. Mills. The army hired Bat and his friend Billy Dixon as scouts, and they rode with them during the Texas panhandle campaign. For the rest of the early 1870s Bat drifted through Colorado, Kansas, Texas, Arizona, and other locations, hunting and scouting.

The next milestone in Bat's career happened in 1876 when Bat shot and killed his first man in a gunfight in Sweetwater, Texas. Bat had become involved with local girl Molly Brennan. When her former lover, Sgt. Melvin King, caught them together in the saloon, he drew on the pair. Molly interposed herself to save Masterson and was shot dead for her

Above: Comanche chief Quanah Parker with his wife Tonasa in 1892. They are standing on the porch of their five-bedroom house.

loyalty. The bullet that killed Molly lodged itself in Bat's hip and disabled him for life, leaving him with a pronounced limp. Masterson then gunned down King, who died the next day.

This cool and calculated barroom brawling in the company of prostitutes was to set the scene for much of Bat's middle life. In the summer of 1876, Bat was drawn back to the notorious Dodge City. At this time, his brother George was bartender of the premier dance hall and saloon in the town, Varieties, and his friend Wyatt Earp was town Marshal. Bat worked as Earp's deputy, patrolling Front Street for several weeks, swinging his walking cane. He left in July to follow the gold rush to Deadwood, but only got as far as Cheyenne, Wyoming, where he worked the gambling trade as a faro banker. In spring 1877, Masterson returned to Dodge for the cattle season. Dodge City had been founded on the Santa Fe Trail, close to Fort

Above: A rattlesnake skin necktie.

Dodge, alongside the Atchison, Topeka, and Santa Fe Railroad. The town had first been populated by buffalo hunters and gradually attracted a rough merchant class, whose business was shipping buffalo hides east. By 1873 the town was already known as a focus of crime, with no organized law, and became known at the "Wickedest City in America." In fact, the town became so violent that its cemetery, Boot Hill, was one of the best-known local landmarks.

A handsome dandy, Bat now joined his brothers Ed and James ("Jim") in this volatile town. Jim was the co-owner of a Dodge City saloon and dancehall, while Ed (the eldest Masterson brother) was assistant marshal to Marshal Larry Deger. Deger and Bat soon came to blows when Bat appeared to be drunk and disorderly, and their relationship worsened when Bat aided and abetted the criminal Bobby Gill to skip town. Both men were thrown into jail and fined for their misdemeanors. Gill was given a railroad ticket to leave Dodge City, but Bat remained. Bat subsequently became a peripheral member of the Dodge City Gang. This was a group of local "businessmen" that consisted mostly of renegade Indian fighters and teamsters. They were eager to exploit Dodge City's loose morals to make themselves rich, and were against excessive law enforcement. When Deger arrested gambler and gang sympathizer Charlie Ronan, gang leader Major James "Dog" Kelley invited Bat Masterson to arrest his boss, along with fellow lawman Joe Mason. This resulted in a bizarre situation where both the town's mayor and marshal ended up in prison.

By this time Bat was a well-known figure in the town. His dark hair and blue eyes, coupled with his conspicuous style of dress (which included a sombrero with a snakeskin hat band, red silk neck scarf, gold spurs, and silver-plated six-shooters) led to him being instantly recognizable. He bought a share in Dodge's Lone Star dance hall, and became part of the town hierarchy. This helped him to be elected county sheriff in November 1877, beating Deger by three votes. Now a fully-fledged lawman at the age of twenty-four, he traded his slightly eccentric ensemble for the tailor-made black suit, bowler hat, and walking cane that were to become his trademark apparel. He appointed Charlie Bassett as his undersheriff and began to tame the town. Ed Masterson also became town Marshal in place of Deger, so that the two Masterson brothers controlled the law not only in Dodge City but in all of Ford County.

Below: Lawrence E. Deger, marshal of Dodge City. He became mayor of the town in 1883.

Just a month after his appointment, a six-man gang of outlaws held up a train in the next county. Bat led a posse that captured two members of the gang without firing a shot. He and his brother Ed captured two more of the gang as they approached Dodge City itself, again without a fight. Despite this restraint, Bat's reputation as a gunfighter helped to put down the inevitable saloon brawls and general lawlessness in Dodge. Many criminals chose to avoid the town, rather than face its gun-toting sheriff. But sadly, Bat was unable to prevent a gunfight between his brother, Deputy Marshal Ed Masterson, and two drunken cowboys in which Ed was gunned down and killed. Never a gunfighter in the same league as Bat, poor Ed had practiced his gun skills by shooting cans off fences, but his draw was too slow to save him. He was buried in the cemetery at Fort Dodge. Bat is said to have shot both men in revenge for his brother's death, killing one and maiming the other. After Ed's death in April 1878, Bat hired his brother Jim as his deputy, cracked down on the use of guns in Dodge, and enforced a 9 p.m. curfew. In January of the following year (1879), Bat was appointed U.S. deputy marshall for the region. At this time, a "turf war" had broken out between two local railroad companies (the Denver and Rio Grande, and the Atchison, Topeka, and Santa Fe), who both wanted to build the line to Deadwood. Bat was obliged to protect the workers of both companies from being killed or injured in shootouts between rival workers. Despite

his effectiveness, Bat lost his campaign for re-election in November 1879, and Jim Masterson was elected town marshal in his place, at a reduced salary of $50 a month. Bat's defeat can probably be attributed to the fact that many Dodge City residents were sick of the influence of the Dodge City Gang and longed for a more peaceful way of life in a town that was not run for the benefit of the saloon owners.

Even at this time, there was a general disaffection with the "frontier characters" of Dodge and their gun-slinging ways, and their "flitting" to other towns was welcome to many.

Left: Dodge City's famous Long Branch Saloon. Built in the late 1870's, Luke Short bought a partial interest in the business in 1883. It was the scene of countless shootings, gunfights, and standoffs.

Unabashed, Bat made his living from the law and gambling (mostly playing faro) for the next few years. He drifted to the boomtown of Leadville, Colorado. By early 1881, he had made it as far as another iconic Western town: Tombstone, Arizona. Here he continued his close friendship with Wyatt Earp, who was the proprietor of the Oriental Saloon in the town. Bat is credited with introducing Earp to drinking and faro, and spent many nights in the Oriental, gambling with poker pals Doc Holliday, Wyatt Earp, and Luke Short. Ironically, Bat was to the leave Tombstone just before the O.K. Corral "incident," returning to Dodge City to support his brother Jim. Jim Masterson had become partners with A.J. Peacock in Dodge's Lady Gay saloon, but had fallen out with both Peacock and Peacock's brother-in-law, Al Updegraff, who had been working there as a bartender. As soon as Bat arrived in Dodge by train at noon on April 16, 1881, a shootout began between Peacock and Updegraff, the Masterson brothers, and Charlie Ronan. The Fort Collins Courier of May 5, 1881, reported how Masterson shot Updegraff through the lung and fatally wounded him. In fact, this is completely inaccurate. Updegraff survived for a further two years until he died of smallpox. Despite the fact that he had almost certainly been fired on first, many townsfolk were disappointed by Bat's involvement in the firefight. The paper reported that "the good opinion many citizens had of Bat has been changed to one of contempt. The parties engaged in this reckless affray were permitted to leave town, though warrants were sworn out for their arrest... there is good reason to believe they will never darken Dodge City any more. " Amazingly, given his reputation, this is Bat's final recorded gunfight at the age of just twenty-seven. He was out of Dodge by nightfall.

In April 1882, Bat became the marshal of Trinidad, Colorado, and remained in the town for a year. But in 1883 he returned to Dodge City to support his friend and fellow Dodge City Gang member Luke Short in the so-called Dodge City War. Short had bought a half share in Dodge's Long Branch Saloon, but the town's Mayor, Alonzo B. Webster, was determined to drive men like Short out of business. Although he had won the 1881 election on the ticket of reforming the town, Webster himself was a saloon owner, and involved in the whiskey trade. Having fired Jim Masterson as city marshal, Webster instructed his own man, Sheriff Louis C. Hartman, to arrest several prostitutes that were working in Short's establishment. Short went to the town jail to try to get them released, and became involved in a shootout with Hartman. Luckily, Hartman was unharmed, but Short was kicked out of town. Outraged by the treatment he had received, Short called on all his old gunslinger friends to come to Dodge to support him. Bat Masterson, Wyatt Earp, Charlie Bassett, Frank McLain, Neal Brown, W.H. Harris, and W.F. Petillon all subsequently appeared to show their solidarity. Terrified by the assembled posse of well-known gunfighters and hard men, Webster negotiated with the level-headed Wyatt Earp to allow Luke Short to return to Dodge City and resume his business at the Long Branch. In fact, despite the potential for violence from the Commission, no one was killed in this stand-off. The most lasting souvenir of the event was the famous double-row photograph of the eight commission

members, taken by C.S. Fly in June 1883. Bat stands at the back, second from the right, easily identified by his trademark bowler hat and well-groomed moustache.

Over the next few years, Bat roamed the boom towns and cow towns of the Old West, including Dodge City, Denver, Trinidad, Reno, and Las Vegas. He gambled, promoted boxing matches, wrote a weekly sports column for a Denver paper, and became a theater producer. True to form, Bat initially ran a faro layout in the Arcade in Denver. Later, he bought the town's Palace Variety Theater, and in 1891, he married local actress Emma Walters. He also established the Olympic Athletic Club to promote boxing in the town. In 1896, Bat staged a boxing match to determine the new heavyweight champion. It was due to be held in El Paso, but when the Texas Rangers were sent in to break up the fight, Bat moved the action to Langtry. The huge purse of $10,000 was won by prizefighter Bob Fitzsimmons. Having staged the fight and protected the prize money, Bat then returned to Denver to write about the bout.

Above: Faro was a popular Western game of chance, played by many famous gunfighters, including Bat Masterson.

Throughout this period Bat remained an upholder of the law, as he swaggered about with his pair of pistols on prominent display. It certainly kept him out of trouble. In one form or another, Bat relied on his gunmanship throughout his adult life. In 1930, Arthur Chapman, writing in the New York Herald-Tribune, explained how Masterson perfected his skills "It was not magic which enabled Bat Masterson to produce some wizard-like effects with the draw. It was hard and unrelenting practice." Evidently, the young Bat and his roommate, "Conk" Jones, practiced gunplay for at least an hour each day, using unloaded pistols to endlessly "draw and click... draw and click" to improve the speed of their draw. Evidently, Masterson developed a strange way of "holstering" his gun, tying it to a string hung around his neck. But this is actually most unlikely. His gun of choice was the .45 caliber Colt revolver, which weighed around three pounds when loaded. Conk and Bat had a brief fallout later in their career, when Conk felt that his friend had taken advantage of a young and unwary poker player. Words were exchanged, but the pair had too much mutual respect to risk exchanging lead. Ultimately, Bat achieved the status of "Doctor of the Draw", and could back his actions with the unspoken threat of his gunmanship. But like many other western gunfighters, Masterson's reputation as a killer was greatly inflated. He was credited with over twenty-seven fatal shootings, but had actually killed only two or three men. His view of gun fighting was nothing if not succinct: "Always shoot first, and never miss."

As the nineteenth century drew to its close, many men of Bat's kind turned to drink and became troublesome to their neighbors. In 1898 there were reports that he, Wyatt Earp, Doc Holliday, Ed Casey, and Doc Brown of Spokane were on their way to Havana to introduce gambling to the island and establish a kind of southern "Monte Carlo." Few welcomed the prospect. Meanwhile, Bat became the victim of a vendetta by Otto Floto, the sports editor of the *Denver Post*. They had been in partnership to promote boxing matches but the relationship had soured. Ultimately, their antagonism resulted in a street brawl in July 1900. Masterson whipped Floto with his walking cane' and the infuriated newspaperman hired a gunman to avenge his humiliation, "Whispering" Jim Smith. Ultimately, Bat was forced to leave the city to avoid further trouble. Bat drifted east to New York, and became a sports writer for the *New York Morning Telegraph*. But he didn't stay out of trouble for long. In 1902, he was arrested and fined for running a crooked faro game in which George H. Snow (the son of the late president of the Mormon Church) lost the then-enormous sum of $16,000. Despite his gambling habit, Bat once more re-visited his career in law enforcement in 1905, when President Theodore Roosevelt appointed him as United States Marshal of New York. On December 15, 1905 *The Elbert County Banner* reported that "Bat Masterson, well known in Denver and throughout the West as a dead shot with a big number of notches on his gun, is to be appointed to the secret service at the White House." Bat kept the job until the following year, when he resigned to pursue his more lucrative newspaper work. Perhaps he also realized that the day of the gunman was over, and moved on with the times. He recounted many of his earlier experiences in his column in *Human Life* magazine and told stories of his well known confederates, including Wyatt Earp and Doc Holliday. He also wrote about Dodge City itself, and described how "gambling was not only the principal, (but the) best-paying industry of the town."

In his final years, Bat spent his time writing columns and visiting gyms. On the morning of October 25, 1921, Bat went to work as usual as the sports writer for the New York Morning Telegraph. Bat sat behind his newspaper desk and wrote the following words with his ink pen, "There are those who argue that everything breaks even in this dump of a world of ours. I supposed these ginks who argue that way hold that because the rich man gets ice in the summer and the poor man gets it in the winter, things are breaking even for both. Maybe so, but I'll swear that I can't see it that way…" These were the last words he ever wrote. He died of a heart attack at his desk, at the age of sixty-eight. The paper described him as a "former Western gunman and resident of Colorado." During his extensive writing career, Bat had churned out more than four million words. Known for his integrity, Masterson asserted that "a sports writer who is not willing to stand by his honest judgment ought to chuck his job and try something else." Masterson's columns were crudely written but full of challenging statements that packed a punch. Damon Runyon, writing about Bat in 1933, said that the former gunman had "no literary style, but he had plenty of moxie."

Above: Bat Masterson attired in his trademark outfit of tailor-made black suit and bowler hat.

Winchester 1866 Carbine

Right: The 1866 Carbine was named the Yellow
Boy after its distinctive brass receiver.

Below: The familiar slot
in the side which re-
ceived bullets. Normal
loading was by thumbing
the shells in.

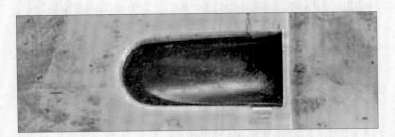

Although designed as a horseback weapon,
the Model 1866 Carbine also saw action in
the hands of gunfighters. Its compact
twenty-inch barrel, with no bolt action or
any other encumbrance, made it swift to
draw and just as easy to stow. It featured a
saddle ring on the left side of the frame for
extra security, and front and rear swivels
for carrying on a sling. The polished brass-

alloy frame and receiver gave rise to its
nickname 'Yellow Boy'. The .44-inch rim
fire cartridge had its limitations when it
came to ultimate power, but this was more
than compensated for by its accuracy and
ease of use. With fourteen shots and a
quick reload action, you could put two
bullets into your intended target in the
time that it took to aim a higher-powered

SPECIFICATIONS

Caliber: 0.44 rim fire
cartridge

Length of barrel: 20 inches

Barrel shape: Round

Finish: Blue Steel Barrel, brass
frame and receiver

Grips: Walnut

Action: Under lever repeating
with 14 shot magazine

Year of manufacture: 1866-91

Manufacturer: Winchester
Repeating Arms Company,
New Haven, Connecticut

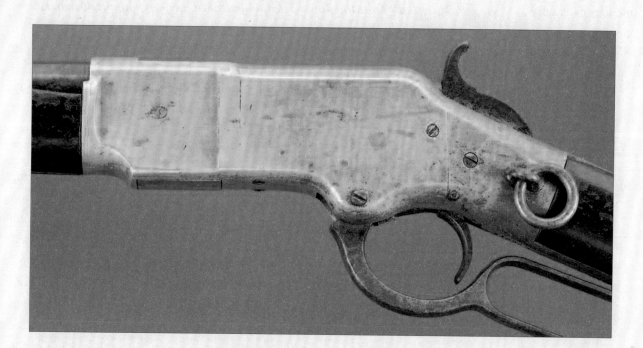

single-shot rifle. This was tremendously useful for a wide range of targets including lawmen and guards. Jesse James used his Model 1866 to hold up trains and banks where the lighter carbine version would have doubtless proved a useful weapon.

Native Americans also aspired to Winchester ownership, as it put them one step ahead of their adversaries in the United States Cavalry. For the most part,

cavalrymen were still using Civil War-issue, single-shot weapons. Indians acquired the weapons either by capturing them from settlers or buying them from unscrupulous white traders. Indian versions were often customized, with brass and nickel-plated studs hammered in to the stock and fore grip, together with rawhide tassels and beadwork. Many examples have survived.

Above: Left side view shows carbine ring. At $40 a time cowhands weren't about to lose this gun.

Texas Jack Omohundro

Opposite page: A dusty cattle herd being driven along the trail. Their average speed was ten to twelve miles a day.

"*My friends, perhaps many of you do not know this man whom we have gathered to honor. No doubt you would like to know something of him, who was one of my dearest and most intimate friends.*"

– Graveside tribute to Texas Jack by Buffalo Bill Cody

"*He was the Mustang King – The Conqueror of Cayuses without a rival. Horses came to him on the end of a lariat… He was a Knight in Silvered Sombrero, defender of women, subduer of bullies… He fought Comanches by the tribe and put them to death or flight. He led cavalry to the rescue of wagon trains. He saved officers' ladies from prairie fires… He had a heart so soft that it never failed the innocent and the friendless.*"

– *New York Times Magazine,* January 4, 1931

John Baker Omohundro was born on July 27, 1846. "Texas Jack's" family home was "Pleasure Hill" in Palmyra, Fluvanna County, Virginia. He was the fourth of John B. and Catherine Omohundro; "Baker" was his mother's maiden name. Buffalo Bill maintained that John was part Powhatan Indian and it is certainly true that he was a natural outdoorsman, scout, and tracker. He was reluctant to make the five-mile journey to school, preferring to fish, hunt, ride and shoot. As soon as he was old enough, he made his way to Texas to become a cowboy. Too young to fight when the Civil War broke out, he enlisted under General J.E.B. Stuart of the Confederate army as a courier and scout in 1861, and became known as the "Boy Scout of the Confederacy."

His elder brother Orville was a lieutenant in the Confederate Army. Ironically, some of John's best friends in later life were to be former Union soldiers. When the Civil War ended, Omohundro sailed to New Orleans and was subsequently shipwrecked on the west coast of Florida. Jack became a schoolteacher in Florida and then moved on to Texas on horseback. He became head of the Taylor ranch in Texas and returned to the cattle drives, negotiating the Chisholm Trail and driving cattle across Arkansas to beef-hungry Tennessee. The state was afflicted by drought and people were virtually starving, so they were extremely grateful for the cattle John drove into the area. This was how he earned his famous nickname. Buffalo Bill described this cattle-driving as tough work. "Life on the plains was a hardship and a trying duty," he noted. It wasn't only difficult, but dangerous. Cattle drivers

were often attacked by Indians, and on one occasion Jack lost seven of his cowboys. At around this time, Omohundro adopted a five-year-old boy who survived when his parents had been killed in an Indian attack by hiding under the floorboards of his pioneer home. Omohundro named him Texas Jack Jr. and taught him all he knew about cattle and horsemanship. Later, the boy was to work in Buffalo Bill's Wild West show with his adopted father and went on to be a showman in his own right, and to discover Will Rogers.

John continued on the cattle drives, and finally met Bill Cody in North Platte, Nebraska. Bill knew his reputation as an expert trailer and scout. They acted as guides for celebrities, including the Earl of Dunraven. Dunraven wrote about his experiences in Yellowstone and the Northwest in his memoirs, The Great Divide. He described Jack as "all life and blood and fire, blazing with suppressed poetry… a great personage." In 1872 they also guided a royal hunt with the Grand Duke Alexei Alexandrovich of Russia and several military men. In December that year, Cody and Omohundro met with dime novelist Ned Buntline. Buntline proposed that the three of them should bring a taste of their adventures on the western prairies to the stage. Buffalo Bill described how "he and I went East to go into the show business. He was the first to do a lasso act upon the stage." He described the opening night of *Scouts of the Prairie* as follows, "The Scouts of the Prairie was an Indian drama, of course, and there were between forty and fifty "supers" dressed as Indians. In the fight with them, Jack and I were at home. We blazed away at each other with blank cartridges, and when the scene ended in a hand-to-hand encounter, a general knock-down and drag-out, the way Jack and I killed Indians was a caution. We would kill them all off in one act, but they would come up again ready for business in the next. Finally, the curtain dropped, the play was ended, and I congratulated Jack and myself on having made such a brilliant and successful debut." *The Boston Journal* said of the pair, "Two finer specimens of manly strength and beauty were never seen on the stage or off the stage." The *Richmond Enquirer* said that "The way the Scouts handle their navy revolvers is the main secret of their success." Unlike other famous westerners that appeared on the show, Jack thoroughly enjoyed his acting career and his pleasant personality held the show together. Others, like Wild Bill Hickok, were much less enthusiastic about their stage antics. He lasted for only one season of the show, from 1873 to 1874, despite his friendship with the easygoing Omohundro. Cody had recruited Hickok to join the play in New York. Hickok had never been East, and was keen to see more of the States. Ultimately Omohundro and Cody paid him off with $500 each and a fine pistol, and Hickok returned to the West. Jack was also popular with the Indians who worked

Above: Grand Duke Alexis Alexandrovich of Russia, with puppy. The Grand Duke was the instigator of the famous royal hunt of 1872.

Opposite page: Texas Jack Omohundro dressed to appear in Cody's show.

Opposite page: Cody's *Scouts of the Plains* show debuted in Chicago in 18972. It was produced by Ned Buntline.

on the show. They called him "White Chief" and the "Whirling Rope."

Scouts of the Prairie was immensely successful, and toured the country. When it reached Chicago, Jack met Josephine (or Giuseppina) Morlacchi, an Italian dancer and actress, who was playing the part of Dove Eye in the show. The pair continued to tour with the show together, strolling down the street, or dining together. They were married on September 1, 1873. The *Rochester Democrat and Chronicle* reported an announcement of their marriage: "The fair actress immediately took a liking to the gallant scout of the prairies, the renowned Indian fighter and buffalo hunter. The affection ripened, until it took the form of a declaration of love on the part of Omohundro, which resulted yesterday in a ceremony which made the twain one." The paper said that Josephine was originally from Milan, and that she was a highly educated, beautiful brunette. Jack himself was equally attractive, with an "aquiline nose, jet black hair, erect form, and piercing eye."

By 1877, Jack was running his own acting troupe, and like many great Western characters and "fighters", he wrote newspaper articles about his hunting and scouting experiences which were published in eastern newspapers and popular magazines.

Sadly, Jack's marriage to Josephine was only to last less than seven years. In 1880, Omohundro died of pneumonia at the tragic age of thirty-three. He was buried in the Evergreen Cemetery in Leadville, Colorado. Josephine was completely devastated and retired from the stage. She died of cancer only a few years later.

After his adoptive father's death, Texas Jack Jr. continued to tour the Wild West Show around the world. It was especially successful in South Africa. Bizarrely, Jack had another posthumous life, as a character in a series of highly-popular dime novels and newspaper articles written by several different Western writers, including Colonel Prentiss Ingraham and Joel Chandler Harris. He featured as a hero of the Confederacy. Herschel Logan published a famous biography of Jack in 1954, *Buckskin and Satin*.

Texas Jack is quite unusual among western gunmen. A brave and resourceful man who was handy with guns of all kinds, he never strayed onto to the wrong side of the law. On the contrary, he was a consummate gentleman, kind and loving, who took in orphans and faithfully loved his wife.

Omohundro was inducted into the Hall of Great Western Performers by National Cowboy Hall of Fame in Oklahoma City, Oklahoma. Sitting alongside such luminaries as John Wayne and Clint Eastwood, he is one of the few real cowboys among them.

Smith & Wesson Model No3

Below: Intricate engraving complements the S&W trademark in brass set into the walnut handgrip.

The .44 Russian was a more powerful version of the Smith & Wesson No. 3 revolver. The gun got its nomenclature through the company receiving a massive order for it from the Russian army. The order absorbed Smith & Wesson's entire manufacturing capacity for a full five years and almost brought the company to the verge of bankruptcy. The gun was manufactured around a special .44-inch internally-lubricated cartridge, specified by the Russian Army. This cartridge gave it excellent power and made the gun a serious rival to Colt's equivalent models of the 1870's. Revolvers manufactured for the Russian military order had an extra hump above the grip and a distinctive spur on the trigger guard.

The No. 3 Model remained in production for many years. This example has been engraved after leaving the factory. Embellishment of this kind was not unusual. The dark blue/black casehardened finish of the barrel cylinderand top-break frame contrasts beautifully with the engraving, which is filled in with gilt to set it off. It is both fancy and deadly.

A holstered brace of these revolvers was serious equipment for the western gunfighter.

Right: The top break action allowed for the whole barrel and chamber assembly to hinge forward for reloading. Note the intricate carved pattern around the pivot pin.

Left: A Work of Art-the beautifully engineered .44 Russian revolver.

SPECIFICATIONS

Caliber: 0.44 Russian

Length of barrel: 6 inches

Barrel shape: Ribbed

Finish: Blue/black steel with gilt inlay engraving

Grips: Checkered walnut

Action: Single action revolver

Year of manufacture: from 1875

Manufacturer: Smith & Wesson, Springfield, Massachusetts

Commodore Perry Owens

Opposite page: John S. Fuller wrote a famous poem about Commodore Perry Owens, describing him as the "Law of the West."

Commodore Perry Owens (named for the famous naval commander) was a gunman who stood square on the side of law and order. But his methods were rooted in the style of the Old West, and soon got him into trouble.

Owens ran away from his Tennessee home at the age of thirteen. Teased for his unusual name, he cultivated a famously flamboyant appearance, with waist-length, strawberry-blonde hair and a neatly trimmed moustache. He started out as a roping and branding cowboy, but also worked as a buffalo hunter and for Wells Fargo. He was considered a dead shot, and became famous for his use of the cross-draw of the brace of pistols he wore around his hips. The technique gave him a split-second advantage over his opponents. For tough jobs, he also carried a Winchester.

While working as a cattle foreman, Owens got into trouble for shooting a Navajo horse rustler. He was tried for the offense, but acquitted. His notoriety helped him to get elected as the sheriff of Apache County, Arizona, where he was responsible for over 21,000 square miles of lawless territory. His reputation for iron nerves ad brilliant horsemanship preceded him. During his time in the job as a single-handed law enforcer, Owens tamed the volatile town of Holbrook, shooting six members of the Snider Gang in the notorious Round Valley Gunfight. He also became involved in the Pleasant Valley War. This was a turf feud between families of cattle ranchers and sheep farmers. Under pressure to serve an arrest warrant on the horse rustler Andy Blevins (who also used the alias of "Cooper"), Sheriff Owens went out to the Blevins family ranch. Unfortunately, Cooper refused to come quietly, and a shootout ensued. Within a minute, Owens had fired five shots, four of which killed Cooper, Sam Blevins, and Mose Roberts, and wounded John Blevins. Owens would probably have been hailed as a hero, except that Sam Blevins was little more than a boy (although he had been armed and ready to kill the lawman). Sam's death turned the tide of public opinion against Owens, and an inquest ensued. Although he was acquitted of any blameworthy conduct, the *Saint Johns Herald* distilled the general mood: "The common people are beginning to think that our territory has had enough of desperadoes as 'peace' officers… [who] shoot whom they please."

Aggrieved by this treatment, Owens scrawled this message on the back of Andy Cooper's tombstone: "Party against whom this warrant was issued was killed while resisting arrest." Owens was relieved of his commission, and the court officials attempted to withhold his outstanding pay until he took this from them at gunpoint.

Leaving his steady job, Owens became a gun for hire on the side of law enforcement. For a time, he worked as a guard for the Atlantic and Pacific Railroad, but later returned to public service as a Deputy U.S. Marshall.

William Clarke Quantrill

Above: A romantic portrait of William Clarke Quantrill.

Opposite page: A daguerreotype of Quantrill made when he was fifteen. Stories of his depravity were already circulating.

William Quantrill was one of the most infamous bad men of the post-Civil War period. Intelligent and good-looking, he was almost certainly a psychopath and a documented mass murderer. Unusually, he was also well-educated and a qualified teacher, but rejected his profession to live by the gun.

Born in Dover, Ohio on July 31, 1837, his parents were Caroline Cornelia Clarke and Thomas Quantrill. The Quantrills were "Free-Soil" Unionists, who believed that a slavery-free America would be a stronger and godlier country. William was the eldest of eight children. Even during his childhood years there were disturbing rumors of cruelty to animals and other children that would indicate that he was already a seriously disturbed individual. Despite this, Quantrill was well-educated, and began his adult life as a school teacher. For several years he taught school in Ohio, but in 1858 he travelled to Utah Territory with a Federal army wagon train. His ambition was to make more money than he had in his teaching job, and his role was to resupply the troops for their on-going fight against the Mormons. Quantrill decided to abandon his profession (at least temporarily), and assumed a completely new identity as Charles Hart, gambler and petty thief. He moved on to Lawrence, Kansas, in 1859 and taught school once more until 1860. By this time he was wanted for horse theft and murder (both capital offenses) and was forced to flee to Missouri. During his time in the South, it appears that Quantrill completely turned his back on his Unionist family background, becoming pro-Confederate and anti-abolitionist. When the Civil War began in 1861 he claimed to be a native of Maryland and enlisted on the Confederate side in the Missouri State Guard. But he soon became disenchanted with army discipline, and within months of joining up he had formed a band of guerilla troops known as Quantrill's Raiders. Their double aim was to be a thorn in the side of the Union and to become rich. At this stage he commanded no more than a dozen men, but they ambitiously robbed mail coaches and Union supply convoys, while attacking Unionist towns, troops, and civilians. Most of this activity took place along the Kansas-Missouri border and often involved

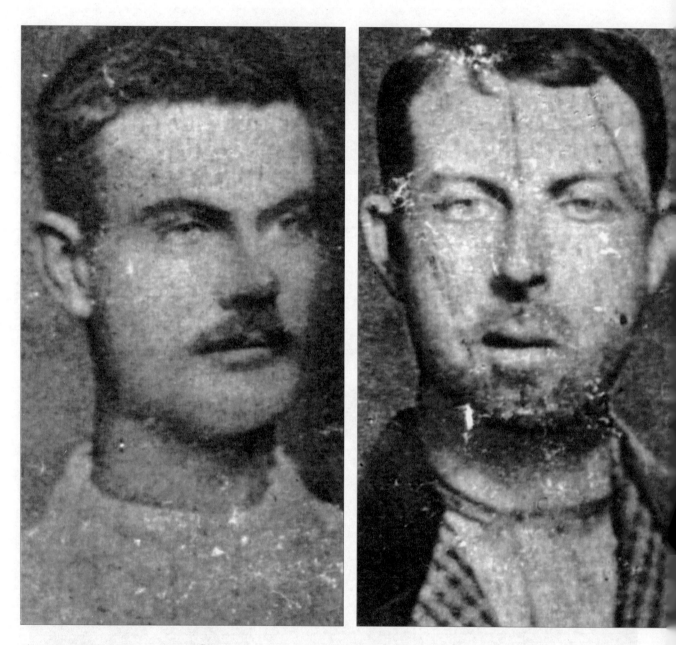

Above: James Younger (left) and Bob Younger (right). Both were captured at Northfield and jailed.

conflict with the so-called Jayhawkers. These were the Unionist equivalent of Quantrill's men: undisciplined and violent guerilla fighters. Despite being mustered into the Confederate army under the Confederate Partisan Ranger Act of August 15, 1862, and rising to the rank of captain, Quantrill was declared an outlaw by Unionist Commander Major General Henry W. Halleck. This had very serious ramifications for Quantrill; if he was captured by the Union, he would be shot rather than being taken prisoner of war. Unfortunately, this proclamation seems to have seriously backfired. Up to this time, Quantrill had behaved as a normal soldier, accepting the principal of enemy surrender. He now moved to a new plateau of instant retaliation, with "no quarter" given to the enemy.

By 1863 Quantrill's Raiders numbered more than four hundred and fifty men, virtually a small army. Bizarrely, the troop also included fifteen-year-old Kate Clarke King, Quantrill's common-law wife, who often dressed as a man and rode with her husband. The Raiders soon escalated their violent anti-Yankee campaign. Quantrill viewed Lawrence, Kansas as a hotbed of pro-Unionist, pro-abolitionists, and a base for Jayhawk raids into Missouri. Another offense in Quantrill's eyes was that the town was also home to Federal Officer James Henry Lane, who had led a brutal attack on Osceola, Missouri and was a leading member of the Kansas Free-Soil campaign. To add fuel to the fire, several women relatives of the Quantrill Raiders had been killed when a prison collapsed in Kansas City. On August 20, 1863, Quantrill assembled his men (who included two infamous pairs of brothers: Frank and Jesse James, and Cole and James Younger) and crossed the border into Kansas. Kidnapping a thirteen-year-old boy, Jacob Rote, from a nearby settlement at Captain's Creek, they forced him to guide them through the moonless night into the town of Lawrence itself.

Above: Cole Younger also rode with Quantrill and was present at the Lawrence, Kansas, massacre.

The Raiders reached the town before sunrise on August 21 and scattered to their pre-arranged positions. The raid was coolly pre-meditated. Weeks before the invasion, Quantrill had sent spies to assess Lawrence's defenses. Thus began one of the worst atrocities of the Civil War. Quantrill's order was "to burn every house and kill every man." Witnesses described the attack as "hell let loose." Men and boys were dragged from their beds and butchered in front of their wives and mothers, even as they begged for their lives and shielded them with their bodies.

Opposite page: The dead
Bloody Bill Anderson, shot
by Union troops.

From a small-town population of around two thousand, the ruffians murdered one-hundred forty-three men and boys, leaving eighty widows and two-hundred fifty orphans. Few of these people had had any real connection to the Union army. The dead included twenty free African-Americans, including a baby. Many had fled to Lawrence to escape slavery, and two black churches had been founded in the town. Firsthand accounts of the massacre mention black townspeople "being pursued with special malignity." A further twenty-two men and boys were wounded by the gang, and many buildings in the town were torched. As well as robbing and looting the town, Quantrill seems to have invented ethnic cleansing. Perhaps the most appalling aspect of the massacre was that Quantrill himself had lived in the town for over six months (posing as Charles Hart) just a few years earlier, boarding at the City Hotel. It seems very likely that he must have known many of the people that his followers murdered and robbed.

The Confederate leadership was stunned by the brutality of the raid on Lawrence and withdrew their support from Quantrill and his "bushwhacker" gang. Leaders of the Union forces were even more outraged. On August 25, 1863 General Thomas Ewing issued his Order No. 11. This was an eviction notice to anyone who could not prove their loyalty to the Union cause. Its effects were completely devastating. Virtually overnight, the population of Cass County dropped from ten thousand to six hundred.

Unrepentant, just two weeks after the Lawrence Massacre Quantrill and his men were involved in a raid on a Union train in Baxter Springs, Kansas, where ninety-eight soldiers were slaughtered. Much to the embarrassment of the Confederate command, Quantrill continued to lead his men behind Union lines in Texas. But Quantrill's guerilla force soon began to disintegrate into small bands of desperados, some led by Quantrill's "lieutenants:" Bloody Bill Anderson, Frank James, and Archie Clement.

Quantrill was killed by Union forces in May 1865, during a raid in Kentucky. By the end of the following year, Anderson and Clement were also dead.

But even after his death, this "Unreconstructed Rebel" was considered a folk hero by many in Missouri, despite the violence that he and his followers had inflicted on so many civilians. Neither were his tactics forgotten by his followers, many of whom became outlaws and criminals. The James Gang and the Cole brothers went on to apply his methods to bank and train robberies with some success.

The first Quantrill gang reunion took place on May 11, 1888, in the City Hotel in Blue Springs, Missouri. Fourteen former Raiders met at an "ice-cream social" on

the lawn of the hotel to honor Quantrill's mother, Caroline Clarke Quantrill. Mrs. Quantrill was touring the sites of her son's "campaign." According to the *Kansas City Journal*, these ex-guerillas were "an intelligent and well-behaved lot of men, and did not seem possessed of any of the bloodthirsty characteristics ascribed to them. If they ever had, the refining influences of twenty-three years of peace and civilization have evidently transformed them into good law-abiding citizens." These meetings continued until 1929, and were attended by such famous gang members as Frank Gregg and John Noland, an African-American scout who had ridden with Quantrill. The last surviving member of the gang, Frank Smith, died in 1932, at the age of eighty-six.

According to Antonio Mendoza, the author of *Killers on the Loose*, mass murderers are "usually people who aspire to more than they can achieve. They feel excluded from the group they wish to belong to, and develop an irrational, eventually homicidal, hatred of that group. Invariably, they choose to die in an explosion of violence directed at a group they feel oppresses, threatens or excludes them." So what had the poor citizens of Lawrence done to deserve the treatment they received at Quantrill's hands?

Opposite page: Noted guerilla George Maddox, sporting a pair of Remington's 1863 New Model Army pistols.

Remington 1863 New Model Army Revolver

Above: The Remington revolver had a solid frame
which gave the gun good rigidity when firing.

Colt didn't have things all their own way. When Samuel Colt set the price for his Army revolver to the U.S. Government at $25 at the start of the Civil War, he didn't bet on Remington setting the price at just half that for a very competitive weapon. Indeed, in some ways the Remington New Model scored over the Colt. It had a solid frame-making for a more rigid barrel and cylinder under fire. The pistol was based upon a design by Fordyce Beals, and was introduced to the market in 1861. It matched the Colt at a caliber of .44 (designed to suit the Union army) and was a weapon highly valued by soldiers and civilians alike. It was a similar model to the Remington Navy, which was a

.36- caliber weapon. 122,000 examples of the Remington Army revolver were delivered from the company's plants at Ilion and Utica between 1861 and 1875, making it second only to the Colt Army in popularity. This meant that there were many examples still in use on the frontier when the Civil War was over.

George Maddox, "a cold-blooded killer" and member of the Quantrill gang, was famously photographed with a loaded pair of .44 Army revolvers. These were clearly his weapons of choice. A further endorsement by William F. "Buffalo Bill" Cody added enormous kudos to Remington's revolver when he asserted, "It never failed me."

SPECIFICATIONS

Caliber: 0.44

Length of barrel: 8 inches

Barrel shape: Octagonal

Finish: Blue

Grips: Walnut

Action: Single

Year of manufacture: 1863

Manufacturer: Remington Arms Company, Ilion, New York

Below: Detail of the finely - machined cylinder and hammer, both of which display a good amount of the original blue steel finish.

Above: The Remington New Model Army Revolver was a major competitor to Colt as the Civil War approached. Its shape, while less elegant than Colt's Army, demonstrated many of the same specifications and proved to be a reliable weapon in action.

Belle Starr

Above: Belle Starr consciously posed as the "Bandit Queen."

"Bandit Queen" Belle Starr was well-known for toting a gun, but preferred to use her intelligence to further her criminal career. She had a life-long association with a cavalcade of famous bad men, including the James brothers and the Youngers, and was wont to use her home as a hideout for criminal gangs, cattle rustlers, and brigands.

Myra Maybelle Shirley was born on her father's farm near Carthage, Missouri, on February 5, 1848. Her father was John Shirley, the black sheep of a well-to-do Virginia family, and her mother was his third wife, Eliza Pennington. By this time the couple was quite prosperous, and raised corn, wheat, hogs, and purebred horses. Belle was one of six children. Her father moved the family into Carthage when the Civil War began and bought an inn, a tavern, a blacksmith's shop, and livery stables in the town. In 1860, his assets were estimated at a considerable $10,000. As the daughter of a well-to-do and cultured family, Belle was educated at the Carthage Female Academy and a private school, Cravens. She was a clever girl, learning Greek, Latin, and Hebrew, as well as playing the piano. But the Shirleys' life took a terrible turn for the worst in 1864 when Union forces burnt Carthage to the ground. Belle's elder brother Bud, who had been a guerilla soldier in the Quantrill Gang, was shot and killed by Union troops in the same year. The family migrated to Scyene in Texas, and it was there that various southern criminals – including the Younger brothers, Jesse James, and various Quantrill members – used their family home as a hideout. It is likely that the Shirley family thought of these men as rebels, fighting some kind of irregular war against the forces of the Union, but it is almost certain that their early influence turned Belle to a life of crime.

Belle married James C. Reed in 1866. Reed was a former Confederate guerilla who had now become a thieving bandit wanted for murder in Arkansas. Their daughter, Rosie Lee ("Pearl") was born in 1868, and their son, James Edwin ("Ed"), was born in 1871. Reed tried to work as a farmer, but became involved with the notorious Starr family (a Cherokee family noted for whiskey-running and stealing cattle and horses), together with the James and Younger gangs. In fact, the couple first lived together at the Indian Territory home of outlaw Tom Starr, just west of

Opposite page: Belle Starr poses with Blue Duck, her Native American husband.

Fort Smith, Arkansas. Jim then moved his young family to Los Angeles, California, trying to avoid his murder charge, but was forced to flee to Texas for passing counterfeit money.

In November 1873, Jim Reed and two accomplices robbed Creek Indian farmer Watt Grayson of $30,000 in gold coins. The family was forced to separate and go into hiding. Belle moved to Dallas, allegedly living off some of the gold from the robbery and operating a livery barn in the town. Belle took to wearing a mannish outfit of buckskins, high-topped boots, a Stetson, and twin holstered pistols. She frequented saloons, drinking and gambling at dice, roulette, and cards. She was also noted for riding through the town while firing her pistols. But she was never glamorous; a contemporary unflatteringly described her as being "bony and flat-chested with a mean mouth; hatchet-faced; gotch-toothed tart."

In 1874 Jim continued with his crime spree, robbing the Austin-San Antonio stagecoach of $2,500. A reward of $7,000 was posted for his capture, and he went into hiding. Belle became a widow when the law finally caught up with Jim near Paris, Texas, on August 6, 1874. He was shot and killed trying to escape.

Forced to earn her own criminal living, Belle left Pearl and Ed with her family and went to live with the Starr family once more. In 1880 she married Samuel Starr. From her new husband's family, Belle learned how to fence goods and animals for rustlers, horse thieves, and bootleggers.

In 1883 Sam and Belle were accused of horse theft by one of their neighbors in Indian Territory, and were brought into Fort Smith to appear before the famous "Hanging" Judge Isaac Parker. Parker sentenced the pair to a year in the Detroit House of Correction. Belle took her punishment, proving herself a model prisoner. But Sam proved much more rebellious and was given hard labor. Both were released in nine months and immediately returned to Indian Territory and their life of crime. In 1886 she was again accused of horse theft, but escaped conviction. But on December 17, 1886 her husband was shot to death by Officer Frank West, who also fell dead in the gunfight.

By now, Belle had taught herself how to manipulate the law and helped acquit several criminals in Judge Parker's court, providing legal advice for Bluford "Blue" Duck (a Cherokee Indian indicted for murder) and her son Ed (charged with horse theft). Blue Duck's sentence of death was commuted to a jail term, while Ed was given a full pardon.

For the final two years of her amoral life, Belle took various lovers, including Blue Duck, Jack Spaniard, Jim Tully, and Jim French. She also married for a third

Opposite page: A studio portrait of Judge Isaac Parker. The "Hanging" judge arrived in Fort Smith in 1875, with a remit to tame the town.

Opposite page: Belle's equally notorious daughter, Pearl Starr. Pearl ran a famous brothel in Fort Smith.

time. This time, her husband was a relative of her second husband. Jim July Starr was fifteen years younger than Belle, but their marriage enabled her to live in Indian Territory.

Her irregular and troubled life was brought to an end on February 3, 1889, two days before her forty-first birthday. She was shot in the back while riding home from Eufaula, Oklahoma. Falling from her horse, she was then shot again in the neck and face. There were several suspects, including her husband and son. Ultimately a neighbor, Edgar Watson, was charged with the offense. It was claimed that Belle had threatened to turn him in for a murder he had committed in Florida. But Watson was acquitted of the crime, and it remained unsolved.

Below: Blue Duck's Colt single-action revolver.

Belle's daughter Pearl buried her mother at Younger's Bend on the Canadian River and erected a smart headstone, using her earnings as a prostitute and madam in Fort Smith. It was embellished with various motifs that Pearl felt represented her mother: a bell, a star, and a horse. She also wrote a charming epitaph:

"Shed not for her the bitter tear,
Nor Give the heart to vain regret;
'Tis but the casket that lies here,
The gem that filled it sparkles yet."

Smith & Wesson Schofield Revolver

After the Civil War, the new U.S. Army decided to adopt a standard-issue cartridge revolver, and fixed on the Smith & Wesson Model 3 for their purpose. Lessons learned in the war had shown that cap and ball black powder revolvers were vulnerable, in terms of both slow loading and unreliability in damp conditions. In 1875 the U.S. Ordnance board granted Smith &Wesson a contract to supply Model 3 revolvers that incorporated improvements to the barrel catch and cartridge ejection, patented by Major George W. Schofield of the U.S. Cavalry. The gun was named after him. The gun was chambered for .45 ammunition, similar to the Colt .45. It had a standard barrel length of seven inches and a blue finish.

Many of the Smith & Wesson Model 3 Schofield revolvers saw service in the Indian Wars and were popular with both lawmen and outlaws in the American West. Reportedly, they were used by Jesse James, John Wesley Hardin, Pat Garrett, Virgil Earp, and Billy the Kid. While the standard barrel length was seven inches, many Schofields were purchased as surplus by distributors who shortened the barrels five inches and refinished them in nickel.

Above: This is the "Second Model" Schofield, which has the circular thumb grip on the barrel latch and no washer behind the retaining pin.

Below: The inspector's cartouche is embossed into the grip. It is still legible.

SPECIFICATIONS

Caliber: .45 S&W

Length of barrel: 7 inches

Barrel shape: Fluted

Finish: Blue steel

Grips: Walnut

Action: Six-round top break single action revolver

Year of manufacture: 1875

Manufacturer: Smith & Wesson, Springfield, Massachusetts

Bill Tilghman

Below: A "Big Fifty" Sharps rifle. These gun were often used in buffalo hunting.

"*He was the man who took a thousand chances, arrested more law gangs, sent more criminals to the penitentiary than any other frontier officer and, with it all, was quiet, soft spoken and gentlemanly.*" – MacLeod Paine

"*The greatest of us all.*" – Bat Masterson speaking about Bill Tilghman.

"*A temperate man who never took a drink.*" – Zoe Tilghman, Bill's second wife.

"*He was the handsomest man I ever met.*" – Marshal E.D. Nix

"*Tilghman would charge Hell with a bucket.*" – Teddy Roosevelt

William Matthew Tilghman Jr.'s career spanned the golden years of the Wild West era and had many of the classic elements of the archetypal gunfighter. He was a dead shot, successful buffalo hunter, saloon owner, rancher, army scout, state senator, and (most essentially) a brave and successful lawman. He was reputed to have earned more reward money than any other law officer in the Old West. But unlike many of the type, Bill was a clean-living, temperate man who believed in the values of fair play and hard work. The March 27, 1898, issue of the *Fort Madison Iowa Chronicle* described him thus: "The officer from Oklahoma is a pleasant gentleman of suave manners, courteous demeanor, and face and eye that show he is not afraid of anything!" Bill was to spend a total of fifty-one years in law enforcement and became the last of the old-time sheriffs.

Bill was born on July 4, 1854, on a hardscrabble farm in Fort Dodge, Iowa, but constant Indian attack forced the family to relocate to Kansas. Like many young men of this era, he grew up as an outdoorsy farm boy, dividing his time between chores, hunting, and fishing. But a chance meeting in the local countryside had a huge impact on the young Bill. Driving the family cart to take his sisters berry-picking, they were approached by a man dressed in buckskins, toting a pair of Colt Navies in his sash, twirling his sleek black mustachios. This impressive dandy was Marshall Bill Hickok. The young Bill Tilghman was thunderstruck, and began to practice target shooting and "drawing" with his father's 1869 Colt Army. Bill's father had been a sharpshooter in the Union army during the Civil War and had been

Left: Bill Tilghman wears a dark shirt and carries a Sharps buffalo gun. He carried his Colt in a reverse-draw flap holster, and wears a cartridge belt. James Elder stands to the right.

partially blinded during his military service. At the age of sixteen, Bill and three of his cousins left the farm to hunt buffalo. Like Bat Masterson, Texas Jack, and thousands of other hopefuls, Bill sought to make his fortune with his "Big Fifty" Sharps. First he joined Bucknam and Rife's buffalo hunting team, then partnered with George Rust to hunt prairie wolves. But in the summer of 1872, and just like the Masterson brothers, Rust and Tilghman won a contract to supply fifty buffalo carcasses a week to the construction workers of the Atchinson, Topeka, and Santa Fe Railroad. Bill was forging a lucrative career on the prairies and persuaded his brother Dick to leave his parents' farm and join him hunting buffalo. But, as was quite common, the hunters were attacked by Native Americans, who were unhappy about the decimation of the buffalo herds. A Cheyenne and Kiowa raiding party launched an attack and killed Dick Tilghman. Devastated, Bill signed on as a cowboy, driving three thousand Longhorn cattle to Wyoming. At the end of the trail, the now twenty-year-old Tilghman decided to ride on to the wild and woolly Dodge City, "the Western Babylon," as it was known. Like many great Westerners before him, Tilghman became a town deputy at $50 a month. But Tilghman found the town too confining, and soon returned to the wide-open prairie spaces. In the winter of 1874, Tilghman hunted with the famous Hurricane Martin around Cimarron, New Mexico, and continued this life for another five years. Over that time, he is reputed to have dispatched over twelve thousand buffalo with his Sharps. But unlike many hunters, who frittered away their earnings on bad women and worse whiskey, by 1875 Bill had saved enough to buy a ranch at Bluff Creek, Kansas. In the same year, he also married a widow by the name of Flora Robinson.

By good fortune, Bill's ranch was next to that of the renowned gunfighter Neal Brown. Like many Western gunfighters, Brown had his own special way of holstering his Colt, in a cross-draw holster concealed in his waistband. The pair successfully worked together on their ranches and in the hide trade. The enterprising Tilghman invested his profits in a Dodge City saloon, the Crystal Palace. It was located next door to the Lone Star Saloon. Henry Garis was his partner in this enterprise. Unfortunately, the proximity of the Lone Star was to prove its undoing. July 4, 1877 was to go down in history as the night when "things blew up at the Lone Star." Groups of cowboys and buffalo hunters entered into a violent brawl. Ultimately, the fracas was subdued by gentleman lawman Bat Masterson. Bill and Henry decided to sell the concern in May 1878. Tilghman reinvested his money in another saloon, the Oasis, which he bought for his brother Frank to run. The local paper joked that the Oasis would serve "Methodist cocktails and hard-shell Baptist lemonade." His

Opposite page: Police Chief Bill Tilghman in later life.

out-of-town business was also in trouble. A Cheyenne war party burned his ranch to the ground. Tilghman and his family rebuilt, but they were wiped out again by the Great Blizzard of 1886. Concerned for his family's safety, Tilghman moved them into Dodge. At around this time, he started working in the law again, as a tracker. He became involved in a New Mexico gunfight in which he shot and killed Arizona Wilson and two of his gang.

In January 1884, Bill was sworn in as a deputy marshal to Marshal Pat Sughrue. Three months later, new Dodge City Mayor George M. Hoover appointed him the town's fully-fledged marshal, with Thomas C. Nixon as his deputy. This was in the post-Dodge City War period, and Tilghman soon became sickened by the political in-fighting between the city's various corrupt factions. He resigned his commission in March 1886. But he was to continue working as a lawman from time to time until the very end of his life. In 1887 he became involved in a notorious gunfight with Ed Prather in Farmer City, Kansas. Drunk and disorderly, Prather started to discharge his gun in the street. Tilghman asked him to take his hand from the gun, but Prather drew instead. Tilghman shot him dead on the spot. Like many other gunmen, Bill evolved a philosophy of gunplay. In his case, he only ever drew his gun (a Colt .38 Special, with a five-and-a-half-inch barrel) if he intended to shoot. When he did shoot, he "aimed at the belt buckle, as that was the broadest target from head to heel." In 1889 he was elected city marshal of Perry, Oklahoma, and was appointed deputy U.S. Marshal in 1892. He moved his family from Dodge City to Chandler, Oklahoma. He also served as sheriff of Lincoln County and was the chief of police in Oklahoma City. At this time, the U.S. government bought two million acres of Indian Territory, with the intention of opening it up to white settlement. As every kind of human poured west, the rule of law was slow to catch up. Bill Tilghman became one of the Three Guardsmen of the Indian Nations, a three-man team of United States Marshals that included Chris Madsen and Heck Thomas. The trio were assembled by U.S. Marshal Evett Nix and worked under his direction. They were also involved with Wyatt Earp, Doc Holiday, Luke Short, and Bat Masterson. These lawmen-gunfighters started to clean up what was to become the state of Oklahoma, arresting or shooting over three-hundred criminals and desperados. These included the outlaw "Cresent" Sam, the Creek Indian Calhoun, and various members of the Doolin Gang ("Wild Bunch"), including Bill Doolin himself as he tried to escape. They also arrested Little Britches and Cattle Annie. The Guardsmen became iconic enforcers of the law, and were said to have even inspired the crimes of men like the Coffey gang, who attempted to rob two Coffeyville, Kansas, banks simultaneously so that they could escape from the Guardsmen's territory.

In 1900, Bill was elected sheriff of Lincoln County, Oklahoma. He also had a model farm in Oakland renowned for its blood stock, Jersey cattle, and Poland hogs. His horse Chant was a Kentucky Derby winner. In 1900, Bill's first wife, Flora, died from tuberculosis after a protracted illness. He remarried three years later, in 1903. His second wife, Zoe Stratton of Ingalls, was twenty-seven years his junior.

In 1904, President Roosevelt appointed Bill a U.S. Marshal and his representative

Opposite page and above: Theodore Roosevelt in 1885. At the time, he was a fledging ranchman. On this page, he poses in his buckskins for a studio portrait, with his gun across his knee.

in Mexico. Roosevelt was hugely impressed by him and asked how "a gunman on the side of the law all of his life was still alive after so many experts had tried to kill him?" Bill replied, "A man who knows he's right has an edge over a man who knows it's wrong!" In fact, it is estimated that Bill had been shot at more than a hundred times in the course of his duties.

His survival skills enabled him to last into the twentieth century, and he became fascinated by the silent movies that were becoming popular. Bill invested some of his money in films about the iconic Western characters he had known and worked with in his colorful career (including the Earp brothers, Doc Holliday, and Bat Masterson). In 1915, he, Nix, and Madsen made the movie *The Passing of the Oklahoma Outlaws*. He also made a second film, *The Bank Robbery*. He interspersed his film work with his work as the chief of police of Oklahoma City.

Tilghman retired in 1910 and was elected to the Oklahoma State Senate. He resigned his seat in 1911, to become head of the Oklahoma City Police Force for a further two-year stint. Retiring once more, Tilghman ran his champion stock ranch from 1913 to 1924. But he obviously missed his time in law enforcement, and in 1924 accepted one final job. He was seventy years of age and had been diagnosed with cancer when he became police chief of Cromwell, Oklahoma. Cromwell was a wild Western town, full of brothels, pool halls, bootlegging, and disreputable saloons. It was known as "the wickedest town in Oklahoma." By this time, Guardsman boss Evett Nix had died from Bright's disease, but the surviving Guardsman Chris Madsen felt that subduing Cromwell would be too much for Tilghman. He warned his slightly younger friend that age had taken its toll, and his draw would have inevitably slowed down.

It was in Ma Murphy's Restaurant in Cromwell that, on Halloween night 1924, a crooked prohibition agent by the name of Wiley Lynn drew a Government 1911 .45 Automatic on Tilghman as Bill tried to arrest him. Although Bill was seventy years old and unwell, the aging gunman still managed to subdue and disarm Lynn, covering him with his Colt .32 Automatic. But for once in his life, Bill broke his cardinal rule and holstered his gun without shooting. Lynn drew a concealed pistol from his pocket and shot Tilghman twice in the chest. Bill was carried to a furniture store next door to the restaurant and bled to death twenty minutes later.

Dave Tutt

hereas some Western gunfighters were defined by the men they killed, poor Dave Tutt was defined for history by the man who killed him, Wild Bill Hickok.

Davis K. Tutt was born in 1839 in Yellville, Arkansas. His family was involved in the violent Tutt-Everett Feud that was to claim his father's life, so the young Dave became familiar with weapons at a very early age. In 1862, he joined the First Regiment, McBride's Brigade Arkansas (Confederate) Infantry. He served for one year and was then appointed to the quartermaster's department as a wagon master. Once discharged from the army, he made his way to Springfield, Missouri, bringing his mother, sister, and half-brother with him. He made his living at the gambling tables there. This is where he came upon the irascible Bill Hickok, who was also playing in the town. Initially friendly despite having been on different sides in the Civil War (Hickok had fought for the Union), the two men soon fell into a bitter professional rivalry. There were also rumors that Hickok and Tutt had fallen out over women. Tutt

Below: A lithograph of Bill Hickok's shooting of the unfortunate Dave Tutt in the Square at Springfield, Missouri.

believed that Hickok had had an affair with his sister and rejected her, while he had been accused of paying too much attention to Hickok's lover, Susanna Moore. Their relationship went from bad to worse. One night, Hickok became irritated by Tutt's ill humor and refused to play with him. Infuriated, Tutt funded and coached other gamblers to "play" with Hickok, hoping to bankrupt him, but his stooges lost every hand to the far better player.

The adversaries continued to spar in public. One night when Hickok was playing at the Lyon House Hotel in Springfield, Tutt confronted him with a debt of $40 for a horse trade. Hickok paid up, but demurred when Tutt asked him for a further $35, which he said that Hickok owed as a poker debt. Hickok insisted that the debt was only $25, and an argument ensued. Tutt grabbed Hickok's watch off the table, saying that he would keep it as collateral until the debt was settled. The watch was a Waltham

Right: The old Greene County courthouse at Springfield, Missouri, photographed in 1865. Dave Tutt fell and died near the courthouse steps.

Repeater gold pocket watch and was one of Hickok's proudest possessions. Hickok probably wanted to draw on Tutt there and then, but the saloon was full of Dave's friends and allies. Humiliated and angry, Hickok warned Tutt not to wear the watch in public, but Tutt insisted that he would sport the trinket the very next day. Hickok's response to this was unequivocal. "Tutt shouldn't pack that watch across the square

unless dead men can walk." He then collected his winnings and left the hotel.

Seemingly unable to refrain from baiting Hickok, Tutt turned up wearing the watch in the town square the next day, July 21, 1865. In the morning, Tutt and Hickok tried to resolve their differences, but Tutt overplayed his hand, telling Hickok that he now wanted $45 to settle the poker debt. Several other men became

"Wild Bill" James Hickok

involved in the argument, including Eli Armstrong and John Orr. They tried to persuade Tutt to accept $35, but Hickok was adamant that he would only pay Tutt the $25 he had offered the previous evening. At this stage, both men agreed that they didn't want to fight, and went off for a drink together.

But at a few minutes before six that evening, Hickok reappeared in the square, this time brandishing his Colt Navy pistol. He called out to Tutt, who was standing alone in the northwest corner of the square, "Dave, here I am." Hickok holstered his already cocked pistol and called out one final warning to the younger man: "Don't you come across here with that watch." By way of response, Tutt drew his pistol. This was a serious mistake. Although Tutt was renowned as a better marksman, no one could break Hickok's nerve.

Colonel Albert Barnitz, Springfield's military commander, witnessed the gunfight from the balcony of the Lyon House Hotel. He said that both men fired "simultaneously… at the distance of about a hundred paces." Tutt shot wildly, but Hickok steadied his gun on his opposite forearm and took careful aim. Bill's bullet hit Tutt straight in the heart, and the broken gambler collapsed near the courthouse steps. As he fell, Tutt cried out, "Boys, I'm killed."

Two days later, Barnitz arranged for Hickok to be arrested and charged with Tutt's manslaughter. Hickok offered no resistance. Giving evidence, medical examiner Dr. Edwin Ebert reportedly stated that Hickok's bullet "had entered (Tutt's body) on the right side between the fifth and seventh rib and passed out on the left between the fifth and seventh rib." This statement indicates that Tutt was standing side-on to Hickok, in the classic pose of the Western duelist.

Hickok's trial began on August 3, 1865, and lasted three days. The case was prosecuted by Major Robert W. Fyan, and Hickok was represented by Colonel John S. Phelps. Hickok claimed self-defense, and Judge Sempronius Boyd allowed the jury to apply the unwritten law of the "fair fight" to the evidence they heard. Hickok was acquitted, but his local reputation was sullied by the killing.

Ironically, though, it was the publicity around the case that attracted Colonel George Ward Nichols, a writer for *Harper's New Monthly Magazine*, to seek out Hickok. His definitive article about the then-unknown gunman and gambler were to secure Hickok's historical reputation as one of the great legends of the Old West. It was published in February, 1867.

Dave Tutt was buried in the Springfield City Cemetery. But in March 1883, Lewis Tutt, a former slave of the Tutt family, disinterred it and reburied him in the Maple Park Cemetery.

Opposite page: This photograph of Bill Hickok was taken by Wilbur Blakeslee of Mendota, Illinois in 1869. It shows him wearing his guns butts forward for a faster draw.

Colt 1851 Navy Revolver

Above: A detail of the hammer action,
frame, and percussion cap "nipples."

SPECIFICATIONS

Caliber: 0.36

Length of barrel: 7 inches

Barrel shape: Octagonal

Finish: Blue steel, brass back
strap and trigger guard

Grips: Walnut

Action: Six shot single action
repeater

Year of manufacture: 1851-

Manufacturer: Samuel Colt,
New York City

The peopling of the West really took off after
the Civil War, and the Colt Navy Revolver had
been a widely used and popular firearm on
both sides of the struggle. Many such weapons
were carried west by their owners after leaving
military service.

Although widely available, at the time of
the frontier the 1851 Navy was to a large
extent becoming an obsolete weapon.

Left: One of Colts cleanest and most elegant designs. An all-time classic revolver.

Below: Beautiful glowing walnut grip framed in brass

The gun was loaded with a swivel ramrod, which charged each of the chambers in the cylinder from the front. A percussion cap was then pressed onto each nipple at the rear of the cylinder. This was all quite a performance in an age when rim-fire metal cartridges were becoming the norm and center-fire technology was just around the corner. Because of these limitations, the gun was only able to use relatively low-powered black powder charges. This, coupled with the modest caliber of .36 inches, meant that its stopping power was limited. But it did have the advantage of being a multi-shot weapon when many firearms were still single shot. It was, for example, the gun of choice of Wild Bill Hickok, who carried a pair of these pistols, butt forward to allow for a "twist" or "underhand" style of draw. Despite what we have written about the gun's modest stopping power, in the hands of a skilled gunman, it was still a deadly weapon.

Wild Bill was able to kill his opponent Dave Tutt with a single shot, two hundred feet away across Springfield, Missouri's town square on July 21, 1865. The gun remains a popular collectors' choice, and many people continue to fire the weapons at black powder ranges and at re-enactments.

Gunfighter Filmography

Opposite page: James Garner as Bret Maverick in 1959. He played the role from 1957 to 1960.

Robert Clay Allison, The "Shootist"

No movies seem to have been made in tribute to the dubious character of Robert Clay Allison, but he does appear in a couple of classic television shows in 1959. First airing on June 15 that year, "Clay Allison" is the ninetieth episode of the long-running series *Tales of Wells Fargo*, which ran from March 1957 to June 1962. Allison is played by Warren Stevens. Clay made a second appearance that year in the sixtieth episode of James Garner's *Maverick* television series, "Full House." In this surreal hour-long episode, Clay Allison appears in company with many other famous westerners (Belle Starr, Cole Younger, and Billy the Kid) as a member of the Bubbly Springs Gang.

Billy The Kid

By contrast, Billy the Kid has been the subject of over fifty different movies, beginning in 1911 with *Billy the Kid*, directed by Laurence Trimble and starring Tefft Johnson. Although many movies inspired by Billy the Kid are of dubious quality (and have put the character in some extremely unlikely situations), there have been some more serious attempts to explore his life and psyche. Several memorable actors have played Billy over the decades. In 1938, Roger Rogers starred in *Billy the Kid Returns*.

Between 1940 and 1943, Peter Stewart, Sherman Scott, and Sam Newfield directed a series of potboiler movies about Billy the Kid. Initially, these featured Bob Steele, who was later replaced by Buster Crabbe.

In 1943, Howard Hughes directed a slightly bizarre study of Billy's life, entitled *The Outlaw*. The film's four main characters are Billy, Doc Holliday, Pat Garrett, and Doc Holliday's girl, Rio McDonald (played by Jane Russell in a succession of revealing outfits). In 1961, Marlon Brando starred in and directed a strange Western adventure called *One-Eyed Jacks*, in which his character, Rio, is heavily based on Billy.

In 1970, Billy featured in the John Wayne movie *Chisum*, where cattle baron John Chisum joins forces with Billy the Kid (played by Geoffrey Devel) to fight the Lincoln County War.

In 1973, classic Western director Sam Peckinpah directed *Pat Garrett and Billy the Kid*, starring James Coburn as Garrett and Kris Kristofferson as Billy.

Young Guns, released in 1988, has been one of the most successful films based on the life of Billy the Kid. Although it does not pretend to document real events,

the movie has a sensible and believable plot. Emilio Estevez plays the part of Billy. A sequel, *Young Guns II,* was released in 1990, also starring Estevez.

Billy the Kid has also become a star of the small screen, with several television credits. In 1989, Gore Vidal's made-for-television movie *Billy the Kid* was shown, starring Val Kilmer. It rejoiced in the tagline, "He was a cold-blooded killer and the all-American boy."

Black Bart

Western director George Sherman directed the below-average *Black Bart, Highwayman,* which was released in 1948. It starred Dan Duryea as the "California stage robber (who) meets European dancer Lola Montez" (played by Yvonne De Carlo). Hardly less amusingly, Black Bart also appears in Mel Brooks' 1974 comedy spoof of Western clichés, *Blazing Saddles*. In Brooks's movie, Bart is a washed-up drunk, locked up in Rock Ridge's town jail, who is then appointed town sheriff. The joke is that he is actually black. Bart was played by Cleavon Little in the movie. In the following year, *Black Bart,* a television spin-off from the movie, was aired. Black Bart is still black, and was played by Louis Gossett Jr.

Butch Cassidy

Butch Cassidy inspired one of the most popular Westerns ever, 1969's *Butch Cassidy and the Sundance Kid*. A winner of four Oscars, the film starred Paul Newman as Butch and Robert Redford as Sundance in one of the most iconic screen pairings of all time. The movie was directed by George Roy Hill. A rather less inspiring film that took Butch Cassidy as its inspiration was released in 2006, Ryan Little's *Outlaw Trail*. Set in 1951, the movie featured Butch Cassidy's fictional grandnephew.

Blackthorn, a kind of sequel to *Butch Cassidy and the Sundance Kid,* is due for release in 2011 or 2012. The movie will feature Sam Shepherd as Butch Cassidy in 1910, as he tries to make it back to America.

The Dalton Gang

The Dalton gang's violent career inspired several movies. The first of these was 1940's *When the Daltons Rode*, which was based on Emmett Dalton's book of the same name. This was followed by *The Dalton Gang* of 1949. Directed by Ford Beebe, the film was a run-of-the-mill Western caper, where two of the Daltons have inexplicably changed their names to Blackie and Guthery. Although Emmett keeps his name, Bob is missing from the film all together. The tagline for the film was "Outlaw Hunt! ... For the most daring bad men of a dangerous era..." It sounds like a "B" movie, and it is. "The Dalton Gang", first airing in 1954, was a half-hour episode of the thirty-nine-episode American television series, *Stories of the Century*.

In 1979, the made-for-television movie *The Last Ride of the Dalton Gang* took a light-hearted look at the gang's final raid on Coffeyville, Kansas. Cliff Potts played Bob, Randy Quaid was Grat, Larry Wilcox was cast as Emmett, and Mills Watson played the part of Bill.

The Doolin Gang

The Doolin gang first appeared on the big screen in 1949, in the *Doolins of Oklahoma*. Directed by George Douglas, the film starts as Bill Doolin (Randolph Scott) arrives late at the Coffeyville Massacre, and covers his outlaw career until he is shot to death. The history series *Stories of the Century* devoted its sixteenth episode to the Doolin Gang. The program was first shown in 1954.

Bill Doolin's character reappeared in the 1981 film *Cattle Annie and Little Britches*. By now an ageing outlaw, Bill is played by Scott Glenn.

Wyatt Earp

Without doubt, Wyatt Earp has been one of the best portrayed gunfighters at the movies. He has been played by a wide range of high-caliber movie stars, from Errol Flynn (*Dodge City*) in 1939, to Kevin Costner in his exhaustive 1994 biography, *Wyatt Earp*. In between, Earp has been brought to the big screen by such luminaries as Randolph Scott (*Frontier Marshall* 1939), Henry Fonda (*My Darling Clementine* 1946), Burt Lancaster (*Gunfight at the O.K. Corral* 1957), James Stewart (*Cheyenne Autumn* 1964, this was John Ford's final film), James Garner (*Hour of the Gun* 1967), and Kurt Russell (*Tombstone* 1993), among others. It certainly says something for the magnetic appeal of Earp's legend that so many big stars have wanted to take on the role of this enigmatic lawman. In March 2011, *Variety* reported that Val Kilmer had been cast as Wyatt Earp in a new movie about the legendary gunman, *The First Ride of Wyatt Earp*, to be released sometime in 2012 or 2013.

Robert Ford

Although Bob Ford figures in many movies about Jesse James, he doesn't get many title credits. One exception is the 2007 film, *The Assassination of Jesse James by the*

Coward Robert Ford. In the movie, Ford's motivation for the betrayal of his friend and idol are explored seriously. Directed and written by Andrew Dominick, the film casts Casey Affleck as the tormented Ford.

Pat Garrett

The character of Pat Garrett has appeared in over twenty movies, beginning with *Billy the Kid* of 1930, where he was portrayed by Wallace Beery. Notable portrayals of the venerable lawman include George Montgomery's in the 1958 film, *Badman's Country,* and James Coburn's in *Pat Garrett and Billy the Kid* 1973. This is by far the most well-known movie featuring Pat Garrett. Set in New Mexico in 1881, the movie features an aging Garrett, hired by the local cattlemen to bring down his old friend Billy the Kid. Director Sam Peckinpah cast James Coburn as Garrett, playing against Kris Kristofferson's Billy. Bob Dylan wrote the score for the film, and plays the part of "Alias." The movie's tagline is "Best of enemies. Deadliest of friends." This is a succinct summation of the action.

A completely unconventional view of Garrett is offered in 1988's *Young Guns*, where Patrick Wayne plays a young Garrett in company with younger versions of many other famous westerners. Most recently, the character of Pat Garrett appears in the 2011 movie *The Scarlet Worm*. Played by Michael A. Martinez, the aging gunfighter makes a brief appearance in this very alternative Western.

John Wesley Hardin

John Wesley Hardin has been featured in several movies and television programs. In the 1951 movie *The Texas Rangers,* Hardin was played by John Dehner. More notably, Rock Hudson took the part of Hardin in the 1955 film *The Lawless Breed*. More recently Hardin was played by Max Perlich in the 1994 *Maverick* movie. On television, John Wesley Hardin was one of the subjects in Jim Davis' highly regarded *Stories of the Century* series, where he was played by Richard Webb. In 1959 Hardin was also featured in an episode of the long-running *Maverick*.

He was back on television once more in 1995's mini-series *Streets of Laredo*. Starring James Garner and Sam Shepard, the series was based on a book of the same name by Larry McMurtry. Hardin was played by Randy Quaid.

Wild Bill Hickok

Wild Bill Hickok has been featured in nearly twenty movies, beginning with the

1923 offering, *Wild Bill Hickok,* in which he is played by William S. Hart. More interestingly, Hickok was portrayed by Gary Cooper in Cecil B. DeMille's 1936 movie *The Plainsman* and by Roy Rogers in the 1940 epic *Young Bill Hickok*. Several films about Hickok were released in the 1950s. Most were undistinguished, but Howard Keel's singing Hickok in 1953's *Calamity Jane* is entertaining. In 1977, Charles Bronson played the gunfighter in the surreal movie *The White Buffalo*. Hickok and Crazy Horse team up and roam the plains together, hoping to dispatch this legendary beast. The 1995 film *Wild Bill* is a far more serious portrayal of Hickok at the end of his career. Jeff Bridges' evocation of the aging sheriff of Deadwood shows a man who is worried about his failing eyesight and fully aware that he is likely to end his days violently.

Doc Holliday

Of all the gunfighters of the Old West, Doc Holliday has had one of the most successful posthumous movie careers. Beginning with *Frontier Marshal* in 1939 (where Holliday is played by Cesar Romero), Holliday has appeared in over twenty films and has been portrayed by some of Hollywood's finest actors. These have included Walter Huston in Howard Hughes's 1943 film, *The Outlaw*, Victor Mature in John Ford's 1946 *My Darling Clementine*, Kirk Douglas in *Gunfight at the O.K. Corral* (1957), Val Kilmer in *Tombstone* (1993), and Dennis Quaid in 1994's *Wyatt Earp*. Holliday has also appeared in several iconic television shows. He had his own episode in Jim Davis' *Stories of the Century*, broadcast in 1954, and was played by Dennis Hopper in *Wild Times*, a 1980 mini-series based on Brian Garfield's novel.

Jesse James

Jesse James was even more successful at the movies, featuring in over thirty different films. In the first two movies in which he features, *Jesse James as the Outlaw* and *Jesse James Under the Black Flag*, the part of James was played by his own son, Jesse James Jr. Over the years, James was played by several distinguished actors including Tyrone Power (*Jesse James* 1939), Roy Rogers (*Jesse James at bay* 1941), Robert Duvall (*The Great Northfield Minnesota Raid* 1972), and Kris Kristofferson (*The Last Days of Frank and Jesse James* 1986). There have also been several novelty movies featuring Jesse, including the comedy Western *Alias Jesse James* (1959), where Bob Hope takes the part, and the unlikely-sounding *Jesse James Meets Frankenstein's Daughter* of 1966.

Interest in the notorious bandit has persisted to the present day, and several

Above: Poster for the 2007 movie *The Assassination of Jesse James by the Coward Robert Ford*, directed by Andrew Dominik.

movies featuring James have been made recently. Colin Farrell is Jesse in the 2001 movie, *American Outlaws*, while Brad Pitt takes the role in 2007's *The Assassination of Jesse James by the Coward Robert Ford*. Given the fact that Jesse was actually such an unappealing personality who came to an ignominious end, it seems surprising that big Hollywood stars have always been so eager to tell his story.

Bat Masterson

Of all the Western gunmen, it may be only Bat Masterson and Bill Tilghman that can be seen on film. His figure appears in 1897's boxing documentary, *The Corbett-Fitzsimmons Fight*, complete with his trademark bowler hat. He has been influencing popular culture ever since, and his character has appeared in several movies. In 1943, Masterson was played by Albert Dekker in *The Woman of the Town*, and Randolph Scott in 1947's *Trail Street*. Between 1958 and 1961, Masterson had the distinction of being the inspiration behind a long-running television series, in which he was played by Gene Barry in one hundred and seven episodes. In 1959, Masterson hit the big screen once more in *The Gunfight at Dodge City*, played by Joel McCrae, where he appears during his time as Ford County sheriff. He reappeared more recently in 1994's semi-biographical movie, *Wyatt Earp*, where he is played by Tom Sizemore.

Bizarrely, Bat was also the inspiration behind the Sky Masterson character in the classic musical *Guys And Dolls*. Played by Robert Alda in the original 1950 production, Sky is a high-rolling gambler who is just about to fly to Havana, Cuba. By the end of the show, he is married to the leading lady, Sister Sarah Brown.

Texas Jack Omohundro

A professional showman for much of his life (celebrated in the Hall of Great Western Performers), Texas Jack Omohundro would almost certainly have been delighted to appear in the movies. Two movies featuring Omohundro were made in the early 1930's. *The Adventures of Texas Jack* (1934) was directed by Victor Adamson, and starred Hal Taliaferro as Jack. 1935's *Texas Jack/ Loser's End* starred Jack Perrin in the title role. Texas Jack's character also appeared in Ray Nazarro's 1953 movie *Gun Belt*. Jack was played by Red Morgan. More recently, Texas Jack Vermillion appeared in Kurt Russell's more serious film, *Tombstone* (1993), played by Peter Sherayko.

William Quantrill

William Clarke Quantrill has appeared in several movies about his life, most concentrating on his part in the shocking Lawrence Massacre. In 1940's *Dark Command*, Walter Pidgeon plays a thinly disguised Quantrill (William Cantrell) against John Wayne's sheriff character. In this version of events, Cantrell is killed during the raid on Lawrence. *Kansas Raider*s from 1950 is something similar. Brian Donlevy is Quantrill, and Lawrence is "aflame again." In 1958's *Quantrill's Raiders,* directed by Edward Bernds, Lawrence is depicted in a "shock-hot saga of night-riding terror" and Quantrill is played by Leo Gordon. In *The Young Jesse James* of 1960, "Charlie Quantrill" is shown having a bad influence on the young outlaw. He is played by Emile Meyer. Ang Lee's much more serious, and therefore much more shocking 1999 film, *Ride with the Devil,* shows a brutal portrait of the Civil War South. John Ales makes a brief appearance as Quantrill.

Belle Starr

Although contemporaries described Belle as being a "hatchet-faced; gotch-toothed tart," this was definitely not how she was portrayed by Hollywood. First represented by Betty Compson in the 1928 movie *Court-Martial*, she went on to be played by Gene Tierney (*Belle Starr,* 1941), Isabel Jewell (*Daughter of Belle Starr,* 1946) and, most improbably of all, by the ultra-glamorous Jane Russell (*Montana Belle*, 1952). Later films that feature Belle's character include 1980's *The Long Riders*, where she is played by Pamela Reed.

Belle has also appeared on television, featuring in an episode of the long-running *Stories of the Century* in the early 1950s (played by Marie Windsor), and in series three of *Dr. Quinn, Medicine Woman*, where she appears as a young and vulnerable outlaw.

Right: 1952's *High Noon* contains another famous duel, between Sheriff Will Kane (Gary Cooper) and bad man Frank Miller.

Bill Tilghman

Like many Western lawmen-gunmen, Bill Tilghman had a second career. His was as a movie director and actor. Beginning with the 1908 film, *A Bank Robbery,* Tilghman became fascinated by the storytelling aspects of film making. His first film was only nineteen minutes long, and featured Frank Clanton, Heck Thomas, Quanah Parker, and Tilghman himself, all playing themselves. The movie was made in Cache, Oklahoma. In 1915, Tilghman made a second film, *The Passing of the Oklahoma Outlaws*. This was his attempt to show the dark side of Western life. It starred E.D. Nix, Chris Madsen, and himself, all appearing as themselves.

After his death, Tilghman continued to appear in the movies. In 1981, he was played by Rod Steiger in the 1981 film *Cattle Annie and Little Britches*. Sam Elliott starred as Tilghman in the 1999 made-for-television film *You Know My Name*.

Dave Tutt

Dave Tutt has not received any title billings at the movies, but his fatal shootout with Bill Hickok has had a huge impact on the western genre. From Gary Cooper's *High Noon*, to Clint Eastwood's *Dollars Trilogy*, their iconic duel has been replayed many times. 1995's *Wild Bill* re-enacts the gunfight, with Robert Knott playing the part of Tutt.

Opposite page: 1966's *The Good, the Bad, and the Ugly* was the final movie in Sergio Leone's "Dollars Trilogy." Clint Eastwood often replays the iconic Western duel, as fought by Bill Hickok and Dave Tutt.

Introduction to the Cowboys

The proud tradition of American cowboying has a very long history that dates right back to the Mexican charros. They, in turn, inherited their skills from the Spanish *conquistadors*, who had arrived in the Americas following Christopher Columbus's discovery of the New World in 1492.

The heyday of the American cowboy stretched from the years following the Civil War through to the 1880s. This was the time of the great cattle drives along the iconic cattle trails. These acted as arteries of cow commerce from the Southern states to America's meat-hungry East and North. The impetus behind the growing cattle trade was simple: there were more cattle than people in the huge tract of land between the Great Plains and California, while the industrialised and heavily-populated northern and eastern states were crying out for fresh meat.

Inevitably, this led to a great increase in the number of men employed in the industry. Although cowhands had been working on ranches in Georgia and Florida before the Civil War, the profession only became familiar to most Americans when they became familiar in the states and territories to the west of the Missouri. In the decades following the war, it is estimated that as many as forty-thousand men worked as cow punchers in the burgeoning cattle industry.

The term "cowboy" itself is thought to have been coined by the greatest cattleman of all, Charles Goodnight. When Goodnight wrote about the ranching methods he used on his extensive J.A. Ranch, he explained how he had employed "a little army of men called "'cowboys'" to care for his hundred-thousand head of cattle. Surprisingly, Goodnight was writing in the mid 1880s, when land enclosure was already threatening the cowhand's traditional role. Goodnight had originally referred to his hands as "boys," and he did indeed have a very paternal relationship with them. At this time, the average age of a western cowboy was around twenty-four.

It could be argued that far from being free to roam the unspoiled prairie, cowboys were actually little more than servants of investors from eastern America and Europe as the cattle business became hugely profitable. But despite this, our image of the brave cowboy persists, that of a strong and resolute individual facing down dangers of all kinds; wild weather, wild beasts, and wild men.

The involvement of capital, especially in the railroad industry, did have a huge effect on the cattle trade. Immensely long cattle drives were now required to bring

Opposite page: The cowboy has become a classic character in American folklore.

Opposite page: This oil painting of a well-equipped cowboy was featured in an early advertisement for Colt.

cattle from the Texan and Southern ranches to the railheads that had sprung up, mostly in Kansas. From here, the animals were loaded onto cattle trucks and shipped to where their meat could bring the highest prices. Generally, this was about ten times what the meat was worth in the South.

The cowboys themselves led tough and largely thankless lives, surviving on meagre pay of around $25 to $45 a month. Few were literate, and most would have struggled to find other forms of employment. Their work was also dangerous; every cowboy had to beware of stampedes, snakes, and drought, but a cowboy's most likely cause of death was from riding accidents. It was relatively common for men to be dragged, thrown, or kicked to death by their own horse. The second most likely cause of death was from pneumonia, hardly surprising when you consider their working and living conditions.

Though it may seem lonely and unrewarding by modern standards, the life of the cowboy seems to carry lasting appeal. We admire their courage and self-reliance, and their freedom to roam across the unspoiled wilderness of the West. The cowboy has become a true icon of the American way of life.

Below: Cowboys worked in all conditions. This one is wearing a pommel slicker.

The History of The Cowboy

Oh, he would twirl that lariat and he didn't do it slow

He could catch them forefeet nine out of ten for any kind of dough

And when the herd stamped he was always on the spot

And set them to milling, like the stirrings of a pot

— from Zebra Dun, cowboy folk song

Opposite page: For many Americans, John Wayne is the epitome of cowboy glamor. In real life, he was admired for his horsemanship and courage.

Of all the West's iconic characters, the cowboy is the most universally recognized and admired. But the cowboy role that has come to symbolize the free spirit of America actually originated in Spain. When the conquistadors imported their cattle handling skills into South America in the sixteenth century, the vaqueros learned how to herd large numbers of horses and cattle across the open lands to forage. These original cowpunchers were usually mounted on horseback, but also rode donkeys, or burros. The Spanish were also responsible for bringing the first Longhorn cattle to America in 1493.

The word "cowboy" (the English-language equivalent of the Spanish vaqueros), made its first appearance between 1715 and 1725. By this time, the cattle industry had become an important element of the North American economy, particularly in the South and West. The "boy" tag was not meant to be demeaning; tough work like this required youth and vigor, and boys as young as twelve were employed in ranch work.

As European settlers imported Longhorn cattle to America, a culture of ranching became established, particularly in the South. Surprisingly, the market for beef meat was very limited at this time, and the animals were mainly bred for their hides and tallow. The State of Texas (independent from 1836), soon became prominent in the American cattle trade. Anglo-Texans drove out many Mexican ranchers from the territory and confiscated their animals. This new breed of Texas cattlemen soon developed its own cowboy traditions. Typically the Texas cowboy was a solitary drifter, who worked for a different outfit every season.

Ranching had been established much longer in California. There were already nineteen rancheros by 1790, and this number was greatly increased by 1836. Spanish mission farmlands were often seized by the Mexican government and huge

Above: A romantic evocation of the life of a cowboy. One man and his horse guard the herd, while the others rest in their dreaming sacks.

Right: The heyday of the cattle trails was between 1866 and 1890.

tracts of land were redistributed to favored ranchers for grazing. More verdant grazing meant that there was less open range, and Californian meat tended to stay in the region. This meant far fewer cattle drives, and more settled living conditions for Californian cowboys, who mostly lived on permanent ranches. Also known as buckaroos, they were considered more skilled in animal husbandry than their Texan counterparts. California cowboys often aspired to someday own their own ranches, get married, and have a family, whereas Texan cowboys were far more likely to stay single and wander the land.

A third type of cowhand, known as the Florida cowhunter, or "cracker cowboy", had a completely different way of working. Spanish settlers had introduced cattle to the state in the sixteenth century, and cowhunters were usually of Spanish or American Indian descent. These men used dogs and bullwhips rather than horses

Right: A small number of well-trained cowboys could control thousands of cows on the trail. They were paid between $25 and $40 a month for their hard work.

Opposite page: Roping was an important skill for a trailhand, and became celebrated in rodeos across the West.

Below: The tough and distinctive Texas Longhorn was well-suited to the cattle drives. The breed lost very little weight along the trail.

and lassos to control the smaller breeds of cattle native to this region. Historically, meat produced in Florida was used to supply the Spanish missions in the north of the state and the island of Cuba, but this meat became of critical importance to the Confederacy during the Civil War. It was so crucial that in March, 1864, the eight-hundred-strong Cow Cavalry (the 1st Battalion Florida Special Cavalry) was formed to protect the cattle from Union raiders.

In Canada, the cattle industry was focused on Alberta and Saskatchewan. Many cowboys working in Canada came north from America. Elsewhere in the Americas, Hawaii had its paniolos, Argentina its gauchos, Peru its chalans, Chile its huasos, and Mexico its vaqueros and charros. Each of these regions had wide-open spaces for grazing cattle, sheep, or horses, and developed its own special herding techniques and traditions.

A fantastic panorama of a cattle drive. The photograph shows the ethnic diversity of the trailhands.

Marlin Models 1893 and 1894

Winchester didn't have it all its own way in the Western market. The Marlin Firearms Company launched its first lever-action rifle in 1881, followed by the Model 1893. The 1893 was the company's first rifle designed for the recently introduced smokeless cartridge. It was offered in five different calibers. The barrels were either round or octagonal, and varied in length between twenty-four and thirty-two inches. Some 900,000 examples of the gun were manufactured. They were marked Model 1893 up to 1905 but this was shortened to Model 93 thereafter. This example is marked Model 93.

The Model 1894 was very similar to the Model 1893, but had a shorter action. This example is in .25-20 caliber and has a twenty-four inch round barrel. Marlin manufactured around 250,000 Model 1894s between 1894 and 1935. Marlin guns were mass-produced and sold at competitive prices. Their marketing strategy is the same today. As a result, the Marlin was a popular cowboy weapon.

John M. Marlin founded
Marlin Firearms in 1870.

Marlin's 1893 was their first rifle specifically designed for the smokeless cartridge.

In 1969 the company returned the popular Model 1894 into production, now chambered for the .44 Magnum. A wide variety of Model 1894s has appeared since then, chambered for various calibers: the .22, .the 38 Special, and the .45 Long Colt. This example is chambered for the .45 Long Colt round. This version of the weapon was first marketed in 1996 and is intended to meet the requirements of the sport of cowboy action shooting. The weapon weighs seven-and-a-half pounds and the tubular magazine holds ten rounds.

The original Marlin workshop was located on State Street in New Haven, Connecticut.

SPECIFICATIONS

Caliber: .22, .38 Special, .45 Long Colt

Barrel: 24-32 inches

Type: Lever-action repeating rifle

Origin: Marlin Firearms Co., New Haven, Connecticut

The Cattle Towns of the West

Below: Cattle were loaded onto eastbound trains at the cattle town rail heads.

The defeat of the Southern states in the Civil War had a great effect on the cattle industry, leading to a kind of cowboy diaspora. When Texans went off to fight in the war, their cattle were left to roam free, and huge herds built up. After the war, there was no market for the five million cattle stranded in the economically crippled South, while the wealthy and industrial North was desperate for meat.

To drive these cattle north was extremely difficult, time-consuming, and dangerous. This meant that cowboy skills were in high demand. Originally, the Texan herds were driven across Missouri on their way to the north and east. But the cattlemen ran into increasing hostility from the local farmers, who objected to the damage that the cattle drives caused. Many also believed that the cows carried a virulent tick that was deadly to their livestock. In effect, this standoff meant that thousands of cattle were marooned in Texas, where they were worth only $4 a head. They were prevented from reaching the North, where each animal was worth in excess of $40.

This economic opportunity was the impetus that inspired an economically and culturally important phenomenon. This was a completely new kind of settlement, the western cattle town.

These towns underwent a boom that lasted for about five years. The major cattle towns were all at the new Kansas railheads: Abilene, Hays City, Dodge City, Newton, and Ellsworth.

Above: It wasn't long before the cow towns had the veneer
of respectability and all the usual amenities.

Abilene, Kansas

Right: Abilene, Kansas in 1879. Most of the town's original buildings were false-fronted wooden structures, but these were gradually replaced by more solid brick buildings.

Abilene was the first of the cow towns of the West. The town began as a small prairie village along the Smoky Hill Trail. Timothy Hersey established it as a stage coach stop in 1857 and gave the town its name, a biblical term that means "city of the plains." At this time, the settlement was no more than a collection of a few wooden huts, but boom times were coming. Texan cattle men had been searching for a safe and accessible market for their wild Texas Longhorn cattle, but did not find themselves welcome anywhere. This staggering economic opportunity was not lost on entrepreneurial cattlemen like Illinois businessman Joseph G. McCoy. He had a vision of a great cattle depot on the plains, from which cattle could be shipped by train to the industrial East.

McCoy persuaded the Kansas Pacific Railroad to build a siding at Abilene, Kansas. In 1867 he opened his Great Western Stockyards at Abilene's railhead, where cattle could be held before being loaded onto the eastbound railroad. McCoy's stockyards were the largest ones west of Kansas City, and were perfectly situated right next to grazing prairies. He then encouraged the Texas ranchers to drive their animals to Abilene. In 1867, the first year of Abilene's great cattle market, McCoy was responsible for shipping 35,000 head of cattle eastwards. By 1871, this had increased to 600,000 animals shipped on the hoof.

Overleaf: A panoramic view of Abilene's High Street. Its dirt road gives way to the open prairie in the very near distance.

In this way, Abilene became the first major end-of-the-line town, situated at the head of the Chisholm Cattle Trail. The town boomed, and the local hotel — The Drovers Cottage — became the headquarters of the cattle bosses and buyers from the East. By 1868, the town's population had swelled with an influx of cowboys, gamblers, pimps, prostitutes, and gunslingers. The usual trouble ensued, and galloping horses

and the sound of wild gunplay became commonplace on Abilene's streets. It soon became one of the wildest towns in the West, and remained so for a couple of years.

Joseph McCoy wrote that these newcomers would "imbibe too much poison whiskey and straightway go on the warpath... At such times it is not safe to be on

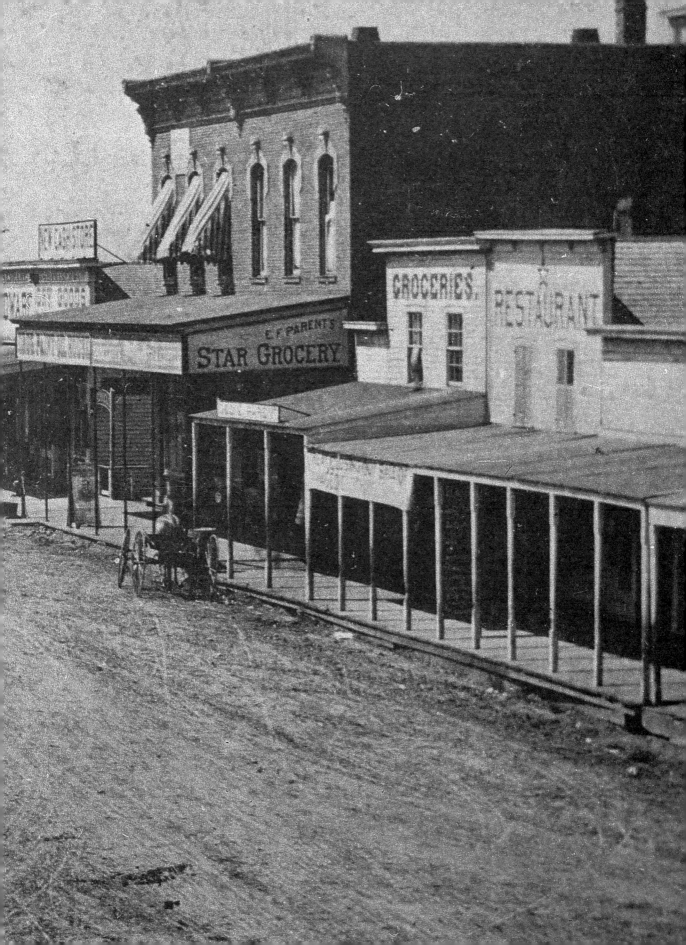

Above: McCoy opened his Abilene stockyards in 1867. The Kansas Pacific Railroad shipped thousands of cattle east from here.

the streets." The Devil's Addiction district of the town was particularly riotous.

By the spring of 1870, the townsfolk of Abilene had had enough of this violence, and decided to suppress it with a newly-appointed marshal and a "no guns" law. But the cowboys came into town as usual, ripped up the anti-gun notice, and demolished the newly built jail. Abilene's civic leaders then tried to employ two police officers from St. Louis, Missouri; legend has it that the two men rode the train into town, took one look around, and returned to St. Louis the same evening.

A man of a much higher caliber arrived later that year, when Marshal Tom "Bear River" Smith rode into town on his famous mount, Silverheels. Smith enforced the "no guns" policy with his bare hands. Smith survived two assassination attempts, but was ultimately murdered and decapitated on November 2, 1870, after just a few months on the job. In April, 1871 Abilene turned to Wild Bill Hickok in the hope that his reputation would bring some order to the town. Hickok's period in office ended ignominiously when he accidentally shot and killed his own deputy, Mike Williams. He was fired from the Abilene job in December that year.

But by the fall of 1871 the tracks had been extended, and the cattle trade was already moving on from Abilene to other Kansas rail towns further along the line, such as Ellsworth, Hays City, Newton, and Dodge City.

Ellsworth, Kansas

Ellsworth was known as "The Wickedest Cattletown in Kansas." Of all the cattle towns, it was said that "Abilene, [was] the first, Dodge City, the last, but Ellsworth the wickedest." The town was named for the nearby Fort Ellsworth, which had been constructed in 1864. In the 1860s, the new Kansas Pacific stockyards at the railhead meant that Ellsworth became a bustling cowtown, filled with cowboys and trail bosses. The railroad cut the town's main street in two. The cattle bosses had pretty much abandoned Abilene by 1872, and Ellsworth took over the business. Like Abilene, Ellsworth became redolent with violence, and the streets rang with the sound of gunfire. Shootings became so commonplace that it was said that "Ellsworth had a man every morning for breakfast." Most of the town businesses were run for cowboys: saloons (including the famous Plaza), dancehalls (including Lizzie Palmer's), gambling halls, and brothels. There was also a famous drovers'

Below: The Kansas Pacific Railroad extended the train line and, by 1872, the cattle business had moved from Abilene to Ellsworth.

Left: The Southwestern Hotel in Caldwell, Kansas. Though not as famous as some of the larger cow towns, Caldwell's position on the Chisholm Trail kept the cattle drives coming between 1871 and 1885.

Above: Ellsworth in 1871. J. Mueller's shop catered for the footwear needs of cowboys driving cattle to the town.

mercantile store — the Old Reliable House — that sold cowboy supplies, clothing, and equipment. Cowboys passing through the town also bought gifts at the store to take home to their families in Texas.

In 1872, Ellsworth's Drover's Cottage Hotel (which had moved there from Abilene) opened, with rooms for one-hundred-seventy-five guests. It was used by trail bosses and stockmen. The transient nature of the town meant that violence was commonplace. Ellsworth's resident population was only 448 people in 1870; by 1880 it had more than doubled to 929. One of the main reasons that genuine settlers avoided Ellsworth was the town's lawless character and bad reputation. Wild Bill Hickok ran for town marshal in 1868, but was beaten to the post by ex-soldier E. W. Kingsbury. Although popular and well-respected, Kingsbury struggled to control the town, even with the help of the local police force. On September 26, 1869 Marshal Will Semans was shot and killed in Joe Brennan's saloon. An outbreak of serious mayhem followed, as the local criminals took advantage of the vacuum in law enforcement. Two local miscreants, known only as Craig and Johnson, were particularly active in terrorizing the town. In the end, they pushed the Ellsworth townsfolk too hard; a group of local vigilantes caught up with and lynched the pair near the Smoky Hill River.

Another famous lawman, Wyatt Earp, worked in Ellsworth briefly. The town's violence and lawlessness came to a head in 1873, when a drunken Billy Thompson accidentally shot and killed Ellsworth County Sheriff Chauncey Whitney. This killing launched a tide of violence, during which it was said that "Hell was in session at Ellsworth." Although Thompson was acquitted of murder, Whitney's killing led to a great deal of hostility towards cowboys, which culminated in a double tragedy. Chief of Police Ed Crawford pistol-whipped Texan cowboy Cad Pierce to death. A short while later, Crawford himself was shot to death in a local brothel. It was assumed that this shooting was a revenge killing for Pierce's death. This tide of violence led to several other shootings, including those of ex-Marshal "Happy" Jack Morco and Texan Ed Crawford.

As the trails began to favor other Kansas towns, Ellsworth's crime rate dropped, but so did the economic activity in the town. Kansas Pacific finally shut down its Ellsworth shipping pens in 1875.

Below: Wichita, Kansas. The ramshackle shops catered to all a cowboy's needs.

Left: This gun shop in Denver, Colorado, sold and repaired firearms for cowboys.

Sharps Buffalo Rifle

The Sharps Buffalo rifle was a legend in the West and had a fearsome reputation. Its long-distance accuracy and tremendous stopping power is celebrated in a classic Hollywood movie scenario. The bad guy confidently rides off into the sunset, while the good guy takes aim unhurriedly. He touches the foresight with spit to provide a gleam of light, and adjusts the vernier backsight. When the good guy squeezes the trigger, the audience is convinced that his adversary has escaped. As it is fired, the Sharps rifle booms loudly. The barrel bucks from the explosive detonation of the heavy .50 cartridge, then silence returns. We watch the bad guy continue his ride into the distance for several long, tantalizing seconds. Suddenly, almost in slow motion, the shot connects with bad man's retreating form. Dead, he slumps from his mount.

Such drama seldom entered the life of an ordinary trail cowboy. His requirements were for a heavy caliber rifle that could bring down large game for the chuck wagon, or a sick steer at considerable distance. The gun could also be used to warn off trouble. The booming report from its large caliber ammunition had an strong deterrent effect on anyone planning to harm the herd.

Sharps Rifle Manufacturing Company was founded by Christian Sharps on October 9, 1851.

This example has a classic thirty-inch barrel. It is smaller than the big .50, but at .45-70, it is still an extremely potent weapon. The .45 lead slug was propelled by a seventy grain charge. Even the standard Winchester at only .44-40 (with forty grains at its disposal) was a mighty gun. The .50 Sharps was simply devastating.

The gun pictured was supplied by J.P. Lower of Denver, the famous western dealer and outfitter. His name is stamped on top of the barrel. The gun has double set triggers and a shotgun butt plate. It also has Lower's special Rocky Mountain buckhorn site that he designed himself, and had made up by Sharps. The tang site is a modified sporting site with a vernier staff added for extra range. The gun was known as "old reliable."

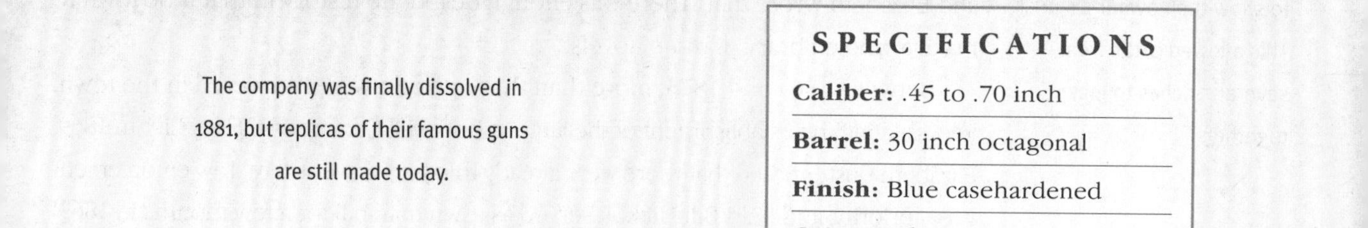

The company was finally dissolved in 1881, but replicas of their famous guns are still made today.

SPECIFICATIONS

Caliber: .45 to .70 inch

Barrel: 30 inch octagonal

Finish: Blue casehardened

Grips: Walnut

Action: Single-shot, breech loading

Hays City, Kansas

Just as in Abilene and Ellsworth, it was the building of the Kansas Pacific Railway that inspired the foundation of Hays City. The entrepreneurial Buffalo Bill Cody and the railroad contractor William Rose founded the settlement of Rome, Kansas, near Fort Hays. The fort had been established to protect railroad constructors from Indian attack. Cody and Rose hoped that the railroad would come to their fledgling town. A rival developer to Cody and Rose, Dr. William Webb, established an alternative settlement on the other bank of the Big Creek. This new town was called Hays City. The railroad bosses favoured Hays City for the end of the new tracks, and Cody and Rose's venture failed. As soon as the railroad reached the new municipality in 1867, Hays City grew rapidly. By the following year, Rome, Kansas, was a ghost town.

As an end-of-the-line town, Hays became the supply point for the territories to the west and southwest. The town was soon full of businesses, including the Gibbs House hotel, the Moses and Bloomfield general store, and a post office. Most of the early town buildings were wooden frame structures, but a stone drugstore soon graced the town. Hays City soon had its first newspaper, appropriately named the Railway Advance.

Just like Abilene and Ellsworth, Hays City was beset by crime and violence from its foundation. This was largely a side effect of the town's role as a railhead for cattle being shipped east. It was also the outfitting station for the wagon trains following the Smoky Hill Trail eastward. As well as the usual casual violence, desperados like Jim Curry also plagued the town. During his stay he murdered several black men, a few townsfolk, and a young boy. Soldiers from the local fort were also involved in violence in Hays City. George and Elizabeth Custer lived at Fort Hays for a while, and Elizabeth wrote that "there was enough desperate history in that little town to make a whole library of dime novels."

Above: Cattle were branded to show their owner's mark. This allowed cattle from several ranches to graze together.

Between 1867 and 1873, more than thirty people were murdered in the town, necessitating the establishment of the famous Boot Hill Cemetery in Hays City. In 1869, Elizabeth Custer noted that there were already thirty-six graves there. Law enforcement was a priority, and Wild Bill Hickok served as town marshal for a few months in 1869. Unfortunately, his effect on the town was less than benign. He managed to kill two townsmen, two soldiers, and wound several others during his employment at Hays City. He was forced to flee the town and was next heard of working in Abilene.

By 1872, the railroad had been built to Dodge City, and the cattle industry had pretty much abandoned Hays City. The town began to establish itself as the center of a farming community, and the trouble moved on to Dodge City.

In 1873, a stone courthouse was erected in Hays City, and a schoolhouse was built by a subscription that raised twelve thousand dollars. In 1875, local luminary H. P. Wilson built an elegant stone residence on Chestnut Street, the Pennsylvania House. Civilization had made it to Hays City.

Newton, Kansas

On July 17, 1871, the Atchison, Topeka and Santa Fe Railroad arrived at Newton. The town was the railhead for the famous Chisholm Trail, the shipping point for the huge herds that has previously been loaded onto the railroad at Abilene. Newton was incorporated as a city of the third class in 1872. The coming of the

Above: Dodge City became known as "the Queen of Cow Towns". The cattle industry moved there when a spur from the Chisholm Trail (which became known as the Great Western Cattle Trail) was diverted to the town. The town's peak years in the cattle trade were 1883 and 1884.

Previous pages: Dodge City became the epitome of the wild Western frontier town. Infamous for its gun-slinging inhabitants, the town became embroiled in the Dodge City War of 1883.

Left: When the cattle trade moved on, Dodge City became a sleepy little town, like any other in western Kansas. The days of the Old West were numbered.

railroad and the cattle drives attracted the usual cast of desperados: gunslingers, gamblers, and prostitutes. The town soon rivalled Ellsworth for bloody violence and lawlessness; it, too, was sometimes called the "wickedest city in the West." Newton's bad reputation was largely due to the notorious gunfight that took place on August 9, 1871 in Perry Tuttle's dance house in the Hyde Park area of the town. Eight men were shot to death in the fracas. Despite this, the town soon became well known for its hospitality. The Hyde Park area boasted fifteen different saloons, included the Do Drop In, The Side Track, and the Gold Rooms.

When the railway moved on to Dodge City in 1872, complete with a branch line to Wichita, the cattle trade moved on with it, and Newton was freed from many of the rough types that had frequented its streets. The reign of the cowboy was over, and the first stirrings of law and order were felt in the town. Unfortunately, Newton's tough times weren't over. A terrible fire occurred on the night of December 8, 1873. The east side of block 38 (the business area of the city) was completely destroyed. The population of the town decreased dramatically in the years following 1872, and did not recover until late in that decade.

Dodge City, Kansas

Dodge City dates from 1871, when Henry L. Sitler built a three-room sod house near Fort Dodge. Conveniently located near the Santa Fe Trail, and with the Santa Fe Railroad rapidly approaching from the east, the town started to boom in 1872, and was to become the Queen of the Cow Towns. The Atchison, Topeka, and Santa Fe Railroad arrived in Dodge City in September 1872. A new cattle trail, the Great Western, branched off from the Chisholm Trail to bring cattle to the railhead, and thousands of cattle were soon passing through the town's stockyards. The peak years of the trade were between 1883 and 1884. George M. Hoover opened the town's first saloon, and the town soon boasted the usual selection of saloons (including the Long Branch), gambling halls, barbers, restaurants, general stores, dance halls, and brothels (including the China Doll). The town even had a bullfighting ring for a brief period in 1884. All of these places of entertainment were designed to take as much money as possible from the cowboys that passed through the town. By 1877, nineteen establishments in the town were licensed to sell liquor.

Dodge City started out as a tent town, and its first trade was in buffalo hides and meat. A good hunter could make a hundred dollars a day. These commodities were loaded into railcars and shipped east. An estimated 1,500,000 buffalo hides were shipped from Dodge City between 1872 and 1878. Businesses such as Robert Wright's Dodge City Hide Yard were very profitable, but indiscriminate hunting meant that the prairie was littered with the rotting corpses of dead animals. The mass slaughter destroyed the huge buffalo herds of the plains. Filthy buffalo hunters and traders filled the town's establishments, and inspired the derogatory term "stinker." Longhorn cattle were the next source of income for the town, and were the main source of business for Dodge City for a period of ten years. Over five million head of cattle were driven through the town on their way to the railroad.

Like all the frontier towns, Dodge City passed through a blazing period of violence and lawlessness. There was no conventional law enforcement in the town, and the number of shooting deaths soon necessitated a local graveyard. (Another) Boot Hill Cemetery was established soon after the town was, and saw continuous use until 1878.

Law and order finally arrived in the town with Bat Masterson, Ed Masterson, Wyatt Earp, Bill Tilghman, and Charlie Bassett. An ordinance was passed that guns could not be worn or carried north of the railroad tracks. These tough law enforcers were especially needed in the summer months when cowboys, cattle buyers, gamblers, and prostitutes flooded the town.

Dodge City was the last of the frontier cattle towns. Fort Dodge was closed in 1882, and the cattle drives ended after the notorious blizzard of January 1886. Tired of the itinerant cowboy population, Dodge City had been advertising for permanent settlers since 1874. At that time, the town had consisted of over seventy buildings, including a school. The settlement of the last of the cattle towns marked the end of the Old West.

The Great Cattle Trails

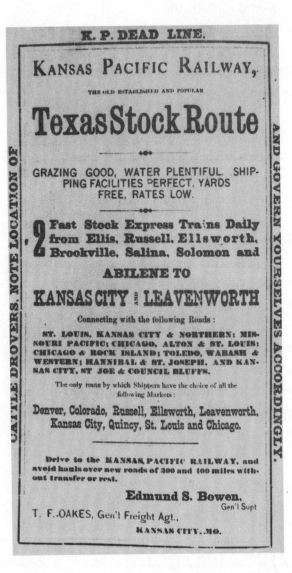

V arious trails, or cattle drovers' routes, were chiselled out of the difficult and dangerous landscape to get cattle to the new railhead towns.

The Chisholm Cattle Trail

One of the main routes that the drovers used to get stock from the Texas ranches to McCoy's Abilene stockyards was the Chisholm Cattle Trail. This famous dirt track was named for Jesse Chisholm. Chisholm was born around 1805 in the Hiwassee region of Texas. His father was a slave trader of Scottish descent, and his mother was a Cherokee woman. After his parents separated, Chisholm was brought up in the Cherokee Nation. Before the Civil War broke out (in which he supported the Confederacy), Chisholm had built several trading posts along what was to become the Oklahoma section of the trail. Chisholm's friendship with the plains tribes and his ability to speak fourteen Indian dialects fluently was essential to the opening of the route. Sadly, Chisholm died from food poisoning from eating rancid bear meat in 1868, and never had an opportunity to drive his cattle along the route that still bears his name.

In fact, the first cattleman to use the Chisholm Trail from San Antonio to the railhead at Abilene, Kansas was O. W. Wheeler (together with his two partners, Wilson and Hicks) in 1867. At this time, Abilene itself was only a six-year-old hamlet. Wheeler succeeded in herding 2,400 steers along the route. Ultimately, Chisholm's dirt track was to be trodden by upwards of five million cattle and one million mustangs. It was served by hundreds of smaller feed trails that drew herds from all over Texas, and became an important financial artery for the region. The trail greatly stimulated the cattle trade and helped the South to recover from the devastation of the Civil War.

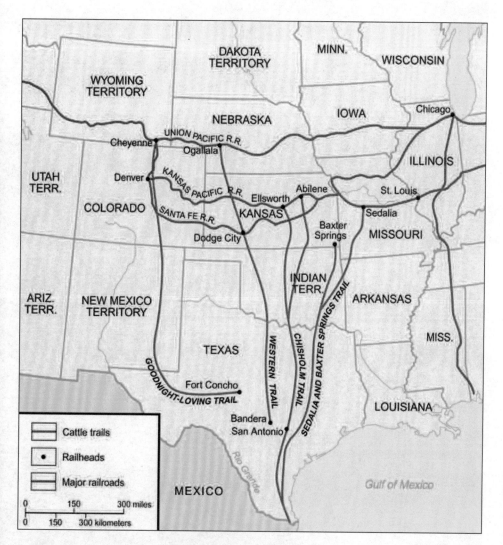

Left: This map shows the cattle trails feeding into the cow town rail heads. They all begin in Texas.

Opposite page: The Kansas Pacific Railway operated between 1863 and 1880. The company operated long-distance lines that were instrumental in opening up the central Great Plains to settlement. Its line from Kansas City to Denver completed the final link in the coast-to-coast railroad in 1870.

In its original form, the Chisholm Trail began in San Antonio, and ended at Abilene. But it was gradually extended further into Kansas; first to Newton, then Wichita, and finally to Caldwell by 1883. The long drive from Texas to Kansas took between two and three months, and was enough to challenge even the most experienced Texas cattlemen. The cattle moved along at around ten to twelve miles a day, which allowed them to graze as they went. The terrain itself was extremely difficult. The herdsmen had to drive the cattle across two major rivers (the Arkansas and the Red), and negotiate various creeks, canyons, mountains, and badlands along the route. Ruthless cattle rustlers and territorial Indians were enough to worry even the most fearless cowboy. At the time, Oklahoma was still part of the Indian Territory. There was also the ever-present danger of stampede

Right: Thirsty cattle raising dust as they swarm to drink. The cattle trails were designed to take advantage of rivers and streams where the herd could be watered.

Right: This cowboy wears a bandana across his mouth and nose to protect him from dust raised by the herd.

Opposite page top: This well-dressed cowboy carries a lasso on his saddle.

Opposite page bottom: The cowhands drove the cattle into a circle at night so they would be easier to protect.

Overleaf: Even today, cowboys drive cattle through the dense scrub and cactuses of the South.

from the capricious Texan Longhorn. The mastering of these diverse problems greatly enhanced the reputation of the Texas cowboy, and he achieved an almost folkloric status. Specialist trailing contractors managed most of these drives, and they recruited bands of cowboys to ride the line. Over the years, these trail bosses perfected an economic system of cattle driving that meant they could get the animals to market for around sixty to seventy-five cents a head. This was far cheaper than sending the cattle by rail. These highly skilled professional drovers included rugged individuals like John T. Lyle, George W. Slaughter, and the Pryor brothers.

The Great Western Cattle Trail

Also known as the Dodge City Trail and the Old Texas Trail, the Great Western Cattle Trail ran roughly parallel to the Chisholm Trail to the west. Its route began in Bandera, Texas, then passed near to Abilene, Texas, and concluded at Dodge City, Kansas. At the time, Dodge City was the cattle capital of the world. The trail was two thousand miles long and ran mostly through Oklahoma. Feeder trails merged into it from several other areas, including the Rio Grande, Wyoming, and Montana.

Famously, Doan's Crossing was the last supply post on the Great Western Cattle Trail before the lands of the Indian Nation. C. E. Doan was the proprietor of the trading post there, and he kept a tally of the beasts moving through. According to

Left: The decimation of the wild buffalo herds left the Indian tribes dependant on cattle for meat.

Below: Trailsmen often lost a few head of cattle to Indian rustlers.

Doan, the peak of the traffic occurred between 1874 and 1886, when five million animals passed along the trail. In 1881, 301,000 head of cattle passed through Doan's Crossing. The largest individual herd to pass through consisted of ten thousand animals. The motivation for driving the cattle along the Great Western Trail was clear. In Texas at this time, cattle were worth ten to twelve dollars a head. In Dodge City, each animal could be sold for around twenty-five dollars. But the trail became increasingly dangerous as the Cheyenne and Arapaho tribes were confined to reservations. Now that the wild antelope and buffalo were nearly extinct, being restricted to these virtually meatless lands effectively meant a lingering death by starvation for the Indians. They tried to survive by demanding a trail bounty of beef from each passing herd. If the trail bosses refused to pay, the Indians retaliated by attacking the drive, or making the cattle stampede (back when the buffalo were plentiful, the Indians would make them stampede over cliffs to kill many animals quickly and easily.)

Opposite page: A cowboy readies his long, knotted *reata* to rope a cow.

Colt Single-Action Army Revolver 1873

The Colt single-action army revolver is one of the greatest handguns in history. Many examples were purchased by the U.S. Army, and the gun was also widely sold on the civilian market. It was particularly popular in the West, where it came to symbolize the cowboy era. The gun dates from 1872, when the U.S. Army held a competition for a new revolver design. The contest was won by Colt. Their entry was accepted for service as the Model 1873 and remained in continuous production for sixty-seven years (between 1873 and 1940). During this time, exactly 357,859 examples were manufactured. The gun was reintroduced into production in 1956. Colt continues to produce small numbers of this revolver, which now carry a high price tag.

There is nothing particularly unusual about the design and construction of the Model 1873, but the inspired combination of simplicity, ruggedness, ease of use, and dependability has made for an enduring and unpretentious classic.

These pearl grips were
probably fitted to the gun
by L.D. Nimschke.

SPECIFICATIONS

Caliber: .45 Colts

Barrel: 4¾, 5½, or 7½ inches

Type: : Single-action, centerfire
revolver

Origin: Colt PFA Mfg Co.,
Hartford, Connecticut

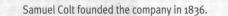

Samuel Colt founded the company in 1836.

Colt is now divided into two parts: Colt
Defense (which serves the military) and the
Colt Manufacturing Company.

The basic Model 1873 was originally produced in three barrel lengths: four and three-quarter, five-and-a-half, and seven-and-a-half inches. This revolver is serial number 181258, a .45 caliber weapon with a seven-and-a-half inch barrel. It has an elegance of line and is especially eye-catching with its re-blued cylinder, barrel, ejector, blackstrap, and trigger guard. This contrasts with the bare metal finish on the frame and the hard rubber grips that show the prancing Colt icon.

Almost since firearms were invented, owners have had a desire for decorated weapons. As in this case, some of these decorations are truly spectacular. This gun began life as a standard Colt single-action army with a five-inch barrel and it is chambered for the 44-40 caliber round. It bears serial number 89332 and records show that it left the Colt factory in 1883. It was then passed to an engraving shop, almost certainly that of L.D. Nimschke. The gun may even be the work of the master himself. Over ninety percent of the available area of the metalwork has been covered with the most intricate patterns, and even the trigger guard is embellished with cross-hatching. The grips are pearl and fit the weapon perfectly.

The Goodnight-Loving Trail

Perhaps the most famous and romanticized cattle trail of them all was the Goodnight-Loving Trail. Charles Goodnight and Oliver Loving formed a partnership when they met in 1866 and started a cattle drive from Young County in Texas to Fort Sumner, New Mexico.

The original purpose of the Goodnight-Loving Trail was to drive cattle to Fort Sumner in Texas. Eight-thousand Navajo Indians were confined there, virtually starving for want of meat. These tribesmen were the responsibility of government agents, who were desperately trying to procure meat for them. Goodnight and Loving knew that this was an exceptional opportunity to make money.

To avoid an Indian attack, the partners decided to drive their herd around the Texas Panhandle, which was teeming with hostile Comanche tribesmen. This involved taking a much longer and completely arid route through what Goodnight called the "most desolate country". Along the route, three-hundred cattle died in the heat and a hundred more thirst-crazed beasts drowned in a stampede at the Pecos River. Goodnight sold half of the surviving herd to the reservation agents. He then continued the drive into Colorado, selling the remaining animals in Denver. The whole escapade netted the partners the huge sum of $24,000, and the reputation for forging the most famous trail route of all time. In the spring of the

Above: Each brand was unique to a particular ranch. Rustlers used ingenious methods to change and disguise them.

following year, Loving and Goodnight returned to Texas to start a new drive. Loving went ahead to scout the trail through Indian country, with just a trusted scout for company. Although he had promised Goodnight to proceed with extreme caution and to move only under cover of darkness, Loving was overcome with impatience and broke cover during the day. Almost inevitably, this led to an attack by the Comanche tribe, in which Loving was seriously wounded. He somehow managed to make his way back to Fort Sumner, only to die there of gangrene. Goodnight sat by the bedside of his close friend for two weeks, until Loving finally expired.

Goodnight kept a promise he had made to Loving and saw to it that his body was buried in Texas. Goodnight described his partner as "one of the coolest and bravest men I have ever known, but devoid of caution."

The Goodnight-Loving Trail originally ran southwest to the Horsehead Crossing on the Pecos River to Fort Sumner. But in 1871, Goodnight extended the route to join up with the Fort Worth and Denver City Railroad at Grenada, Colorado. From here, many cattle were sold to hungry gold diggers. Ultimately, the trail went as far as Cheyenne, Wyoming.

A traditional scene that has hardly changed from the early days of the cattle drives.

Right: An early photograph of a Montana cattle ranch. The cattle have been contained in pens.

Charles Goodnight

Below: Charles Goodnight made his fortune from the Texas Longhorn.

The greatest real-life cowboy of them all, Charles Goodnight was born in Macoupin County, Illinois in 1836, but his family trekked west in 1846, the so-called Year of Decision. He was to become the best-known cattle rancher ever, celebrated as the "father of the Texas Panhandle." Historian J. Frank Dobie wrote that Goodnight "approached greatness more nearly than any cowman of history." In 1856, Goodnight started work as a cowboy, but as war approached, he joined the Texas Rangers in 1857. Later, he fought with the Confederacy during the Civil War. When hostilities ceased, his first great cattle-driving enterprise was the famous "making the gather." During the war, thousands of cattle had roamed loose across the South. The gather was a round-up of the huge Texas Longhorn herd, which was then driven to the railroad heads. This task completed, Goodnight turned his hand to more conventional enterprise.

Charles Goodnight had a huge influence on the culture of the West, and is even credited with having coined the modern use of the term "cowboy." He had a close, almost paternal relationship with his men, and forbade them to drink, swear, or play cards. This inveterate plainsman was a cattle industry pioneer, who made a huge contribution to the hugely lucrative practice of driving cattle to market. He developed an economic and efficient method of droving that is still in use today.

Under his management, the drive usually started after breakfast and continued until a midday lunch. Towards evening, the trail boss would scout ahead for a safe place to bed down for the night. A herd of three-thousand cattle needed between twelve and fifteen drovers, including the trail boss, cook, and wrangler. The status of the cowboys themselves was determined by his place on the drive. The most important men were the lead riders, who guided the herd at the front. The outriders at the flanks were next in rank, followed by the drag riders at the back of the herd, who ate a lot of dust and comprised the bottom of the pecking order. Goodnight also instituted nighthawk watches, where two-man teams took turns guarding the herd, circling round the animals on horseback to keep them together. Although a herd usually moved at around ten to twelve miles a day, speeds of up to twenty-four miles a day could be achieved in good conditions by expert drovers.

Overleaf: A humorous evocation of life on the trail. Cookie runs from a stampeding cow that has overturned the coffee pot onto the camp fire.

Above: The King of the Cowboys, Charles Goodnight, was
born in 1836 and died in 1929. He was one of the first men
to see the financial potential of the cattle industry.

The Goodnight-Adair Partnership

The Goodnight-Adair partnership became one of the most successful associations of capital and ranching know-how in the West, and provided a pattern for many smaller enterprises.

John George Adair was born in Ireland in 1823. He was a Protestant of Scottish-Irish descent. Adair was an intelligent man who attended the prestigious Trinity College University in Dublin and trained to join the British Diplomatic Service, but ended up going into business instead. His family were Irish landowners, and Adair himself built the magnificent Glenveagh Castle in County Donegal, Ireland. Adair had soon realised the huge opportunities offered by western expansion, and he opened offices in both New York City and Denver, Colorado. In 1869, Adair married a well-connected American widow, Cornelia Wadsworth Ritchie.

Adair met his second-most-important partner, Charles Goodnight, in Denver in 1874, when both men were taking part in an organized buffalo hunt. Goodnight opened Adair's eyes to the fortunes that could be made from large-scale ranching, and persuaded Adair to invest in a massive ranch. The two partners were to sign two five-year-long partnership agreements. The J. A. Ranch (named for Adair's initials, at Goodnight's suggestion) was bought with Adair's capital, and Goodnight was to manage the concern at an annual salary of $2,500. The ranch was located in a beautiful area in the Palo Duro Canyon in the Texas Panhandle, and was liberally supplied with plenty of water, timber, game, and fantastic grazing land. At its height in 1883, the ranch covered 1,335,000 acres, and the partners owned over a hundred-thousand grazing cattle. Goodnight became an important Texas cattleman, and became a co-founder of the Panhandle Stockman's Association in 1880. The aim of the association was to improve cattle breeding and repel the threat of rustlers. Goodnight himself preserved a herd of native bison on his ranch, and crossed these with domestic cattle to produce the "cattalo."

Although Goodnight appreciated Adair's financial backing, he thoroughly disliked his hard-drinking, fiery-tempered personality. He was also frustrated by Adair's more conservative approach to land acquisition. Despite these differences, the partnership between the two men was extremely successful. By the end of their first five years together, the partners had made $510,000. In fact, Adair only visited the J. A. Ranch three times before he died in 1885, so Goodnight did not have to suffer too much of his company.

Adair was no more popular in his native Ireland, where he had cleared many families from his property to beautify the setting of Glenveagh Castle. On the night before his burial in Killenard, Ireland, the local people threw a dead dog into his open grave. Two years later, a lightning bolt shattered his memorial stone into a thousand pieces.

After Adair's death, his wife Cornelia took over the partnership with Goodnight, and they worked together until 1888. Things between them were not always smooth, as Cornelia was fairly opinionated about how her money should be spent. At this time, Goodnight decided to leave the partnership to buy his own slightly smaller concern. He bought the 140,000 acre Quitaque Ranch, where he grazed twenty thousand head of cattle. By this time, Goodnight had realised that the days of the lucrative open range were numbered, with the advent of the Fort Worth and Denver City Railroad, arable farming, and barbed wire-fenced enclosures.

Left: Cookie was a highly valued member of the trail team. The chuck wagon was a great help to him in his work.

The Chuck Wagon

Charles Goodnight first introduced the iconic chuck wagon in 1866. Texas rancher, cattle king, and co-founder of the famous Goodnight-Loving trail, Goodnight understood the huge importance that cowhands placed on "larrupin' good" victuals.

Overleaf: An early photograph of trailhands gathering around the chuck wagon for coffee. Note cookie working on the drop-down flap.

Above and opposite page: The chuck wagon was not only a work station, but was also a means of transporting food along the trail. Closed up, it could be drawn along by a horse or an ox.

The first chuck wagon was constructed from wood and drawn by oxen. The chuck box, sited towards the rear of the wagon, had a hinged lid that dropped down to become the food preparation area. The box also contained various drawers and compartments, which held the cooking equipment (Dutch ovens, skillets, and the all-important coffee pot) along with various easily-preserved staples such as cornmeal, flour, dry beans, jerky, dried fruit, molasses, coffee, sourdough starter, and chilli peppers. Often second only in importance to the trail boss, the chuck wagon "cookie" not only used the materials packed in the wagon, but also foraged for locally available game and produce. Chuck wagon cooks make brief appearances in many Westerns, and are often comedic characters. John Wayne's 1972 film The Cowboys, for example, features a chuck wagon chef named Jeb Nightlinger. On the ranch, Cookie usually slept in the cookhouse rather than the cowboy bunkhouse. Wagon cooks often enforced respect for their food stores with the edge of their skillets.

Unsurprisingly, meat was a large component of the grease-hungry cowboy diet. Although they had a ready supply of fresh beef, the trail diet was livened up with venison, wild turkey, squirrel, quail, duck, rabbit, and grouse. Cookie might also collect herbs (especially sage), acorns, buckwheat, nuts, greens, and wild berries along the trail. By the 1880s, some canned goods were available to chuck wagon cooks on the northern range, including tomatoes, peaches, and condensed milk. These luxuries had migrated to the southern range by the 1890s. But although authentic chuck wagon recipes sometimes include fresh dairy products and eggs, these were not in general use before the 1920s.

Cowboys often sought to work for the bosses with the best trail cooks, and even described their trail work as "riding the grub line." Western writers such as Louis L'Amour, were quick to celebrate the mythical powers of chuck wagon cooks to charm the least promising ingredients into appetizing meals. Retired cowboys who settled down to ranching missed not only the freedom of the trail, but chuck wagon coffee and biscuits cooked on an open fire. By the same token, unskilled cooks were reviled and heaped with unfriendly epithets, including belly cheater, grub worm, gut robber, and pot rustler.

While bunkhouse cooks had access to a greater range of equipment and foodstuffs, they could not rival the esteem accorded to a good cook on the open range. Trail bosses rewarded these men with better wages than those of the regular cowboys. While some cowboy dishes — like possum roast and rattlesnake soup — may have lost their appeal over the years, many chuck wagon recipes still sound mighty appetizing. Here are just a few of the most well known: cowboy sausages and sweet taters, Texas camp bread (the recipe dates from the 1850s), spotted pup dessert (mostly rice and raisins), chuck wagon beans, buffalo steaks with chipotle-coffee rub, chuck wagon stew, Missouri-style barbecued ribs, and Indian breakfast.

Opposite page: Chuck wagon coffee and camp bread were an essential part of the trail diet.

Left: Cookie used the chuck wagon to keep his condiments and cooking utensils safe and clean.

Another hugely important part of a cowboy's diet was coffee. Coffee was served from the chuck wagon throughout the day. An apocryphal coffee recipe instructs that two pounds of good strong coffee should be wetted down with a little water and boiled for two hours. A horseshoe should then be thrown into the mixture. If the horseshoe sank, the coffee should be boiled some more.

The most famous brand of cowboy coffee was Arbuckle's. The Arbuckle Brothers of Pittsburgh, Pennsylvania produced pre-roasted coffee beans that became hugely popular in the Old West. Their recipe for good coffee was to throw a handful of their ground beans into a cup of water. Before the Civil War, coffee was sold green, and the beans had to be roasted in a skillet

Below: A Dutch skillet was often stood on the camp fire embers to cook a nourishing stew.

Opposite page: A magnificent Texas Longhorn. This breed of cattle comes in a range of colors, including yellow, black, brown, red, or white.

over the campfire before they could be used. A single burned bean could ruin a whole batch. John and Charles Arbuckle developed a patented method of roasting coffee beans and sealing in their flavor and aroma with an egg and sugar glaze. The coffee was then sold in patented airtight, one-pound packages. These bore their highly distinctive red, yellow, and black labels, which were printed with the Arbuckle name and their flying angel trademark. Many cowboys didn't even know that other types of coffee existed. Arbuckle's packages became synonymous with coffee on the trail, and were a huge and instant hit with chuck wagon cooks. Brilliant marketing men, the Arbuckle brothers also introduced collectible coupons into their packaging that could be redeemed for useful stuff like razors, neckerchiefs, and wedding rings. They also included a peppermint stick in each pack of coffee, which chuck wagon cooks often used as a reward for any cowboy who would agree to take over the coffee grinding duties.

Goodnight's innovative chuck wagon became one of the most iconic and useful pieces of Western equipment. Used on the cattle drives for decades, a modern form of the chuck wagon is still in use.

Cattlemen like Goodnight changed the fortunes of the whole region. Having made several fortunes and gone bust several times, he finally died at his ranch at the age of ninety-three. Rumor has it that he had survived for years on a diet of coffee, beef, and Cuban cigars.

Below: The leader of the herd was often belled so that the other animals would follow it.

The Texas Longhorn

Charles Goodnight and many other cattle barons made their fortune off the Texas Longhorn.

Texan stockmen created the breed by cross-breeding feral Mexican cattle and domesticated animals from the East. This resulted in tough, long-legged animals that required little water and could withstand blizzards, droughts, and dust storms. The toughness of the Longhorns meant that they lost very little weight along the cattle drive. The breed is best known for their towering horns, which can measure seven feet from tip to tip, and are used both for defense and attack. The Longhorn is also famous for its diverse coloring; their hides may be yellow, black, brown, red, or white. Although these beasts are known for their gentle and intelligent dispositions, they also have a highly developed survival instinct. They have an exceptionally strong sense of smell, which makes it easy for a cow to locate her own calf.

Longhorn bulls, on the other hand, are notoriously mean, and it takes very little provocation to turn one into a serious threat, both to other bulls and to humans. Only a very well-armed cowboy stood a chance against an angry Longhorn bull.

The Longhorn breed has retained its popularity over the years. In addition to their lean, low-cholesterol meat, the animals are prized today for their historic ties to the Old West. Longhorns are the official large mammal of Texas. The most expensive Longhorn ever was sold for $170,000.

Colt Lightning

SPECIFICATIONS

Caliber: Various ranging from .22 to .50-95

Barrel: 20, 22, 24, 26, and 28 inches

Type: Tubular magazine, slide-action rifle

Origin: Colt Armaments Manufacturing Co., Hartford, Connecticut

A medium-frame Lightning carbine with a twenty-inch barrel. The gun is in .44 caliber and has a saddle-ring

The Colt Lightning was designed by William Mason in 1877 and produced by the company between 1877 and 1909.

The Colt Lightning Magazine Rifle was first introduced in 1884. It was the first slide-action rifle to be manufactured by Colt. Based on two master patents registered to W. H. Elliott in 1883, the weapon was produced in three frame sizes. The small-frame version was available only in .22 caliber, while the medium- and large-frame versions were produced as both long-barrel rifles and short-barrel carbines. In addition, a special version of the medium-frame version was produced for the San Francisco Police department. The largest round for the large-frame rifle was the .50-95 Express. This gun earned the nickname Express model for all of its caliber versions. The Lightning was marketed by Colt as the rifle companion to the 1873 Colt Single-Action and the 1878 Double-Action revolvers. The operation of the action with the left hand or off hand was considered a positive improvement on the lever-action rifle. The magazine held either twelve or fifteen rounds depending on caliber. The Lightning Magazine Rifle would sell nearly 200,000 pieces before the model was retired in 1904.

Many examples of this handy weapon found their way out West.

A large-frame Lightning, chambered for a .40-60 cartridge. The gun has a twenty-eight-inch barrel.

The End of the Trails

Opposite page: Joseph Farwell Glidden patented barbed wire in 1874. He formed the Barb Fence Company and became a millionaire.

The heyday of the cattle drives and the trails they used was between 1866 and 1890. Originally, the drives were a major stimulant to the burgeoning railroad network, but as the railroad tracks extended into previously uncharted territory, the need for long and dangerous cattle drives was gradually diminished. They were virtually obsolete by the 1890s. The advent of refrigerated railroad cars in the 1880s meant that, by the end of the century, fresh beef could be transported all the way to Europe by train and ship.

A combination of railroad expansion, the introduction of barbed wire-fenced pastures, and irrigation windmills gradually tamed huge stretches of the Western plains. Barbed wire was invented by Illinois farmer Joseph Farwell Glidden, and patented by him in 1874. This was a cheap and portable fencing material made from twisted wire with spaced coiled barbs. It was used to segment the open prairies of the West into enclosed grazing land and made a huge impact on the society and economy of the region. Ranchers could now isolate their cattle and control breeding. Although the material can cause hide injuries to livestock, it is still widely used today. It was barbed wire that finally closed down the Chisholm Trail in 1884, and drastically reduced the open routes available to the Western trails.

The era of the trails had lasted for around twenty-five years and exerted a great influence on the life of the frontier.

Below: Glidden used a coffee mill to form the first barbs, which he attached to a length of wire. His invention changed Western ranching forever.

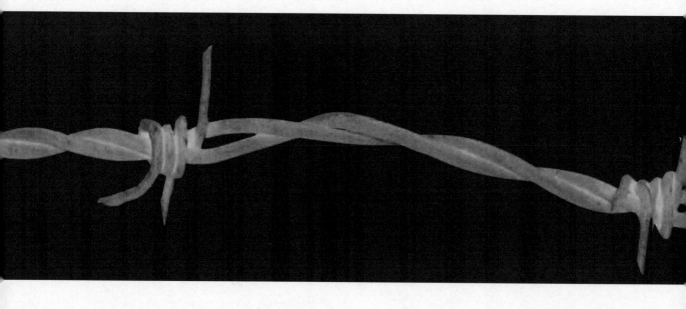

Right: Ranchers used Glidden's "devil's rope" to enclose thousands of acres. This effectively ended the days of the trails and the open range.

Above: William Edenborn refined Glidden's concept and invented a humane fence wire that did not harm cattle.

The End of the Open Range

The changes that Goodnight recognized resulted in a shift away from cattle grazing on the open range towards fenced-in ranching. Before it was enclosed, the open range was a huge area of public-domain land in the central and northern Great Plains. It sprawled across several states including Texas, Kansas, Montana, Nebraska, North Dakota, South Dakota, and Wyoming. The years of open-range cattle grazing were brief, thriving between around 1866 and 1890. This cow country was free from farmers, fencing, and grass-eating sheep, but it was not completely unmanaged. Where water was in short supply, wells were drilled and dams constructed. Windmills were also built to pump up underground water so that ranches did not need to be sited near a river or stream. Individual cattle herds were branded to show who owned them. This meant burning a specific logo onto the cow's hide with a hot iron rod, usually on the left hip. Branded cows could be separated into different herds at round-up time and driven to market.

For a couple of decades, open range grazing was hugely profitable, and attracted many investors from the United States and Europe. The government supported the cattle industry by banning fencing of the range lands, and awarding contracts to feed the reservation-bound Indians to cattle companies.

The end of the open range was hastened by the terrible conditions of 1886 and 1887. A toxic combination of desperate overgrazing of the prairie grasses by non-native species of cattle (by an estimated thirty-five to forty million animals) and atrocious weather conditions led to an ecological disaster. There was an extreme drought in the spring of 1886, followed by a scorching summer when temperatures on the prairie soared to 109 degrees Fahrenheit. The following January (1887), a tremendous winter storm hit the region, and temperatures fell to forty-three degrees below zero. A devastating famine ensued, and it is estimated that over half of the cattle on the prairie succumbed. Many cowboys also perished from cold and hunger. Effectively, the days of the wide-open spaces were numbered. Many cattle operations were bankrupted and investors ruined.

The need for private individuals to manage the land properly, rather than exploiting it, meant that ranching of enclosed acres became much more widespread. Publicly owned grazing land was gradually enclosed. Almost nothing of the open range remained by 1890.

This change in the way the prairie was managed was also helped by the

Left: Even barbed wire did not stop problems erupting between farmers and ranchers.

pacification of the Plains tribes. On the positive side, enclosure went some way to slow down the decimation of the wild buffalo. This more business-like approach to raising cattle also meant that ranches became sound financial investments for savvy entrepreneurs and their financial backers, like Charles Goodnight and his investor, John G. Adair. Huge fortunes were made, and it is estimated that by 1885, just thirty-five cattle barons owned one-and-a-half million cattle between them. About two-thirds of the western lands were now being used for grazing.

Not everyone was happy about the cattle ranchers' domination of this entire region. Writing in 1955, Bernard DeVoto wrote a damning description of this system. "The cattlemen came from Elsewhere into the empty West. They were always arrogant and always deluded... They kept sheepmen out of the West... [and] did their utmost to keep the nester, the farmer, the actual settler, the man who could create local and permanent wealth out of the West... the big cattlemen squeezed out the little ones wherever possible... frequently hiring gunmen to murder them."

The move to ranching also led to a changing focus for cowboys, who became more orientated towards animal husbandry than herding. Their new duties included feeding, branding, ear marking, and basic veterinary care. They were also responsible for maintaining the ranch-land, its water supply, and its boundaries.

The end of the cattle drives brought a gradual end to the male-dominated live of the West. Trail life slowly gave way to the more traditional family life of farmers and settlers. The frontier itself was declared ended in 1890, but thousands of square miles of the West remained unsettled for many years.

Overleaf: The winter storm of January 1887 became known as "the Great Die-Up" because it killed so many grazing animals. Many humans were also lost.

Remington Model 1890

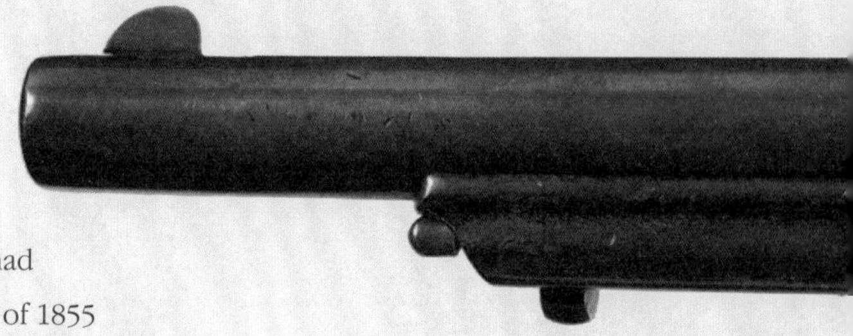

The Remington New Model Army Revolver proved to be serious competition for Colt's output during the Civil War. Over 120,000 guns were delivered. As the Civil War came to an end, it became clear that the metallic cartridge had superseded the percussion system. The Rollin White patent of 1855 prevented other manufacturers from using bored-through cylinders until 1869 when the patent expired. Its expiration led to a rush of new revolver designs at the beginning of the 1870s, and many percussion conversions. First rimfire and then centerfire ammunition was used. The most successful of this generation of guns was the Colt Model 1873.

Remington's answer to the Colt model was its Model 1875 Outlaw, a heavy army-caliber revolver. Originally made for Remington's own .44 caliber centerfire cartridge, Model 1875s were then produced in .44-40 and .45 long Colt calibers. This cartridge revolver retained Remington's signature triangular web under the ejector rod. Whilst this feature was extolled as a

SPECIFICATIONS

Caliber: .44 and .45

Barrel: 7 and 5 inches

Type: Six shot, single-action cartridge revolver

Origin: Remington Armory, Ilion, New York

Remington Model 1875 Outlaw Revolver

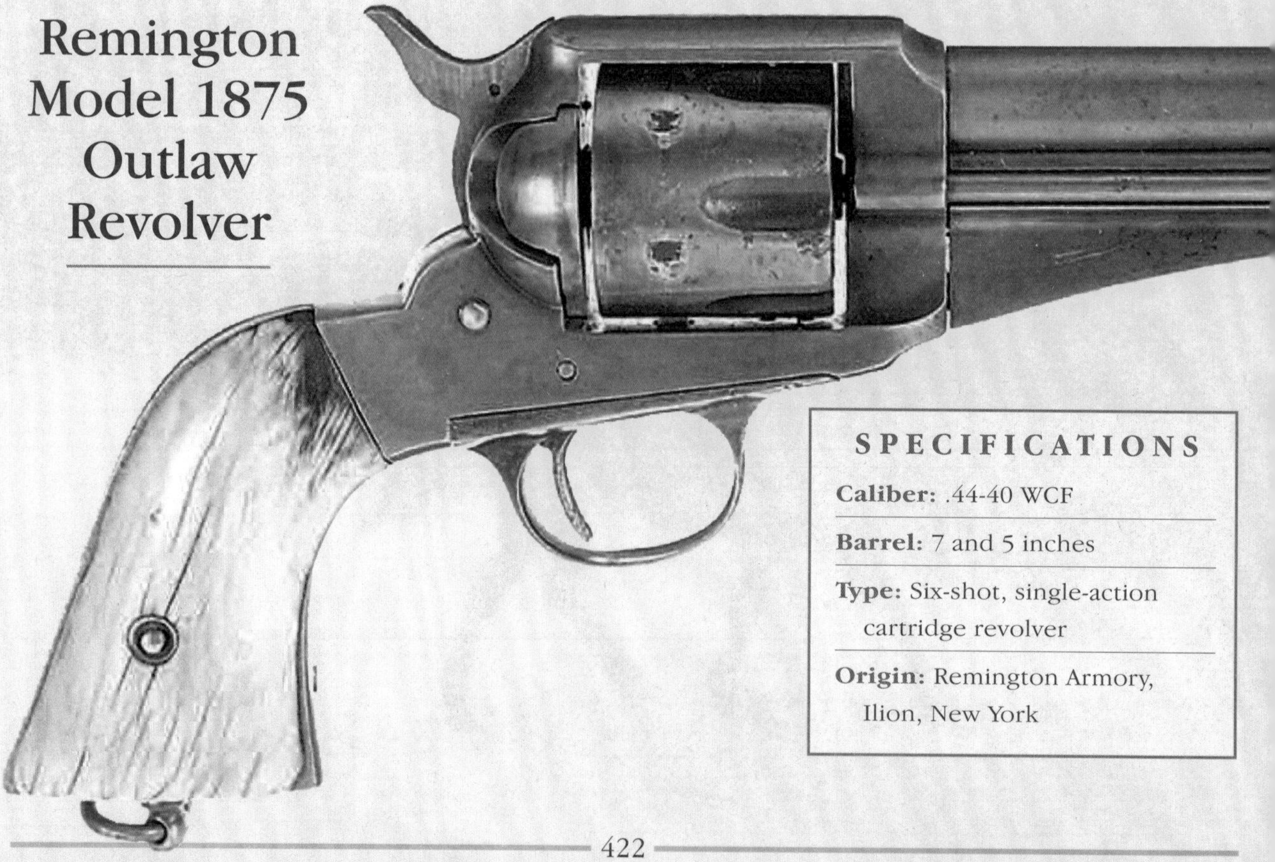

SPECIFICATIONS

Caliber: .44-40 WCF

Barrel: 7 and 5 inches

Type: Six-shot, single-action cartridge revolver

Origin: Remington Armory, Ilion, New York

was just 25,000 units. The gun was used extensively in the West and its owners include outlaws like Frank James, a fact that probably contributed to its name.

positive virtue in barrel location and firing accuracy, it always imparted a clumsier outline to the Remington than that of the more attractive Colt.

The gun was finished in nickel plate or blued. Grips were in oiled walnut, mother of pearl and ivory. Although an effective weapon, the total production of the Model 1875 Outlaw

Remington is the oldest company in America that
is still making its original product.

In 1888, E. Remington & Sons went bankrupt, and the company changed its name to Remington Arms. Before the arrival of the Model 1890, a few Model 1888s were produced, though officially there was no such model. Closely resembling the Colt Model 1873 Single Action Army, this shorter-barreled revolver finally removed the triangular web under the barrel. Available only in .44-40 caliber, the 1890 came with a five-inch barrel. Fewer than five-hundred examples were made between 1888 and 1889.

The official Model 1890 was manufactured between 1891 and 1894. Exactly two-thousand twenty examples were produced, making this a fairly unsuccessful gun. These days it is extremely collectible. Available with either five- or seven-inch round barrels (roll-stamped Remington Arms Co.) the gun came with a choice of hard rubber or ivory grips, and had a blued or nickel-plated finish. A lanyard ring was a popular factory-fitted accessory for this gun as shown on this example.

Cowboy Kit

A cowboy needs wide-open spaces.

A cowboy needs wild, untamed places

A cowboy needs untrammeled trails.

A cowboy needs grassy hills and dales.

Paul Harwitz, A Cowboy Needs

Above: Cowboy equipment is instantly recognizable.

One of the most recognizable aspects of the classic American cowboy was (and is) his classic outfit and equipment. The kit evolved over many years, with practicality as the ultimate goal. Many of its elements were derived from the original outfit of the Mexican vaqueros; aspects of this cowboy kit were adapted for the many different regions of the American West and the challenges posed by their climates and terrains.

Traditionally, the cowboy wore a wide-brimmed hat to protect his face from the sun, wind, rain, and snagging branches. The brim usually measured between four and six inches, and was inspired by the Spanish sombrero (which took its name from sombra, the Spanish word for "shade"). They were high-crowned to keep the head cool in hot weather. A "stampede string" under the chin kept the hat in place in windy weather and during rough riding. The "stampede string" was a long leather lace that ran half way round the crown of the hat then through a hole on each side; the ends were knotted under the chin or at the back of the head. The original cowboy hats were so regionally variable that it was said that you could tell where a cowhand came from just by the crease in his hat. The most famous maker of cowboy headgear was John Batterson Stetson, a professional hatter who popularized a felted version used by generations of cowboys, the iconic "Boss of the Plains." The hat was so successful that Stetson built a large national

Above: The classic wide-brimmed cowboy hat was derived from the Mexican sombrero.

corporation on its popularity. "The Boss of the Plains" was adopted by many famous westerners, including Buffalo Bill, Annie Oakley, Calamity Jane, and Will Rogers. The infamous ten gallon hat was created for Buffalo Bill Coady as an exaggerated stage prop for his Wild West Show. Stetson continued to make the model for particularly flamboyant cowboys. Contrary to the name, the hat was never able to hold ten gallons of anything.

The properly-attired cowboy wore a bandana around his neck, which was also known as a wild rag, a mascada, or kerchief. An authentic wild rag was usually made from silk and was between thirty-six and forty-four inches square. The usually red fabric was folded into a triangle and tied at the back of the neck. Although it was often elaborately knotted, these ties had to release quickly

Above: An early cowboy hat.

Above: The Boss of the Plains became the iconic headgear for cowboys.

Left: A low-crowned cowboy hat.

Right: The classic bandana was also known as a wild rag, mascada, or kerchief.

Right: The cowboy boots on the left have the traditional square toe. Those on the right are round-toed.

in dangerous situations to prevent the rider from being dragged by his scarf. The natural silk fabric of the bandana was chosen for practicality: it was warm in winter and could be used to mop the face or cover the mouth on the dusty summer trails. It could also be used as earmuffs in cold weather and to protect the eyes from snow blindness. In the summer, the cloth protected cowboys from deadly sunburn. The bandana might also be used to hold a hot pot or branding iron, or employed as a makeshift tourniquet or sling in case of injury.

Horsemen have always needed protective footwear, and have often preferred boots with a higher heel. Some early riding boots were based on the English Wellington, a plain leather boot with one-inch heels and straight tops. Cowboys wore high-topped boots to protect his lower leg from chafing during long hours in the saddle. Originally, cowboy boots had square or rounded toes (cowboy boots with pointed toes did not become the standard until the 1950s). These narrower toes helped the cowboy to get his feet in the stirrups, and their high heels kept them from slipping through them. The heels also provided a brace when the cowhands were roping. The boot soles were usually made from slick, smooth leather to stop them catching when dismounting, but they also wore hessian boots. The famous Coffeyville-style cowboy boot was first made in Coffeyville, Kansas around 1870. These boots were usually made from smooth black leather and equipped with a low Cuban heel. The front of the boot (the "graft") was made higher than the back of the boot, and was often in a contrasting color. Texan cowboys often had a Lone Star motif inlaid in the boot. With the prevalence of cowboy radio shows in the 1920s and '30s, cowboy boots became fashion items, with their design becoming more colorful and intricate in the 1940s and '50s. When line-dancing became popular in the 1990s, rhinestone and precious stone inlays became popular. Cowboy boots continue to be highly popular.

Many working cowboys fitted their boots with spurs (la espuela). Spurs are u-shaped devices attached to the heel of the boot by the spur strap; a small metal neck or "shank" sticking out of the spurs is used to poke the horse's sides as a means of steering. Spurs were used to give tired legs a stronger action. Western spurs were often made from metal, and often had a small, serrated wheel attached

Left: Cowboys used spurs to give their tired legs stronger action.

at the end of the spur's shaft. Known as the rowel (or la rodaja or la estrella in Spanish), the wheel or star turned as the rider's heel touched the horse's side. Jingle bobs were also attached to the rowel. These were partly decorative and made a bell-like ringing sound when the spurs moved. They supposedly kept the cowboy's horse alert. Cowboy boots were adapted for each different region, and special boots were made for certain jobs. Roper boots with flat heels were used for working in arenas and for walking, while laced packer boots were made from heavy leather for cold weather hiking and really hard riding.

Above: Many cowboy spurs were equipped with a rowel, or star, that turned as the heel touched the horse.

Right: Levi Strauss was born in Bavaria, Germany, in 1829. He sailed to New York at age eighteen. In January 1853, Strauss became an American citizen, sailing to the West that March.

LEVI STRAUSS & CO.
QUALITY CLOTHING XX
501   W 33 L 30

Left and below: Winters on the trail could be just as cold as the summers were hot, so a cowboy needed a selection of weather gear.

Most cowboys wore sturdy denim jeans to prevent tangling with brush or equipment, and were among the first groups of Americans to popularize this practical garment. Levi Strauss opened his eponymous company in San Francisco in 1853, and gained the patent for his famous reinforcing rivet in 1873. The inside leg seams of cowboy jeans were rolled so that they wouldn't rub his legs when he was on horseback. Cowboys often rolled their Levis up at the bottom in the traditional "four-horse roll" cuff. It was said that polite cowboys used the four-inch turn-ups for their cigarette ash when ashtrays were hard to find.

Further protection for the legs against weather and brush was offered by chaps (correctly pronounced as "shaps"). These were a highly important part of the cowboy rig that were worn over jeans. The terms were derived from the Spanish las

Right: Cowboys wearing various styles of chaps.

Below: A pair of angora chaps, or "woolies." The leather batwing chaps have been embellished with decorative leather patches.

chaparreras, or chaparejos. They were based on the armas of early Spanish and Mexican riders who wore them when they were herding cattle. Essentially, these were two large pieces of cowhide attached to the horn of the rider's saddle stock. These apron-style chaps gradually evolved into the more elaborate versions worn by the American cowboy, which were closer to the leather leggings worn by the Indians. Chaps came in many different styles and varieties, each tailored for the local conditions. Shotgun chaps, for example were tight fitting garments that could be worn as trousers. They had no snaps or rings but often had full length zippers. By contrast, batwings were long chaps with big leather flaps, fastened with rings and snaps. These were often worn by rodeo cowboys. Angora chaps or "woolies" were covered with long Angora goat hair and were usually lined with canvas. They were used as protection against the cold in Wyoming and Montana and the open prairie country. They appeared on the Great Plains in the late 1880s. Chinks were short chaps, or leather riding aprons, and were often fringed. They were favored by cowboys in Texas and the southwest. They sometimes wore chinks with their pants tucked into high boots. Texan cowboys also wore shotgun chaps or stovepipes. These were straight, narrow leggings, popular in the 1870s. Better at trapping body heat, they were especially useful in cold and windy weather. In the summer, Texan cowboys often preferred batwing chaps. These were cut wide, with a flare at the bottom. Usually made from smooth leather, they allowed for greater air circulation than stovepipes, making them much cooler. Armitas were a Californian version of chinks made by hand. When wearing chaps, cowboys often wore chap guards on their spurs to prevent them from fouling the rowel.

On their hands cowboys wore thick hide gloves, sometimes decorated with long leather fringes. They might also use leather wrist cuffs for protection against brush and branches, to prevent wear to their shirtsleeves, or to stop a rope from fouling. Leather jackets were also popular with men riding the trail and might also be decorated with long fringes. For bad weather, there was the pommel slicker, a long

Above: These leather gloves have the classic leather cuffs and fringing favored by cowboys.

Left: A diverse mix of cowboys wearing a wide selection of gear. Almost all wear a hat and kerchief.

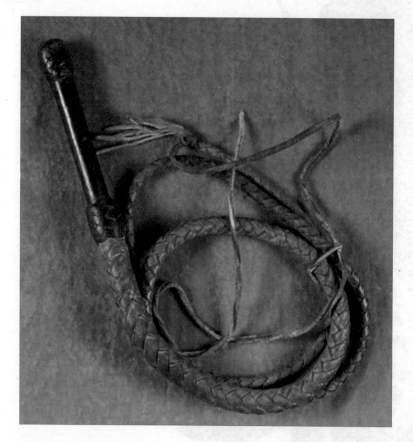

Above: A braided leather cowboy whip, mostly used for its cracking sound, which could drive or direct herds as needed.

Below: Various lasso nooses used for catching cattle.

waterproof coat designed to protect the rider and his saddle from rain and snow.

Every working cowboy also carried a modest selection of equipment. These were often packed into his so-called "war bag" (or "possibles bag"). These typically contained a spare set of clothes, ammunition, playing cards, the bill of sale for the cowby's horse, his makins (see section Cowboy Lingo), and personal effects like a harmonica some precious letters from home. On the trail, a cowboy would also carry a bedroll. This was a roll of blankets or comforters for sleeping in, and was also called a "dreaming sack", "sugan", "soogan", or "hot roll." In bad weather, a cowboy might also pack a teepee or small canvas tent to take shelter in. These became popular from the 1880s onwards and are still in use today. They are sometimes called range teepees or teepee tents. A cowboy was also likely to carry a quart (from the Spanish word la cuarta). This was a short leather strap or braided whip, which often had a handle attached to it, used to increase a horse's speed. A loop was usually attached to the handle so that a rider could wear it around his wrist, or hang it over the saddle horn.

Because of the nature of a cowboy's work, ropes of various lengths and materials were a very important aspect of his kit. A lariat or lasso (Spanish el lazo) was made from braided rawhide or hemp. A hondo, or loop, was attached to one end, and the other end was passed through this. This kind of rope was also known as a "lash rope", "string", or "catch rope". When made from braided hide, the lasso was known as a reata, "riata", or "skin-string". Different hides made ropes of a different texture and stiffness. Bull hide, for example, made a very stiff rope, used for heel roping. Mexican cowboys kept their reatas supple by tying them between two trees and rubbing them first with lemon juice and then with beef fat (suet). Reatas could be very long indeed, up to eighty feet or more. A rope made from plant fiber (such as Manila hemp, sisal, or cotton) is called a sogo. The term in taken from the

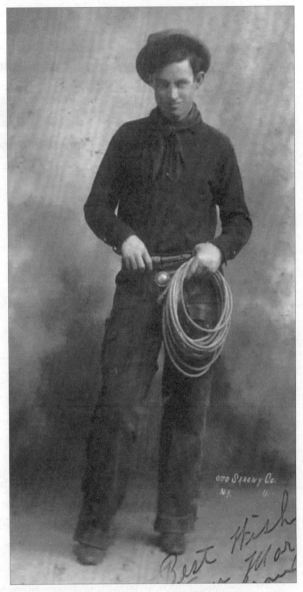

Above: A cowboy poses with his carefully coiled rope. He probably sent copies of this studio photograph to friends and family back home.

Spanish la soga, from which our word, "lasso," is also derived. Other ropes were also popular in cowboy country. Maguey is a Mexican style rope made from agave fiber. "Pigging strings," as they were known in the Great Basin, were short lengths of rope that cowboys carried in their chaps or on their saddles. This kind of rope was pretty much universal, though known by many different terms, including "hoggin' string" in Texas, a "tie-down rope" in the Southwest, and a "short line" in British Columbia, Canada. A cowboy often mounted a useful catch rope on his saddle, attached by a leather rope strap. Standard cowboy roping maneuvers included the backhand flip, forefooting, heeling, the pitch, and the hoolihan. Many cowboys also carried a metal marlin spike for punching holes and unlacing leather, among many other uses.

Although every cowboy aspired to own an expensive pistol, they were more likely to carry old Civil War guns, like the Spencer Repeating Rifle. The ultimate cowboy weapon was Winchester's 1866 Carbine. This more sophisticated weapon used rimfire cartridges, and its relatively compact barrel (twenty inches) made it

Colt Model 1877 Thunderer

Western outlaw John Wesley Hardin used both the "Lightning" and "Thunderer" versions of the Model 1877.

The Model 1877 D.A. was Colt's first foray into the field of double-action pistols. It appeared three years before Smith & Wesson produced their first double-action gun. Originally called the New Double-Action Self-Cocking Central Fire Six-Shot Revolver, the Model 1877 was designed by Colt's well-known employee, William Mason. Mason also designed the famed Single-Action Army Model of 1873. The double action gave the Thunderer a much faster rate of fire. Gunfighters and cowboys alike loved the gun for this reason.

At first sight the gun looks a lot like the famous Peacemaker, except for its signal rear-offset "birds head" grip. The grip was made from either hard rubber or walnut and gave the gun its very distinctive look. The frame is somewhat smaller than that of the Single-Action, and the section of frame in front of the trigger is cut away slightly. Many cowboy cap pistols from the 1930s were modeled on this gun. In use, the Model 1877's action proved over-complicated and hard to repair. Despite this, some 166,000 examples were made between 1877 and 1909. It is not recommended to fire original examples today.

This version of the Thunderer was chambered for .41 Colt ammunition. It came in two barrel lengths, three-and-a-half and four-and-a-half-inches. The nickel finish is in beautiful condition; the gun is unlikely to have been used on the trail for too long.

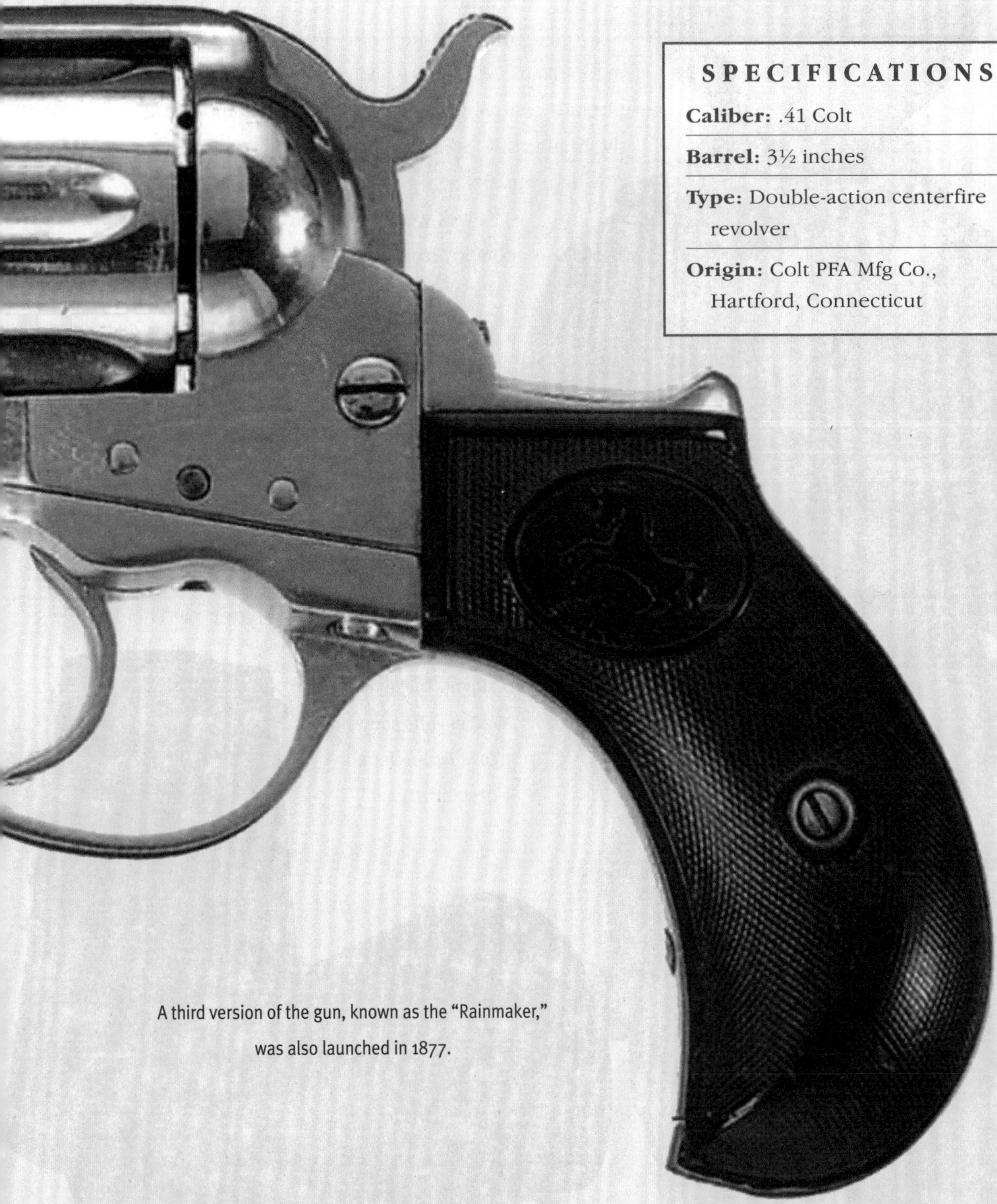

SPECIFICATIONS

Caliber: .41 Colt

Barrel: 3½ inches

Type: Double-action centerfire revolver

Origin: Colt PFA Mfg Co., Hartford, Connecticut

A third version of the gun, known as the "Rainmaker," was also launched in 1877.

easy to stow in a saddle scabbard. With no bolt action, it was quick to draw and fire straight from the saddle. Larger-barreled guns, like the Henry Rifle, were also highly regarded on the plains. As well as warding off trouble, cowboys used their weapons to control varmints and shoot game. Heavier rifles, like the Sharps and Spencers, were usually used for larger targets like buffalo.

Knives were also an intrinsic part of every part of cowboy's equipment, and many carried the famous Bowie knife. Jim Bowie originated his unique curved steel blade in the very earliest years of the nineteenth century. Born in Kentucky in 1796, James Bowie was a prominent frontiersman who fought in the Texas Revolution, dying at the Battle of the Alamo in 1836. During his short but active life, Bowie became notorious for his ability as a knife fighter and was credited with designing the knife that bears his name. But in a letter to The Planter's

Right: These riveted leather cuffs show how cowboys preferred decorative gear.

Opposite page: This casual cowboy wears his holster in the cross-body draw position.

Left, above, and below: There is now a thriving market for Western cowboy memorabilia.

Above: The Hermann H. Heiser Saddlery Company of Denver, Colorado, was renowned for its leather gun belts, holsters, saddles, and tack.

Above: The heavily tooled leather of this gun belt and matching holsters demonstrates how cowboys spent their pay.

Right: A Buscadero fancy holster rig designed for a pair of Colt Peacemakers. Despite its deep decorative tooling, the main purpose of this holster is a speedy draw. There is nothing to impede the rapid removal of the gun it holds.

Fancy holsters were made all over the West, including Texas and Colorado.

Colt Model 1872

Colt patented their centerfire revolver
cartridge in 1871. They developed it for use
by the United States Army.

This weapon is a prime example of how even a major manufacturer renowned for its innovation can get things horribly wrong. The U.S. Army had already decided that its future handguns would have a solid frame (i.e. they would have a top strap). It was clear that for both the military and civilian markets the future lay with the centerfire cartridge. Despite this, Colt produced a weapon without a top strap that was chambered for the .44 rimfire round. It was produced with five, seven, and eight-inch barrels, and had a smooth-sided cylinder chambered for six rounds. The gun was engraved with a naval scene. The overall design is reminiscent of the earlier generation of Colt weapons that were widely used during the Civil War, such as the 1860 army model. Seven-thousand examples of the Model 1872 were manufactured between 1871 and 1872. By Colt standards, the gun was a failure. The Model 1872's main significance is that it was Colt's first original design for a metallic round, as opposed to a conversion. The gun paved the way for the Single-Action Colt Army of 1873. Due to the low production figure, well-preserved examples of the Model 1872 are hard to find. Many of the original guns went to the American frontier where they were hard-used.

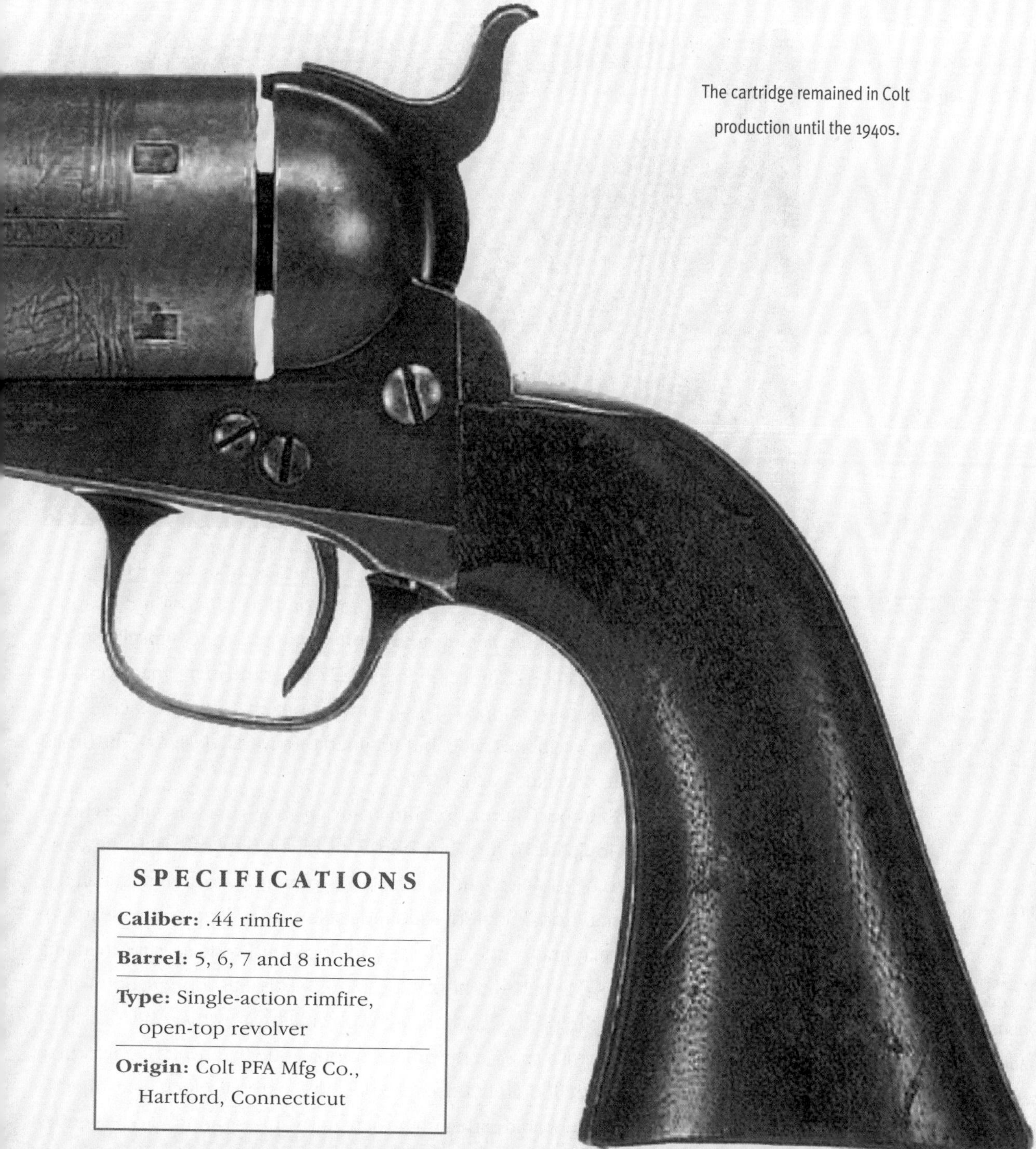

The cartridge remained in Colt
production until the 1940s.

SPECIFICATIONS

Caliber: .44 rimfire

Barrel: 5, 6, 7 and 8 inches

Type: Single-action rimfire,
   open-top revolver

Origin: Colt PFA Mfg Co.,
   Hartford, Connecticut

Right: Cowboy horses were bred to be small and light and to have good "cow sense."

Advocate, James's brother Rezin Bowie maintained that he had designed the blade. In either case, the Bowie knife was designed to be a combination tool and weapon, for use when camping, hunting, fishing, and fighting. James Bowie himself used an early version to win his famous Sandbar Fight of 1827. Over the years, many versions of the unique blade were developed. These varied from six to twelve inches long and one-and-a-half to two inches wide, but retained the overall design of the broad blade that tapered to a wicked curved point.

Perhaps the most important relationship in any cowboy's life was with his horse (caviada or caballa in Spanish). Cowboy horses used a variety of special tack and saddles, designed to be practical and comfortable to men who often spent all day in the saddle. The traditional Western saddle (la silla) had a deep secure seat with a high pommel (la teja) and cantle, and was equipped with wide stirrups, hanging from stirrup leathers. Many had a horn (la cabezal). This was a projection (often bent forward) above the pommel, where a cowboy might stow his rope, or dally it (wrap it counter-clockwise to hold the animal or object he had roped). Californian slick horns were left deliberately uncovered by any material (such as rubber or leather) so that the rope would slide rather than grab. This is thought to be gentler for both horse and cattle. Some Western saddles also had more than one cinch (or girth) to keep them stable, and might have a night latch, or safety strap, for the

Opposite page: The traditional Western saddle has a deep seat and high pommel to keep sleepy cowboys from falling out of it.

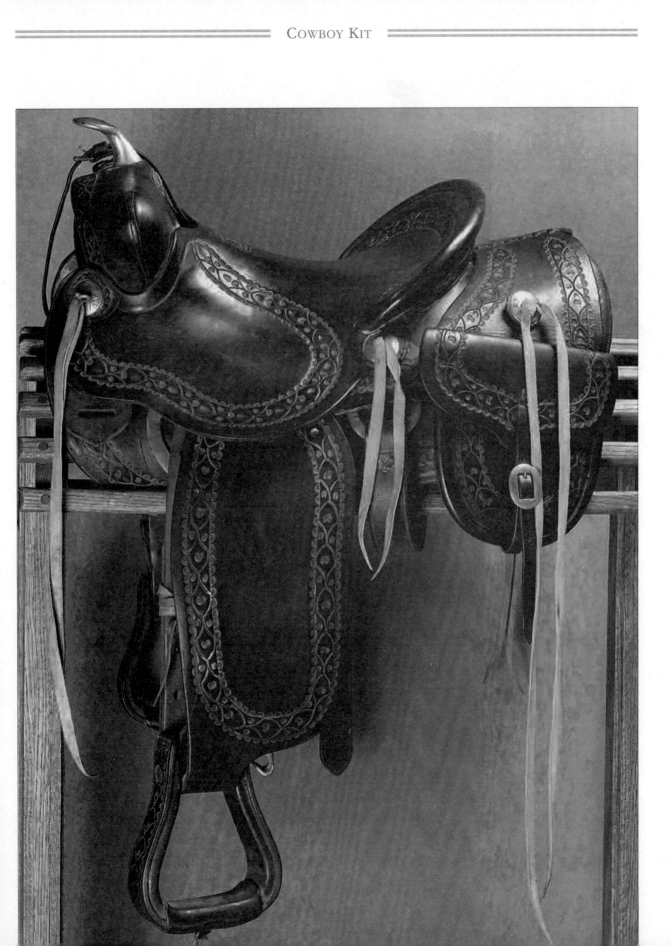

Above: The metal rings on this saddle were used to secure a cowboy's equipment.

rider to hang onto. Padded bucking rolls were also sometimes attached to the front of the saddle to help the rider stay put if he became tired or distracted. Keepers or leather ties were also attached to many saddles to secure loose equipment. The comfort of the horse was also considered. The saddle was made with a wide saddletree that distributed the rider's weight over a greater area of the horse's back, and a woolen horse blanket or pad would be placed under the saddle to prevent it chafing and rubbing. It also kept the saddle clean. These horse blankets were often woven by Native Americans or imported from Mexico. They were known as el cojin or el bastes in Spanish. Saddle bags, or las cantinas, were made from canvas or leather and placed over the rear extensions of the saddle to carry extra gear. At first Western women rode side-saddle, but when they needed to do real ranch work they began to ride astride.

Stirrups varied widely from area to area and from job to job. Oxbow stirrups were particularly thin straps of metal or leather, and preferred by bronco riders. Bell stirrups were much wider and comfortable for longer rides across the big country. Cowboy stirrups were often fitted with tapaderos, or taps. These were stirrup covers designed to protect the rider's feet from brush and the weather. They were available in different styles to accommodate local conditions, including eagle bill, bulldog, and monkey nose.

At the business end of the horse, the Western bridle is usually equipped with a curb bit and has long split reins to give the rider as much control as possible. Bits are metal mouthpieces used to steer the horse. A great many variations were available, with different shapes and degrees of severity. These include half-breed, spade, snaffle, curb, and ring bits.

Western horse tack seems infinitely variable, with many different adaptations for regional conditions, but perhaps the most bizarre example are the snowshoes that Sierra horses used to wear in winter. These prevented horses from "post holing" in the snow. Young horses quickly learned the strange gait needed to

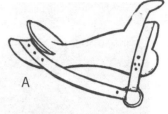

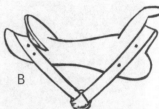

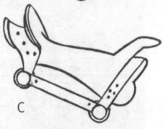

Right: Saddle styles varied from region to region.

Above: Comfortable soft leather stirrups.

Right: This saddle used long leather ties to secure the cowboy's kit.

accommodate the shoes, but even older animals could be trained to use them safely. Invented in Plumas County, California, around 1866, horse snowshoes were sometimes worn by horses pulling sleighs.

The horses themselves were specialized, too. Cowboy horses were bred to be small and light, and to have good "cow sense." Essentially, this meant knowing how to control moving cattle. Many cowboy mounts were wild mustangs

Above: Saddle bags or *cantinas* were made from either leather or canvas. A cowboy used them to carry his personal gear.

and broncos descended from Arabian horses left behind by the Spanish explorers in the sixteenth century. They had completely adapted themselves to the Western habitat, and when they were captured and tamed they were highly valued for their endurance and intelligence. Quarter horses were also popular with trail-riding cowboys. They were the first all-American horse breed, and became the iconic mount of the West. In the nineteenth century, other famous breeds — like the Tennessee Walker, the Morgan, the Chickasaw, the Virginia Quarter-Miler, and the Paint —were selectively bred to ensure their suitability for the cattle drives.

Left: A Mexican saddle blanket. These were used to stop the saddle from chafing the horse and to keep the saddle itself clean.

Cowboy Working Conditions

Right and below: Branding was used from the early days of ranching. The iron brands were heated in a fire.

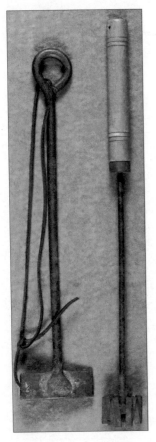

On the trail, a boss could earn around $125 a month, but an ordinary cowboy would be lucky to clear $40. $25 was more usual. Although food and coffee would be provided, the working hand had to supply his own clothes and equipment. This almost always meant that he also had to provide his own mount. Cowboys on the trail worked extremely long days of up to fourteen hours, and were used to sleeping for just six hours a night.

Ranch-based cowboys and cowboys in between trails usually lived together in communal bunkhouses. Also known as the "doghouse", "dive", "shack", "dump", "dicehouse", or "ram pasture", this was usually a barrack-like building with a single large, open room that was used for eating, sleeping, relaxing, and entertainment. When nature called, the cowboys used an outhouse. Indoors, each man had a narrow bed or cot and very little privacy. The bunkhouse was usually heated with a single wood stove.

Even today, ranches beyond the reach of a daily commute often provide bunkhouses for their staff. But these are comparatively luxurious, with electricity, heating, and indoor plumbing.

Right: Prairie weather conditions could be very challenging, even for Longhorns.

Right: This simple cowboy
bunkhouse would be a
very welcome sight on
the prairie in mid-winter.
A wood-burning stove
was used to heat the
room and to cook.

Cowboy Lingo

Opposite page: A cowboy tries to deflect stampeding cattle by waving his saddle blanket. His horse looks alarmed.

Acorn calf: an under-sized, sickly calf

Air the paunch: to vomit

Airing the lungs: cursing

Canned cow: canned milk

Cowpuncher: a long pole used to push the cattle into rail cars, also applied as another name for cowboys

Die-up: widespread destruction of cattle, usually the result of a natural disaster like a blizzard or drought

Greenhorn: a derogatory term for an Easterner unschooled in the ways of the West

Horse wrangler: an inexperienced cowboy who took care of the horses

Judas steer: an obedient steer used to quietly lead the other cattle to slaughter

Little Mary cowboy: the driver of the calf wagon, which was used to transport newborn calves

Mail order cowboy: a derogatory term meaning an immaculate, urban cowboy

Makins: the cigarette papers and tobacco used to roll cowboy cigarettes

Night Hawk: the unlucky cowboy chosen to stay awake at night to guard the saddles

Tenderfoot: an inexperienced cowhand

Ethnicity of the Cowboys

Opposite page: Western cowboys came from a range of ethnic backgrounds. Liberated slaves were attracted to the freedom of the open range.

Below: Around a third of cowboys were from Mexico.

Although the most popular image of the western cowboy is of a young white man from Texas or the Southeast, this does not reflect the varied backgrounds of the men who rode the trail. After the Civil War, many soldiers from both sides of the conflict rode west to start new lives or returned to their former lives on the range. The war also had an impact on the ethnic composition of the profession.

Some newly-freed black Americans were attracted to the freedom of riding the range and the relative lack of racial discrimination in the West. Many former Buffalo Soldiers also became cowboys, putting their riding skills to good use. As many as five-thousand men (or one-quarter of the men riding the line in Texas) were African-Americans. In fact, many of the most famous cowboys were black. These men included George Glenn (who rode the Chisholm Trail in 1870), Charlie Willis (the "Singing Cowboy"), and John Ware (the highly respected rancher).

It was a black cowboy, Texas Bill Pickett, who introduced steer wrestling to the sport of rodeo. Pickett was born on December 5, 1870 in Taylor, Texas, the thirteenth child of a former slave. He was to become known as the greatest cowboys of his day. Not lacking in courage, Pickett developed a technique of wrestling steers to the ground. His technique involved biting the sensitive lip of the animal. He subsequently adopted the stunt name of the "Bulldogger." In 1921, Pickett went on to star in two western movies, The Bull Dogger and The Crimson Skull. He died in 1932 after being kicked in the head by a wild bronco.

Nat Love was another famous African-American cowboy. Love was born in 1854, in Davidson County, Tennessee. His father was a slave foreman, and Nat himself was born a slave. Sadly, his father survived for only two years following his emancipation. Soon after his father's death, Love won a horse in a raffle, which he promptly sold. Sharing the money with his widowed mother, Love used his share to make his way to Dodge City, Kansas, to find work as a cowboy. He was hired as a hand on the Duval Ranch in Texas, and became one of the most admired cowboys in the West. Known as an expert horseman, roper, Indian fighter, marksman, and bronco rider, Love became known by the soubriquet of "Deadwood Dick". Love's

Above: Fifteen percent of Western cowboys were African-Americans.

personal motto reflected his considered outlook on life: "Every time you shoot at someone, plan on dying."

In the years after the Civil War, many Native Americans also became cowboys. Good men were in short supply at this time, and many hands were required to manage the massive cattle drives from Texas to the West. Native Americans were ideally equipped for this work, being experienced horsemen and accustomed to driving herds of buffalo and deer. Faced with depleted buffalo herds, many Indians had been forced to find an alternative way of life, with some becoming cowboys and ranchers. Men from several Indian tribes took up this line of work, including the Creeks, Seminoles, and Timucuas.

The Mexican cowboy tradition stretches right back to the Spanish conquistadors, who introduced horses and cattle to America. The men who herded these animals were the first vaqueros, or Mexican cowboys. They developed their skills of roping, branding, bronco riding, and rounding up cattle. Today, these skills are showcased in charreadas, a special kind of Mexican rodeo where the charros (Mexican cowboys) entertain the public. The original charreadas were held in the Mexican state of Jalisco, and were highly influential on the early rodeo competitions.

By the 1890s, it is estimated that an average of fifteen percent of cowboys were of African-American origin, around a third were from Mexico, and a fifth were Native Americans. If these figures are accurate, then as few as three in ten cowboys would have been white.

Regardless of their racial backgrounds, most cow- hands came from the poorer social classes. Cowboy life was always hard, often dangerous, and the pay was meager. On top of this, the profession carried a lowly social status. Their melancholy permeated the rich cowhand culture, whose songs and poems have been passed down to us.

Opposite page: The tradition of Mexican cowboying goes all the way back to the conquistadors.

Winchester Model 1885

This is a standard Winchester High Wall Model 1885 sporting rifle. It has a thirty-inch .38-55 caliber barrel. Notice how the frame angles sharply upward, leaving the tip of the hammer spur visible.

SPECIFICATIONS

Caliber: .45 centerfire, .14 rimfire

Type: Single–shot rifle

Origin: Winchester Repeating Arms Co., New Haven, Connecticut

Oliver Winchester and several other shareholders created the Volcanic Repeating Arms Company in 1855. After the Civil War, he re-named it the Winchester Repeating Arms Company.

Life on the trail was dangerous, and a cowboy needed a rifle both for self-defense and for hunting. Winchester weapons were a popular choice in the West; their guns had a great reputation for being rugged and hardworking. Being mass-produced also meant that they offered good value for their cost. During the 1880s, single-shot rifles became more popular. Compared to repeating rifles, they are less wasteful of ammunition, easier to maintain, and more accurate.

The Winchester Model 1885 is a single-shot rifle with a falling block action designed by John M. Browning. Two popular models of the gun were produced. The Low Wall version showed an exposed hammer and fired less powerful cartridges. The High Wall used stronger cartridges. Its steel frame covered most of the firing hammer when viewed from the side. Officially, both guns were marketed by Winchester as the Single-Shot Rifle. The Model 1885 was offered with an extensive choice of calibers (including .45 centerfire and .14 rimfire types) as well as a wide variety of barrel lengths. These were either round or octagonal to match the caliber. Finishes and extras were available at additional cost.

The frame of this gun slants more gently forward and upward, at the same angle as the top of the wrist. As the hammer and breech are visible, we know that this is the Low Wall version of the Model 1885.

The Cowboy Code and Culture

Below: This cheerful band of cowboys appears to be hurrahing the town.

The most crucial "equipment" that every cowboy needed was strength of mind and body. The unspoken cowboy code of loyalty, honesty, common sense, and toughness came to be highly regarded. A true cowboy spoke little, but meant what he said; he was a strong man who chose to be gentle. These cowboy virtues have been embodied in many fictional characters, on the page and on screen, and remain powerful today. The cowboy code was a blend of Victorian and frontier values, and even retained a nod to the chivalric code of the Middle Ages. Their hazardous work and tough living conditions in isolated areas bred a tradition of self-dependence and individualism. A high value was placed on personal honesty.

1. Never pass anyone on the trail without saying, "Howdy."

2. When you leave town after a weekend of celebration, it is perfectly acceptable to shoot your pistols in the air and whoop like crazy. This is known as hurrahing a town.

3. When approaching a cowboy from behind, give a loud greeting before getting within pistol shot range.

4. Don't wave at a man on a horse. It may spook the animal. A nod of the head is the proper greeting.

5. After you pass someone on the trail, don't look back at him. This implies mistrust.

6. Riding another man's horse without his permission is completely unacceptable.

7. Never shoot an unarmed man. Don't shoot women at all.

8. A cowboy is pleasant even when out of sorts. Complaining is for quitters, and cowboys hate quitters.

9. Always be courageous. Cowboys hate cowards.

10. A cowboy always helps those in need, even strangers and enemies.

11. A horse thief may be hung without trial.

12. Never try on another man's hat.

13. Never shake a man awake. He may shoot you.

Above: This wide-eyed cowboy is saving his breath for breathing.

14. Real cowboys are modest. Braggarts are not tolerated.

15. A cowboy doesn't talk much. He saves his breath for breathing.

16. No matter how hungry and weary he is after a day in the saddle, a cowboy tends to his horse's needs first.

17. Curse all you want, but only around men, horses, and cows.

Although cowboy wages were low (an average of a dollar a day, plus food) the lifestyle attracted men from many different backgrounds and ethnicities as the cattle industry expanded.

Cowboy music dates from the heyday of the trail drives and cow camps, and are full of nostalgia, raw sentiment, death, fighting, and humor. The song titles are deeply evocative, and many form a part of country music culture to this day These songs include "The Texas Cowboy," "Blood on the Saddle," "The Old Cow Man,"

Above: These cowboys have removed their spurs and made themselves comfortable.

Opposite page: Cowboys taking a well-earned break by the river.

"The Streets of Laredo," "The Call of the Plains," and "The Drunken Desperado." These assorted cowboy verses carry some hint at the different emotions carried by the songs: wistful, tragic, and funny in turns.

It is also true that trail cowboys sang to the cattle at night. Songs like "Old Dan Tucker," "In the Sweet By and By," and "The Texas Lullaby" soothed jittery cows and reduced the likelihood of dangerous stampedes. Stampedes (the word comes from the Spanish estampida) were one of the most serious problems to beset cattle trails. Longhorn cattle were well-known to be more nervous than domesticated cattle, especially when being driven across unknown territory. Thunder and lightning were one of the most common causes of stampedes. If the cattle started running, cowboys were expected to jump into the saddle and try to head them off. This was an extremely dangerous job in the dark, so a full night of singing and patrolling the herd was worth the effort, if it meant avoiding a stampede. The job was usually

Opposite page: Cowboys bedded down near the smoldering embers of cookie's fire, next to the chuck wagon.

undertaken by two men, who circled around the herd on horseback at a walking pace, taking it in turns to sing verses of their cowboy melodies.

I'm wild and woolly and full of fleas,
I'm hard to curry below the knees,
I'm a she-wolf from Shannon Creek,
For I was dropped from a lightening streak
And it's my night to holler — Whoo-pee!
– from "The Drunken Desperado"

There was blood on the Saddle, blood all around
And a great big puddle of blood on the ground
The cowboy lay in it, all covered with gore
Oh pity the cowboy, all bloody and dead
A bronco fell on him and mashed his head.
– from "Blood on the Saddle"

Ho! Wind on the far, far prairies!
Free as the waves of the sea! Your voice is sweet as in alien street
The cry of a friend to me!
You bring me the breath of the prairies
Known in the days that are sped,
The wild geese's cry and the blue, blue sky
And the sailing clouds o'er head.
– from "The Call of the Plains"

Guitar playing was also popular among cowboys out on the range and in the bunkhouse. It was said that cowboys from Mexico and Spain first established the tradition. Guitars were ideal instruments for mobile cowboys, being inexpensive and small enough to fit into saddle bags. The image of cowboys strumming their instruments in the flickering light of the campfire is surely one of the most iconic. Over the years, cowboy guitarists developed their own style of playing, a hybrid of folk and country music with its own distinctive chords.

The famous guitar manufacturer Martin and Company has produced a range of guitars to honor the tradition of cowboy players. They launched the first guitar in

the series, the Cowboy X, in 2000, decorated with a painting of a traditional campfire scene by the Western artist Robert Armstrong. The model shown is a 2002 model, the Martin Cowboy III, which is decorated with an Armstrong painting of a typical ranch scene, complete with ranch hands, a cowgirl, and a bucking bronco.

Cowboy music is not the only art that celebrates the romance of trail life. Beginning in the 1880s, Wild West stage shows also enshrined and perpetuated the cowboy legend.

The Wild West Shows

Opposite page: Buffalo Bill Cody understood the appeal of cowboy skills.

The cowboy legend of the Old West was first commercially marketed by the "Wild West" shows of the day, including Buffalo Bill Cody's *Wild West Show*, which ran between 1884 and 1906. These shows were the first form of entertainment to take their inspiration from the lives and skills of the cowboys. Cody's show celebrated the most skillful and entertaining aspects of a cowhand's work, together with other aspects of the traditional West. Among his vignettes of Western life, Cody's show included a staged battle between cowboys and Indians. In fact, this is historically inaccurate; although cowboys would defend their cattle from rustlers of any ethnicity, most armed confrontation took place between the United States Cavalry and Native Americans. Cody's entertainment also included an

Below: Cody's famous show ran for more than twenty years.

COL. W. F. CODY. "BUFFALO BILL."

Stacy

WILD WEST

CORNER 9TH ST & 5TH AVE.
BROOKLYN.

Right: Buffalo Bill surrounded by the cast of his show. The photograph shows an interesting blend of real cowboys and real Indians.

Opposite page: Cody was a master showman and knew exactly how to promote himself.

on-stage buffalo hunt, and an attack on the Deadwood stagecoach. The show also featured real-life Western characters such as Sitting Bull, Wild Bill Hickok, and Annie Oakley.

Impresario Pawnee Bill (Gordon William Lillie) presented a similar, rival Wild West show. Lillie launched *Pawnee Bill's Historic Wild West Show* in 1888. It starred his wife, May Manning, who was featured as a horseback sharpshooter. In 1908 Hickok and Lillie (who also ran a buffalo ranch) joined their creative forces to announce their *Two Bills Show*.

Above: Buffalo Bill's Wild West shows drew huge crowds of varied spectators.

Another Western showman, Joe Miller, founded the *101 Ranch Wild West Show* in 1905. The Miller family owned a huge 110,000 acre ranch in the Indian Territory of Oklahoma. Their neighbor, showman Gordon Lillie, inspired Joe Miller and his brothers to produce a Wild West show of their own. Joe was the star performer in the show, which also featured Bill Picket, Tom Mix, and even an aging Buffalo Bill.

A former soldier, scout, and bison hunter, Buffalo Bill Cody made his stage debut in Chicago, Illinois, in 1872. He starred alongside the legendary Texas Jack Omohundro. Cody's stage show made him an international celebrity and an American cultural icon. Mark Twain commented that his show gave his audiences "a last glimpse at the fading American frontier."

The Winchester Model 1873

SPECIFICATIONS

Caliber: .44-40

Barrel: 30 inch round, 24 inch round, octagonal, or round-octagonal, 20 inch round

Type: Tubular magazine lever-action rifle

Origin: Winchester Repeating Arms Co., New Haven, Connecticut

A standard Model 1873 saddle-ring carbine, fitted with a twenty-inch round barrel. This gun was made in 1889.

This rifle is a late-production Model 1873 Trapper's Carbine, made in 1909. It has a shortened sixteen-and-a-quarter-inch round barrel.

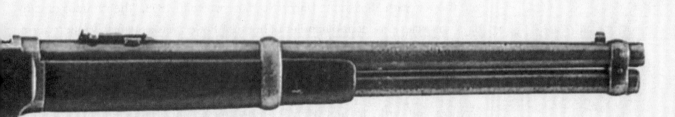

The Model 1873 offered three advantages over the Model 1866. First, it had a stronger frame. The original frame had been made of iron, but after 1884 was constructed from steel. Secondly, the 1873 had a dust-cover over the action. Thirdly, and perhaps most important of all, most 1873s were chambered for the .44-40 round (although other calibers were available). This was the same ammunition used by the Colt Frontier Six-Shooter, a version of the company's "Model P" type single action revolver and meant a man could carry one set of ammunition for these two popular firearms. This was particularly useful in the rigorous environment of the frontier. The Model 1873 was awarded the well-deserved title of "The Gun That Won the West."

Like the Model 1866, the Model 1873 was sold in three versions. These were a musket with thirty-inch round barrel, a sporting rifle with a twenty-four-inch barrel (which could be round, octagonal, or combination round-octagonal), and a carbine with a twenty-inch round barrel.

There were the usual minor changes over the production run, which mainly involved modifications to the dust-cover. When production ended in 1919, around 720,000 Model 1873s had been sold.

The Rodeo

Opposite page: The original rodeos grew out of a mixture of cattle wrangling and bull fighting. They showcased skills that were first used by the sixteenth-century conquistadors.

The idealized view of the cowboy and his professional skills that was first showcased in the Wild West shows was also perpetuated by the rodeo. This more realistic form of Western entertainment has become a durable and popular cultural phenomenon. To us, the rodeo seems like a window into the world of the traditional cowboy. But it actually pre-dates the days of the frontier by over a century. The first rodeos were held back in the early eighteenth century, when the Spanish ruled the West. These shows celebrated the authentic cowboy chores of tie-down roping, horse breaking, bronco riding (broncos are unbroken horses), branding, and team roping.

When the policy of Manifest Destiny emerged in the nineteenth century, the Western cattle business boomed. A huge amount of meat was required to feed the growing American population. Cowboys were in demand, and cowboying became a more valued profession. The rodeos of the later part of the nineteenth century celebrated the vital skills of these tough and resourceful men.

Rodeo became more widespread in the years following the Texas Revolution and the war with Mexico. As Harris Newgate wrote in 1858, "the vaquero of early days was a clever rider and handler of horses." Rodeo was a Spanish vaquero term, meaning "round-up" and did not acquire its modern meaning until 1916. The first rodeos were called "cowboy competitions," or "cowboy tournaments."

These early competitions were inspired by the skills cultivated by professional cowboys and cattle drovers. They soon became an important element of Western life. They were particularly popular with working cowhands as a means to demonstrate their skills and supplement their low wages. By 1851, rodeos had legal status in California, where the *Act to Regulate Rodeos* stated that each ranch should hold a rodeo each year. The first organized rodeo was held at Cheyenne, Wyoming, in 1872. Ten years later, Buffalo Bill Cody held the first commercial rodeo in Platte, Nebraska.

In 1888, the first professional rodeo competition was staged at Prescott, Arizona. This was the first tournament to charge an entry fee and award prizes. At this time, rodeo stars often performed in Wild West shows, like those of Cody and Lillie, as well as rodeos.

Almost from the beginning, rodeos were dogged by controversy around animal welfare, which was an issue for many people and animal welfare groups.

Above: Bucking bronco competitions grew from a cowboy's need to stay in the saddle under any conditions — it could be a matter of life and death in a stampede.

By the 1920s, rodeos were becoming increasingly fashionable, with trick roping being the most popular element of most shows. In 1923, Tex Austin hired the New Yankee Stadium for a ten-day event that awarded $50,000 in prize money. This was double the prize money offered at the Madison Square Garden rodeo in the previous year. Even during the Great Depression, rodeos maintained their large audiences, and many contestants earned between $2,000 and $3,000 a year. At the time, this was more than a teacher or dentist could expect to earn. The Texan promoter Col. William T. Johnson staged rodeos all over the United States and increasingly professionalized the sport. His events included bareback and bronco riding, steer wrestling and riding, and calf roping. By this time, rodeos had changed from a participation sport into a spectator event, and there was an increasing tendency towards general entertainment to be included in the format. In 1939 Gene Autry sang *"Home on the Range"* in the Madison Square Garden annual rodeo, and this tradition of mixing glitz and showmanship into the sport continued for decades. Under Autry's influence, rodeos also became increasingly patriotic events, especially during World War II.

After the war, the influence of individual promoters like Autry, Austin, and Johnson waned, and the sport of rodeo became increasingly regulated and controlled by large associations. Prize money also became much higher. In 1953, a total of $2,491,856 was available to be won. By 1983, this had increased to over thirteen million dollars. In 1976, Tom Ferguson became the first rodeo cowboy to earn more than $100,000 in a single year.

The 1970s were a period of unprecedented growth in the popularity of rodeos, and in 1989, the Texas Cowboy Hall of Fame was opened at Fort Worth, Texas. Despite this, the sport has continued to be dangerous, with a smattering of fatal accidents.

Participation in the sport of rodeo has now become a lucrative profession. Each year 7,500 contestants compete for over thirty million dollars in prize money in over 650 American rodeos. Although modern rodeo is only loosely based on the classic skills of the Western cowboy, it still requires extreme courage, strength, and expertise. Many rodeo events remain substantially unchanged. These include bull riding (the most popular event today), steer wrestling, calf roping, and bareback bronco riding. All of these activities are as potentially dangerous as they ever were. There are now several Rodeo Associations which run the sport, and cater to various niche groups. Although rodeo has always been a relatively inclusive sport, with participation by African Americans, Hispanics, and Native Americans from the early

Below: Steer-roping was also a crucial cowboy skill.

Right: Steer roping (also known as steer tripping) is a skill still showcased in rodeos. A professional steer roper can catch and tie an animal in around ten to fifteen seconds.

Right: Things don't always go according to plan, and rodeo work can be very dangerous.

days, these organizations now include the International Gay Rodeo Association and the All-Indian Rodeo Cowboys Association.

The profile of the participants has changed dramatically from the illiterate cowhands of the early years. Today, nearly a third of all rodeo riders have college degrees, and less than half of rodeo performers have ever worked on a ranch.

Cowgirl Rodeo Stars

The image of the female cowboy owed much to Annie Oakley's role as a sharpshooter in Buffalo Bill Cody's *Wild West Show*. Born Phoebe Ann Mosey, Oakley was born on August 13, 1860 in Woodland, Ohio. Her extraordinary abilities as a sharpshooter propelled her to become the first American female superstar. When Annie's father died while she was still a child, she began trapping and shooting game to help support her family. Gaining some notoriety for her fantastic marksmanship, she joined Buffalo Bill's *Wild West Show*, where she was billed as "Little Sure Shot." During her lifetime, Oakley taught over fifteen thousand women to shoot to defend themselves. She also became an early movie star.

Although cowboying remained an almost exclusively male profession, women were often involved in running family ranches. Some of these women also gravitated to the rodeo scene. By the 1920s, cowgirls performed in many rodeos as relay racers, trick riders, and rough stock riders. By 1928, at least one third of all rodeos had competitive events for women. Unfortunately, the 1929 death of the famous rodeo performer Bonnie McCarroll in a bronco riding accident caused many

Western shows to drop female events. Women were encouraged to participate as rodeo queens rather than athletes. When Gene Autry founded the Rodeo Association of America in the same year, it was created as an all-male entity.

When high unemployment struck in the Depression, more traditional gender roles were reasserted, and women became rodeo figureheads rather than participants. The restrictions of World War II were particularly devastating for rodeo women. Gene Autry held particularly conservative views about gender roles, and excluded women from all rodeos that he controlled. Effectively, Autry's influence meant that real cowgirls were banned from rodeos. In 1942, Fay Kirkwood staged an all-women rodeo in Bonham, Texas, but this was a showcase of women's rodeo skills, rather than a competitive event.

But there were always women that challenged their gender roles. Connie Douglas Reeves was born in 1901 in Eagle Pass, Texas. When the Great Depression forced her to leave law school, she became a teacher and riding instructor at Camp Waldemar at Hunt, Texas. It is estimated that Reeves taught over 30,000 women to ride at Camp Waldemar. She and her husband became sheep and cattle ranchers, but she continued to teach at the camp. In 1997, she was to become the oldest member of the National Cowgirl Museum and Hall of Fame. Reeves died in 2003, at the age of 101, when she was thrown from a horse. Reeve's hands-on motto was, "Always saddle your own horse."

In 1948, a professional women's rodeo association was finally created in San Angelo, Texas. The Girls Rodeo Association was founded with just thirty-eight members. This quickly grew to a membership of seventy-four. Many of these were women ranchers who had been forced to manage family operations while their husbands fought in the war. In its first year, the G.R.A. staged sixty women's events. In 1982, the organization was re-named the Women's Professional Rodeo Association. The Women's National Finals Rodeo is now held each year at the Cowtown Coliseum in Fort Worth, Texas.

Above: Rodeo has become a widely used cultural reference in different media.

Cowboys in the Movies

Opposite page: Errol Flynn appeared in four Western movies between 1940 and 1950. Although Flynn was best known for playing Robin Hood, his cowboy films were also popular.

The early Wild West shows etched the traditions of the working cowboy into the public mind, and were the forerunners of the Western movies that superseded them in the 1920s.

In fact, Western movies featuring cowboys were one of the first staples of the film industry, and they are still popular with today's cinemagoers. Cowboy characters were popular from the earliest days of the cinema, and their working environment and way of life became familiar to millions of moviegoers. The first movie cowboys represented a wide range of stereotypes, from the violent maverick to the honorable hero. The first cowboy movies of the silent era spawned several stars, including Art Acord, William S. Hart, Jack Hoxie, and Fred Thomson. Not all of these actors made it through to the next generation of talking pictures. In the 1930s, film sound technology made a new generation of clean-cut singing cowboys hugely popular. Gene Autry was the archetype of this new style of artist. Not only was Autry a fine singer, but he became heavily identified with his on-screen persona, and conceived his own "Cowboy Code." His basic credo was that a cowboy never shoots first, never takes unfair advantage, tells the truth, helps people in distress, and is always a patriot. Autry's clean-cut image suited the times, and propelled him to enormous popularity. Autry's lyrical character debuted in 1934's *Old Santa Fe*. He went on to make over a hundred films in his long and successful career, making the singing cowboy character hugely popular. Several actors subsequently adopted this persona, including Bing Crosby (in *Rhythm on the Range*, 1936), Tex Ritter, Bob Baker, and William Hopalong Cassidy Boyd.

In the 1940s, Roy Rogers succeeded Gene Autry as the singing King of Cowboys. He had played Autry's sidekick, Frog Millhouse, in many movies, but took his first lead in *Under Western Stars*. Rogers also went on to have a long and distinguished career on screen and television, and was one of the first stars to inspire a marketing phenomenon. He endorsed many products, including cowboy dolls, novels, and a comic strip.

Cowboy movies had an extremely positive effect on the film industry itself at this time, both economically and creatively. As the talkies surged onto the market, a whole new generation of cowboy movie stars began to hit the big time. They included such luminaries as Sunset Carson, Lane Chandler, Tom Mix (considered to be Hollywood's first cowboy megastar), and Gary Cooper. Cooper starred in

Above: Jimmy Stewart played several cowboy roles, including one in the 1952 film *Bend of the River*. The movie was directed by Anthony Mann and written by Western novelist Borden Chase.

1929's *The Virginian*. Considered by many to be the first modern Western (it was also one of the first talking cowboy pictures), *The Virginian* was directed by Victor Fleming. The film was the third screen version of Owen Wister's classic Western novel. Gary Cooper's character is a ranch foreman, beset by the all-too-familiar problem of cattle rustling. Manly, assertive, and decent, Cooper's character is one of the earliest film portrayals of the cowboy ideal.

The next round of cowboy actors from the 1940s and 1950s included Glenn Ford, James Garner, and John Wayne himself. The availability of many of the finest cinema actors ever to grace the screen made the 1930s, 1940s, and 1950s the Golden Era of Western movies, many of which revolved around cowhand characters.

John Ford's 1939 film *Stage Coach* is important for many artistic reasons, but is best remembered as the movie that projected John Wayne from B-movie Westerns to true stardom. Wayne was to become the most iconic movie cowboy of all time. Veteran film director Howard Hawks often cast Wayne as in cowboy roles. Hawks's 1948 movie *Red River* stars Wayne. It tells the story of the first cattle drive along the Chisholm Cattle Trail, fictionalized by writer Borden Chase.

Errol Flynn was another major Hollywood star whose career included a stint as a film cowboy. *Dodge City* (1939) was an early Technicolor movie in which he co-starred with Olivia de Havilland. Flynn plays a lone cowboy, with the action taking place in the Longhorn cattle center of the world, the last of the great cow towns.

In the 1950s, famous film cowboy Clint Eastwood began his career playing Rowdy Yates in the long-running television series *Rawhide*. It was his passport to becoming one of the most iconic movie cowboys ever. As his career progressed, Eastwood went on to play more complex and ambiguous cowboy characters in

Sergio Leone's so-called Spaghetti Westerns. Leone made an important contribution to the character of the screen cowboy in his movies by redefining their "look" as ragged and dusty rather than pristine and salubrious.

In the 1960s, the classic cowboy movie went through more difficult times and underwent several re-interpretations. One of the more questionable was 1965's not-very-funny comedy *Cat Ballou*. The movie tracks the adventures of a rancher's daughter (Jane Fonda) who hires a gunfighter (Lee Marvin) to protect the family acres. But the genre survived such indignities, and the 1970s saw the release of one of John Wayne's final offerings, the classic movie *The Cowboys*. When his ranch

Above: During his career in movie Westerns, Stewart wore the same hat and rode the same horse, "Pie."

Right: John Wayne played several cowboy characters during his long career, including the starring role in 1930's *Big Trail* and 1935's *The New* Frontier.

Left: In 1970's *Rio Lobo*, John Wayne's character Cord McNally returns several ranches to their rightful owners, and bankrupts the local villain, Ketcham.

Right: John Ford (right) made several cowboy films, or "horse operas," as John Wayne called them.

Below: Dean Martin played the drunken cowboy gunfighter in *Rio Bravo* (1970).

hands abandon him to join the gold rush, Wayne's character, Wil Andersen is forced to train up a group of schoolboys as cowhands so that he can drive his cattle the four-hundred miles to Belle Fourche, South Dakota.

Far from dying out, the classic cowboy movie has continued to evolve over the decades to reflect contemporary concerns and attitudes. The 2005 film *Brokeback Mountain* explores the complex sexual and romantic relationship between two (male) cowboys, and became one of the highest-grossing romance films of all time. Interestingly, the iconic bloodied shirts from the film are housed at the Autry National Center. Clean-cut singing cowboy Gene Autry founded the center in 1988 to explore the diversity of the people of the American West.

Below: Director John Ford's Western movies transformed John Wayne into the archetypical Western cowboy. He played variations on the role throughout his long career.

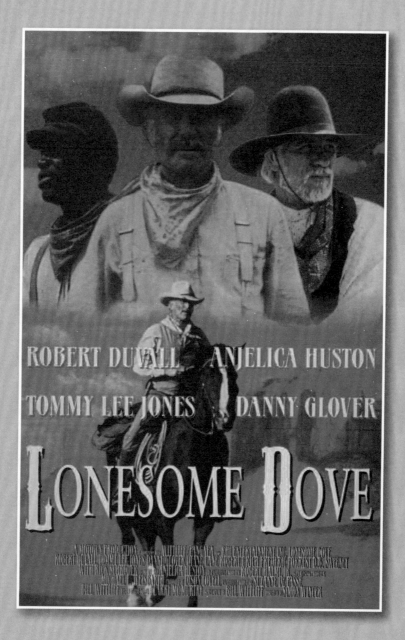

Above: The story of *Lonesome Dove* revolves around the Hat Creek
Cattle Company and its owners and ranch hands. One of them, Joshua
Deets, is an ex-slave working as a cattle drive scout and tracker.

Left: In 1960's *Magnificent Seven*, seven cowboys-turned-
gunslingers defend a village from a Mexican bandit chief.
The movie was directed by John Sturges.

Cowboys on the Small Screen

Opposite Page: Hopalong Cassidy was the creation of Clarence E. Mulford. William Boyd played the character. His NBC show was the first network Western television series.

Below: Roy Rogers and his wife, Dale Evans.

From the early days of television, the cowboy also became a mainstay character of small screen entertainment. Early cowboy-inspired shows were the direct descendants of radio Westerns. Like their movie counterparts, these early television shows often featured so-called "singing cowboys," including Gene Autry, Roy Rogers, Rex Allen, and singing cowgirl Dale Evans.

The popularity of Western themed television shows continued for years, finally peaking in 1959, when cowboy-inspired programs occupied no fewer than twenty-six primetime slots.

The very first network television Western, *Hopalong Cassidy*, aired on June 24, 1949. Based on Clarence E. Mulford's clean-cut cowboy character, the original shows were re-edited B-movies. But these were so successful that the NBC network commissioned some original half-hour episodes. These were immediately successful, rating seventh in the 1949 Nielsen ratings. A radio version was also launched. The show's longstanding success inspired several other cowboy shows for children, including *The Gene Autry Show* and *The Roy Rogers Show*. *The Roy Rogers Show* ran for a hundred episodes between 1951 and 1957. This NBC show also starred Roger's real-life wife, Dale Evans. Dale Evans wrote Rogers's signature theme, *"Happy Trails."*

NBC's *Bonanza* was another iconic cowboy series. Running for fourteen years between 1959 and 1973, the show followed the fortunes of the Cartwright family, who lived on the one-thousand-square-mile Ponderosa ranch in Lake Tahoe, Nevada. *Bonanza* was the first hour-long serial to be shot in color, and starred Pernell Roberts and Lorne Green. Between 1962 and 1971, NBC ran a second cowboy series, *The Virginian,* alongside *Bonanza*. The action of

Best Wishes
Tom Mix

SPURR
HOLLYWOOD

Opposite page: Tom Mix starred in over one-hundred-sixty cowboy movies in the 1920s. He was named an honorary Texas Ranger in 1935.

Left: Clayton Moore starred as the Lone Ranger. His catchphrase was, "Hi-ho, Silver!"

The Virginian was set in the 1880s, and revolved around the business of another large ranch, the Shiloh. James Drury played the Shiloh's tough ranch foreman (and the eponymous Virginian), while Doug McClure remained his loyal top hand, Trampas, for the entire series. Alongside both shows, NBC ran a third ranch-based series, *The High Chapparal*. The series was set in the Arizona Territory of the 1870s, and featured Leif Erickson as rancher Big John Cannon. The show ran for four seasons between 1967 and 1971.

Left: Gene Autry began his career as "Oklahoma's Yodeling Cowboy".

In 1959, the CBS network had launched its own cowboy series, *Rawhide*. The program is now most famous for launching Clint Eastwood's career. Eastwood played the role of Rowdy Yates (who he later described as "the idiot of the plains"). Set in the 1860s, *Rawhide* portrays the challenges faced by a group of cowboys driving their herd along the Sedalia Trail. On the series, about twenty-five drovers (of whom Yates is one) control three thousand head of cattle. This is probably more men than would have been used in real life.

Along with regular series, the networks also produced a number of made-for-television movies featuring cowboy characters. A good example of this would be 1991's *Conagher.* Based on Louis L'Amour's novel, the story revolves around a ranching family and their fight against cattle rustlers, Indian attack, and marauding gangs.

Above: *Gunsmoke* was an iconic television western series of the 1950s. It starred James Arness as Marshal Matt Dillon, policing an area dominated by ranchers.

Opposite page: Clint Eastwood starred as cowboy Rowdy Yates in the 1950s television series *Rawhide*.

Left: Roy Rogers became the most heavily marketed and merchandised singing cowboy of all time.

Right: James Garner starred as cowboy Bret Maverick in ABC's television series, *Maverick*.

Above: Dan Blockner, Lorne Greene, and Michael Landon starred in *Bonanza*. The action centered on a family-run ranch.

In all its different forms, the Western has not only been a foundation of American popular culture, but has also played a huge part in shaping it. Starting in the written form and evolving into movies, radio, and television, Westerns have been a staple of American entertainment for nearly two centuries. The formats and revenue generated by the Western genre have influenced a huge swathe of popular culture, and continue to do so. Westerns have not only revealed a fascinating aspect of American culture and history to an enthralled world, but have also helped to remind us of the origins of America life itself.

Above: The cast of *The High Chaparral*, with
Leif Erickson in the center.

Above: This Hubley twin holster set of toy cowboy guns dates from the 1950s.

Right: Western television series inspired the sale of cowboy cap pistols like this one.

Above: Toy frontier and scout rifles from Hubley, shown with a Buffalo Bill scout rifle from Daisy-Heddon.

Left and right: Toymakers Marx and Esquire made these two versions of bounty hunter Josh Randall's gun.

Below: Toy Derringers were popularized by television Westerns.

Above: The 1950s cap gun craze led to a sudden flourishing of different firing systems.

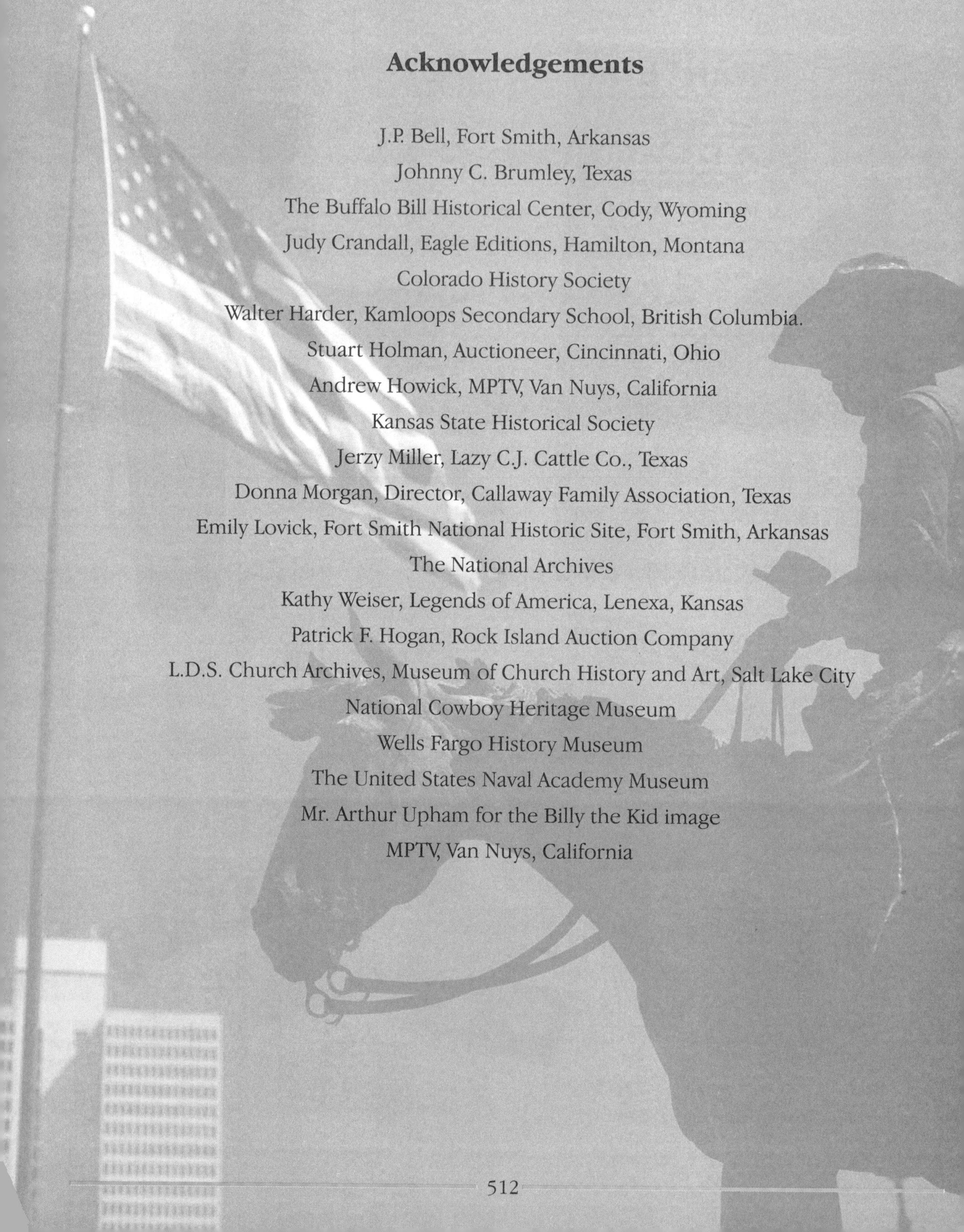

Acknowledgements

J.P. Bell, Fort Smith, Arkansas

Johnny C. Brumley, Texas

The Buffalo Bill Historical Center, Cody, Wyoming

Judy Crandall, Eagle Editions, Hamilton, Montana

Colorado History Society

Walter Harder, Kamloops Secondary School, British Columbia.

Stuart Holman, Auctioneer, Cincinnati, Ohio

Andrew Howick, MPTV, Van Nuys, California

Kansas State Historical Society

Jerzy Miller, Lazy C.J. Cattle Co., Texas

Donna Morgan, Director, Callaway Family Association, Texas

Emily Lovick, Fort Smith National Historic Site, Fort Smith, Arkansas

The National Archives

Kathy Weiser, Legends of America, Lenexa, Kansas

Patrick F. Hogan, Rock Island Auction Company

L.D.S. Church Archives, Museum of Church History and Art, Salt Lake City

National Cowboy Heritage Museum

Wells Fargo History Museum

The United States Naval Academy Museum

Mr. Arthur Upham for the Billy the Kid image

MPTV, Van Nuys, California